Leadership I

**Principles Forged in the Crucible of Military Service
Can Lead Corporate America Back to the Top**

Leadership In Action

**Principles Forged in the Crucible of Military Service
Can Lead Corporate America Back to the Top**

Gregory J. Slavonic, Rear Admiral, U.S. Navy (Retired)

Jacksonville, Florida ♦ Herndon, Virginia
www.Fortis-Publishing.com

Leadership In Action

Principles Forged in the Crucible of Military Service Can Lead Corporate America Back to the Top

Greg Slavonic, Rear Admiral, U.S. Navy (Retired)

ISBN 978-0-9845511-7-0 (hardcover version)
ISBN 978-0-9845511-6-3 (trade paperback version)

Library of Congress Control Number: 2010939245

Published by Fortis Publishing
Jacksonville, Florida—Herndon, Virginia
www.Fortis-Publishing.com

Manufactured in the United States of America

Dedication

"The very essence of leadership is its purpose. And the purpose of leadership is to accomplish a task. That is what leadership does – and what it does is more important than what it is or how it works."

— Colonel Dandridge M. Malone

This book is dedicated to the many men and women with whom I served during my 34-year Navy career.

I've traveled many miles from the Tonkin Gulf in 1972 off the coast of Vietnam—to Saudi Arabia, the Red Sea and Northern Persian Gulf supporting *Operations Desert Shield* and *Desert Storm* in the First Gulf War—to my final wartime tour in 2004 in support of *Operation Iraqi Freedom* where I crisscrossed Iraq.

I learned much from everyone and shared many experiences both good and bad. I am proud to have served with each of you. You each are heroes and greatly influenced my writing of this book.

Contents

Contents (continued)

Contents (continued)

Acknowledgements

"Nearly all men can stand adversity, but if you want to test a man's character, give him power."

— *Abraham Lincoln*

To write a book of this nature requires a total team effort. I could not have been successful with this project without the help of many friends and shipmates who contributed their expertise, time and hard work. I want to say thank you to:

My wife Molly, who stood with me as we worked through this endeavor, sacrificed much and gave of her time to review the manuscript, even while preparing for our daughter's wedding and our first family vacation.

To my daughter Kara for assisting with the editing and reviewing of this book. And to my daughter Maggie for her help with the layout and design of the book and cover.

To the many who assisted with reviewing the manuscript and generating additional ideas including, Commander (Retired) Tucker McHugh, U.S. Navy, Stephen Reel, Bruce Day, and Major John "Wolf" Wagner, U.S. Army. I also owe a big "thank you" to my former Executive Assistant Lieutenant Commander (Retired) Penny Cockerell who provided encouragement, advice and support for this project and to Rear Admiral Vic Beck who assisted me greatly prior to his deployment of Afghanistan. You are all heroes.

To the team at Fortis Publishing who carried out my vision, particular president (and senior editor) Dennis Lowery. His patience, wisdom, insight and experience helped me navigate the many hurdles in publishing a book. His entire team was a pleasure to work with and always available to answer any question or concern which arose along this journey.

Last but certainly not least, thank you to the authors of these chapters for sharing your experiences with all us. Thank you for giving me your friendship and trust while producing this book.

Foreword

"With integrity you have everything....without integrity you have nothing."

– *Winston Churchill*

In 1971, I enlisted in U.S. Navy. I wanted to see the world and see the world I did, plus much more. Later that year the seeds were planted for this book. The premise and concept has grown over the years into what you are about to read.

In early February 1972, I reported aboard my first ship the attack aircraft carrier USS CONSTELLATION (CVA-64). The ship was operating in the Tonkin Gulf off the coast of Vietnam launching daily air strikes into North Vietnam.

I learned quickly, life as a Seaman Apprentice aboard an 82,000 ton, floating city with almost 5,000 men had many challenges. Positioned at the bottom of the Navy food chain, my first assignment was not on the Signal Bridge (I graduated from Signalman "A" as a Signalman Striker) but rather was sent to "mess cooking" duties for almost 80-days. This was a normal assignment for the most junior sailors reporting aboard a ship.

I soon found out leadership was often "do as I say" and not as "I do" and quickly realized men are not only put in charge of other men, but responsible for their lives as well. Some men were prepared to lead while others were not. At the end of the day – leadership – was a key factor in accomplishing any task, mission, and achieving the objective.

These were turbulent times for the Navy and our Nation. The U.S. was engaged in a long, unpopular war. The draft was taking our best and brightest to war. It was only after careful reflection some years later that I realized this early military experience would be the foundation for my own leadership development. It changed me and would shape my life for the next 34 years in the Navy/Navy Reserve. It provided a unique opportunity for me as I rose from the Navy's lowest rank, Seaman Recruit, to flag rank of Rear Admiral. Little did I know the journey was just a beginning.

The actual tipping point that triggered plans for this book occurred the fall of 2008, when the United States faced the worst economic situation in more than 50 years precipitated by a failure of leadership by many leaders across government, financial institutions, and many businesses. The lack of doing the right thing allowing power, greed, selfishness to override common sense and logical decision-making. Failures such as Enron Corporation, Bernie Madoff hedge fund fraud scandal, etc., and there are many more which appear daily in local and national newspapers. Failures of leadership at the top but also by the next tier of leadership down the chain of command. And more importantly – the tremendous void where ethical behavior, character and doing-the-right-thing was expected but not present, led to the worst economic catastrophe we have faced as a nation since The Great Depression.

As a Nation, we weathered that great depression, several wars, internal conflict and many cultural-changing events. Now we face a bigger and more devastating challenge that not only effect the current generation but has long-term impact on future generations as well. Strong leadership is needed—and I believe there is much to learn from a historical perspective from the experience of proven and successful military leaders of the present and past.

* * *

The chapters within this book show how opportunities to test and stretch individuals (whether young or old) with leadership potential are important. Such practices can, prepare people for small-and-medium-sized leadership jobs. But developing people for increasingly responsible leadership roles requires more work (mentoring) on the part of senior executives, often over a long period. That work begins with efforts to spot people with great potential early in their careers and to identify what will be needed to develop them. Again, there is nothing magic about this process. The methods the military use is surprisingly straightforward. The military culture goes out of their way to develop young men and women at lower levels so they can lead at a high level. Senior leaders can judge for themselves who has potential and what the development requirements of those people are. To do that requires a clear sense of purpose to determine who has leadership potential and what skills are needed to develop men and women in the military. Planning for that development is sometimes done as part of a formal succession or retention planning; often it is more informal. In either case, the key ingredient appears to be an intelligent assessment of what feasible development opportunities fit each individual's needs.

The chapters in this book are written by military leaders who are some of the "best of the best" and brightest leaders the military has produced in the past 75 years. They understand how to develop/mentor future leaders and how to lead people – whether in peacetime or during combat.

They distinguished themselves by earning some of the highest awards a Nation can bestow on it military leaders/warriors. These decorations include–the Nation's highest award, The Medal of Honor, Air Force Cross, Silver Star, Distinguished Flying Cross (with Combat "V" for valor), Bronze Star Medal with Combat "V", Combat Action Ribbon, Combat Infantry Badge, Purple Heart and Prisoner of War Medal.

The contributors include: General David Petraeus, U.S. Army; Lieutenant General Don Wetekam, U.S. Air Force (Ret); Rear Admiral Doug McClain, U.S. Navy; Rear Admiral Tom Zelibor, U.S. Navy (Ret); Major General Irene Trowell-Harris, U.S. Air Force (Ret); Captain Tom Hudner, U.S. Navy, (Ret); Colonel Wesley Fox, U.S. Marine Corps (Ret); Colonel David Scott, U.S. Air Force (Ret); Colonel Chuck DeBellevue, U.S. Air Force (Ret); Commander Dan O'Shea, U.S. Navy Reserve; Tom Faught, USMC and former Assistant Secretary of the Navy. Plus, chapters on Commander Lloyd "Pete" Bucher, U.S. Navy (Ret), written by Lieutenant "Skip" Schumacher, his Operations Officer and Lt. Colonel Jim Zumwalt, U.S. Marine Corps (Ret) has penned a chapter on his father Admiral Elmo Zumwalt, U.S. Navy (Ret). And, finally, a unique chapter written by Rear Admiral Joe Callo, U.S. Navy Reserve (Ret), has written an interesting piece on Captain John Paul Jones, one of history's most successful naval commanders and certainly one of our nation's most illustrious heroes and a key figure in the history of the United States Navy.

I chose to profile these colleagues for their acts of integrity, character, and ethics during their careers, plus their experiences – in several cases - where their astounding courage and heroism were displayed. I've personally had the good fortune to observe many of these individuals in high-stress situations, and watched how they led and mentored our best and brightest young leaders. They share some of their personal leadership experiences, insights and reflections in this book.

Individuals make up our military history—they are the "players" on the stage of historic events. They bring experiences that the reader will find fascinating, compelling and helpful as they navigate through their own personal career development whether in a corporate/business environment, politics or the military.

These leaders have all risen through the ranks; have led men and women, and share with the reader their leadership stories on what made them successful and how their success can be a guiding light to challenges facing leaders in corporate America today. Combined they have over 450 years of military service to their country. Many have taken lessons from their highly successful military careers and transferred these skills to engage in equally successful civilian careers. The reader will see the pressures associated with their jobs and the style and determination with which they endured to be successful. Each understands how to lead men and women….they lead from the front. Several have operated at the "tip of spear" and dealt with situations that tested their mettle as a leader and as a human being. They now share part of their story.

Quality Leadership is the cornerstone for every successful organization. Whether applied in the military or a corporate environment, their stories will make the reader stop, think and ask, "How can I incorporate these skills and traits into my own leadership style"; "how can I become a better leader"; or "how can I better develop or mentor members of my staff."

Leadership in Action | *Principles Forged in the Crucible of Military Service Can Lead Corporate America Back to the Top*, resounds with timeless lessons on the most cherished of virtues – integrity - and is a powerful reminder of the strength of the human spirit and the determination to be successful. The book will look at the various key leadership traits woven throughout the chapters and how these traits/principles can apply to business culture and daily life. The ability to endure in any situation or circumstance often times requires what you will read and discover in these pages. The leaders in this book chose to wear the cloth of this great Nation. They aspired to the creed that Gene Kranz, former flight director at NASA stated at a crucial period in space history - *"Failure is not an option."*

In these chapters, the reader will learn the importance of:

- Leading by example

- Integrity

- Character

- Ethics and ethical behavior

- First impressions when meeting your troops or employees

- How attitude in any situation is crucial when addressing any problem

- Physical fitness in daily life

- It's not what happens in life but how one deals with it

- How good leaders instill confidence in others

- A common thread throughout the book - Taking care of your people

- One of General Colin Powell's' rules - "Sometimes being responsible means "pissing people off"

- A basic understanding that, "Hope is not a strategy" - you need a plan (road map) to success

These and other points will be discussed as you read the chapters. Often times the debate is whether leaders are made or born. I espouse the line of thinking that leaders are made, developed and formed through their environment.

The goal for this book is to make one think and challenge everyone in a position of leadership. It is a must read for young leaders who need guidance and role models. Corporate America and our political leaders most of all need real-world leadership lessons and examples. All who are hired to lead organizations or are elected to political office will find valuable lessons and insight from the stories you are about to enjoy. *Would that they read and learn as well.*

Greg Slavonic
Rear Admiral, U.S. Navy (Retired)

Introduction

Kenneth J. Braithwaite

Rear Admiral, U.S. Navy

"The supreme quality for leadership is unquestionably integrity."
— *General Dwight D. Eisenhower*

Leadership is arguably the most important quality an organization needs in order to be successful. Any organization whether a private corporation, a public agency or a nation must have competent leadership in order to advance its objectives.

History is resplendent with examples of those whose leadership skills advanced their respective institutions. This is especially true in times of crisis or challenge, but it is also true during times of relative calm or peace. In strong leadership, decisions are either made or not made, challenges rendered or reserved by and through the capabilities of those who are entrusted to lead.

What exactly is leadership? Can it be defined in simple skill sets or in the measure of what the individual achieved in either battles won, total margins achieved or the advancement of society in whole? Can its essence be captured in a sentence, a paragraph or an entire book? Many efforts attempt to quantify exactly what constitutes leadership. Books and more books have been written throughout the ages to define leadership, to capture it, package it and then pass it on to succeeding generations – all in an effort to advance those that seek out the special tenets of a successful leader.

Entrepreneurs such as those I recently visited with at West Point are working to create programs where the lessons of leadership can be passed on in two, three day and even week long programs designed to advance the management teams of the organizations which participate in that respective program. What evolves from these efforts is the defining importance of the concepts of leadership and what they mean to us as a society. The progress of any component of our society will not happen without leaders. But can leadership be learned or is it inherent in the individual by birth and "refined" by the lessons learned in the classroom, boardroom or battlefield?

In the annals of history, many names come to mind of those generational leaders whose abilities changed not only the course of the institution they led, but also more often than not, the course of history itself. Alexander the Great, Horatio Nelson, Alexander Carnegie, Theodore Roosevelt, Winston Churchill, Lee Iacocca, Mikhail Gorbachev...are easily some names that the world can look to with admiration and respect for their achievements. But there are also successful leaders who used their concepts of leadership for personal reward or individual glory—with power and wealth their only objectives. Their legacies are of course stained with the reflection of time. But in their day, they achieved great power that also altered the course of world history, territorial boundaries and business.

We have discovered through analysis that the tools of leadership can be used in myriad ways to affect the direction by which an organization proceeds. Science, art or inherent in an individual from birth, the skills of leadership will define not only the individual but also the institution they lead. To master or merely practice leadership, the student needs to examine the lessons of leaders. While not all encompassing, the historical vignettes of others experience can surely provide a foundation to further their study. It is therefore in understanding the concepts and influence by the student of leadership that either they can advance their respective institutions or not by the abilities, they practice and master.

In my career, I have been fortunate to have several mentors who guided me in charting my course through life. They, more times than not, did that by personal examples of leadership. They demonstrated it in their actions. One in particular, Rear Admiral Joseph C. Strasser, U.S. Navy (Retired) United States Naval Academy Class of 1962 and later President of the Naval War College, taught my classmates and me an invaluable lesson in the 'art of leadership". I recall as if it were yesterday, his sage words when he told some of us lucky enough to listen to his advice while at Annapolis, that during our Naval careers, we would have good leaders and not so good leaders, ones we should aspire to emulate and others we should learn never to replicate their mistakes. He charged us all to keep a little journal and to mark down in it when we observed someone doing something that inspired us and encouraged us in our service…something as simple as asking how our children (by name) were doing. Likewise, he instructed us to write down when we felt we were being poorly led, either by lack of judgment, egotistical behavior or plain lack of character. Then during our careers, we should pull out that little book and review it to ensure we were following the right course. I have to admit, I long ago misplaced my little green book, but I attempted to memorize most of the traits of those that demonstrated inspiring leadership. In turn I sought many times to emulate them and in so doing hopefully inspire those who were entrusted to my leadership. I learned during my career, in the lessons of others we can and will find precepts of leadership that serve us well.

The author of this book is one of those mentors who inspired me in my service. During his naval career he consistently led by example and took the time to demonstrate what I would call a caring leadership that made you feel not only valued but also appreciated for what you brought to the Team. Having started his career out at the very first "rung of the ladder" as a Seaman Recruit, it was not surprising that he would climb all the ranks possible to retire as a Rear Admiral. His leadership style I would surmise was developed, cultivated and honed by learning from those around him. And although he never served with Rear Admiral Strasser, he too learned similar lessons along the way and has since passed them onto to succeeding generations of naval leaders.

It is his effort herein to bring to light the stories of others who demonstrated different but similarly inspiring leadership when the situation called for them to step forward. These are not world leaders or corporate giants but everyday people who stood up to a challenge and demonstrated leadership during challenging times. They are ordinary professionals who when confronted with extraordinary situations remembered the lessons they had learned along their course in life.

Thankfully, they had the fortitude of character to practice these valuable lessons at what would surely be the right time. In so doing, they led their institutions to not only achieve their objectives but also to excel when others would surely fail. These concepts of leadership will always have value and will serve those that lead in the future as they served these leaders in the past.

Rear Admiral Kenneth J. Braithwaite, U.S. Navy
Chadds Ford, Pennsylvania

Profile

As the Navy's Vice Chief of Information Rear Admiral Kenneth J. Braithwaite serves as the principal Navy Reserve liaison and advisor to the Chief of Information having responsibility for formulating strategic communications counsel to the leadership of the Department of the Navy. Concurrently, he serves as the head of the Navy Reserve (NR) Public Affairs program and as an adjunct advisor to the Commander, Navy Reserve Force.

A 1984 graduate of the United States Naval Academy, Braithwaite was designated a naval aviator in April 1986. His first operational assignment was to Patrol Squadron 17, NAS Barbers Point, Hawaii. He flew anti-submarine missions tracking adversary submarines throughout the Western Pacific and Indian Ocean regions.

In April 1988, Braithwaite was selected for redesignation as a public affairs officer (PAO) with his initial tour aboard the aircraft carrier USS AMERICA (CV-66). He had additional duty as PAO to Commander Carrier Group 2 and Commander, Striking Force 6th Fleet. He made both a North Atlantic Treaty Organization (NATO) Force deployment to the North Atlantic operating above the Arctic Circle and a Mediterranean /Indian Ocean cruise where the battle group responded to tensions in the Persian Gulf. In 1990, he was assigned to the staff of Commander, Naval Base Philadelphia as chief of Public Affairs.

Braithwaite left active duty in 1993 and immediately resumed naval service in the reserve where he served with numerous commands from Boston to Norfolk.

Additionally during this time he earned a master's degree in Government Administration in April 1995 with honors from the University of Pennsylvania.

In October 2001, Braithwaite assumed command of NR Fleet Combat Camera Atlantic at Naval Air Station Willow Grove, Pa. During this tour, the command was tasked with providing support to the Joint Task Force (JTF) Commander, Guantanamo Bay, Cuba. In March 2003, Braithwaite deployed for Operation *Iraqi Freedom* with a portion of his command in support of naval operations to capture the port of Umm Qasr. Following this tour, he served as commanding officer of Navy Office of Information New York 102.

Most recently, Braithwaite served as Commander, Joint Public Affairs Support Element-Reserve (JPASE-R) from October of 2004 to October 2007. In this role, he commanded a 50-person joint public affairs expeditionary unit that was forward deployed to support Joint Combatant Commanders in time of conflict. While in command and following the devastating earthquake in Pakistan in 2005, Braithwaite was deployed to Pakistan as part of the Joint Task Force for Disaster Assistance serving as the director of Strategic Communications working for both the JTF Commander and the U.S. Ambassador in Islamabad.

His decorations include the Defense Meritorious Service Medal (with oak leaf cluster), Meritorious Service Medal, Navy Commendation Medal (5) with Combat "V", Navy Achievement Medal, Combat Action Ribbon and numerous campaign and service medals. In his civilian career, Braithwaite is senior vice president, Hospital and Healthsystem Association of Pennsylvania where he leads the Delaware Valley Healthcare Council in Philadelphia.

Chapter 1

Gregory J. Slavonic

Rear Admiral, U.S. Navy (Retired)

Webster defines leadership as *"Influencing people by providing purpose, direction, and motivation while operating to accomplish the mission and improving the organization."*

About Leadership

> *"In war, three quarters turns on personal character and relations; the balance of manpower and materials counts only for the remaining quarter."*
> — *Napoleon I*

Individuals at many different levels within many different walks of life created the series of events, which led to the challenges that currently beset our great Nation. These leaders in business and government didn't understand key (and some would say – basic) lessons of *leadership* or if they did — they chose to allow their personal interests to take precedence over their responsibilities.

It has often been said, *"The corporate world buys leaders, while the military develops/grows its leaders."* What the next several chapters will provide is an insight into what senior military leaders feel is important when leading "from the front" and having to make tough decisions.

Corporate America

Most U. S. corporations today are over managed and under led. There is great need to develop and exercise leadership at many different levels.

The military culture/environment doesn't wait for leaders to come along. People with leadership potential are sought out to provide them career experiences designed to develop that potential. Indeed, with careful selection, mentoring, nurturing, and encouragement, these same leadership skills and philosophies that the leaders in this book share—are transferable to business organizations or the government. When companies understand the fundamental difference between leadership and management, they can then begin to groom their top people to provide both.

Organizations should know that strong leadership with weak management is no better, and is sometimes actually worse, than the reverse. Just because an individual is, say a superb sales person, it does not equate to having the necessary leadership skills to lead a sales staff. The challenge is to combine strong leadership and strong management and use each to complement the other. It all starts with leadership.

Corporations and government organizations today bear a heavy burden. With a struggling economy, staffing challenges, Board pressures to ensure the profitability of the enterprise, strong leadership is critical. Coping with complexity and with change—shapes the characteristic activities and development of a leadership style. Since change is often a function of leadership, being able to generate high-energy behavior is important in order to cope with the inevitable barriers to change. That is a responsibility of leadership.

How many times do we hear someone say – "he (or she) is a born leader."

Individuals are not all born with the same leadership potential. Just as all individuals, do not have the ability play basketball like Kevin Durant, Chris Paul or Jerry West. Or sing like John Mayer, Carrie Underwood, or Faith Hill. A person is a product of their environment and as such will develop a foundation that will affect the rest of his/her life. Successful motivation ensures that they will have the energy to overcome obstacles. The military does a tremendous job providing motivation to young leaders. The leaders who have written chapters in this book will share many of the motivational techniques that have helped them.

I'm amazed every day how leaders are unwilling to accept responsibility for their actions. They are more concerned with their reputation and position within the organization and forget about the importance of their actions. They feel that since they are in a senior position they are above everyone else or above the law. Every day we see individuals in the media, government, entertainment, business and sports who have a "miss-step" or a failure of judgment, and find themselves unable to deal with the truth. When this occurs…the ripple, affect creates problems throughout an organization.

Good leaders motivate people in a variety of ways. They always communicate the organization's vision. Most discussions of vision are critical elements to leadership. Leaders who articulate their vision are strategic thinkers who are willing to take risks. Many leaders in this book have taken risks – risks that could have resulted in a life or death decision –for themselves or for those under their leadership. Remember, military leaders are raised in a culture where finishing second is an unacceptable outcome. There is too much to lose if you do.

These leaders in this book will share many bedrock leadership principles that are transferrable skills, which leaders can apply within any organization. These can be the foundation for developing successful leaders and a successful organization. General George Washington, the father of our Nation, created what he called "Rules of Civility" and chose to articulate all 101 of these rules when he was only sixteen years old. Many are timeless and useful to any leader today:

- Treat everyone with respect

- Keep your promises

- Be considerate of others

- Be responsible for your actions

- Have integrity

- Maintain high ethical standards

- In the final analysis – it is all about *Character*

- When a person does their best and fails, do not criticize him

- When you must give advice or criticism, consider the timing, whether it should be given in public or private

- Do not be quick to talk about something when you don't have all the facts

- Actions speak louder than words

An area, especially important to me, which has allowed me to engage with all levels of individuals I have served with, is maintaining a regular physical fitness program. Training, running or exercising with the troops has allowed me to have out-of-the-office conversations, that are beneficial (and sometimes essential) to the well-being of personnel and aided in accomplishing their duties or mission. Maintaining a level of fitness and physical appearance is something very important—to me—and in how others perceive you. How many times have we seen overweight or "out of standard" leaders in their uniform or business attire? In the Navy, fitness was a requirement and I was often miffed when I saw senior leaders who did not exemplify proper physical fitness standards. The men and women under them had to perform and pass certain standards and so should their leader. So such a leader was not an example that met with respect. In my opinion, one of the quickest (and surest) ways to earn the respect of those under you is physical training and fitness—meeting the standards expected.

While deployed to Iraq in 2004, I rose each morning at 0500 and went for a one hour run along the perimeter wall within the Green Zone, which separated the compound from the Tigris River. As I departed my trailer, I would look to my right and usually see General David Petraeus leaving his trailer too, beginning his morning run but heading in a different direction. I would regularly meet up with my running partner Sgt. Addie Collins who would accompany me. At the midpoint of our run, we would cross paths with General Petraeus and his PSD (personal security detail) who ran with him. Without fail, he would always have a morning greeting and we would continue our separate way.

After the run, I would head for the gym for a few pushups, set ups, treadmill, etc. and who would already be there, General Petraeus, lifting weights and visiting with the soldiers. It was not uncommon for a young soldier to challenge him in push-ups. I soon found out…don't bet against General Petraeus.

Courage is the father of every great movement or moment in history. I have always felt courage and leadership go hand in hand. No one is born with courage. It is an acquired virtue. You learn to play football by playing football and so I believe courage is acquired through practice. And when practiced it becomes stronger. Individuals don't follow titles and authority…they follow courage. Today, I believe people who work for you – young and old - are looking for someone who has the courage to look them in the eye and tell them the truth. Cervantes' wrote, *"He who loses wealth loses much; he who loses a friend loses more; but he who loses courage loses all."* Telling the truth and being honest with others whether in the military or business can be practiced. But the least course of resistance – or easy thing to do is to not be truthful with a friend or employee. This is takes courage.

To the above point, I always surrounded myself with a small team of individuals whose opinions I value and respect. I trusted their counsel and knew they would always provide me with "ground truth" whether I wanted to hear it or not. They were not hesitant to tell me if I made a mistake. Bottom line, I respected my staff and what they brought to the fight and I greatly appreciated their candor and insights. What is especially troubling to me is to see leaders who pride themselves on being good leaders and how well they relate with the troops but in reality did not. A four-star once told me how he was a "soldier's soldier" – this was so far from the truth it was embarrassing but this is not uncommon with those who are leaders at many different levels.

An important military technique to develop leaders is to support your personnel's efforts to realize their vision by being a mentor and role model. It's proven that good leaders, help people grow and develop personally and professionally. A leader's moral compass should—no— must possess character, integrity, commitment, conviction, credibility, honor and a strong sense of ethics. Leadership affects the organization's objectives and well-being. Individuals want guidance by those they respect and from those who have a clear sense of purpose. This sense of direction comes by conveying a strong vision of the future.

> *"If we were going to pick a characteristic that is most critical for the Navy in leadership, it is accountability. You need to think through, as an officer, what you believe in, and you need to make sure, particularly with what you do, that your standards are both impeccable and irrefutable and never blurred."*
> *Naval Justice School,*
> *Newport, R.I. – June 14, 2006*

Each organization has its own distinctive culture just like the Army, Air Force, Navy, Marine Corps or Coast Guard. It is a combination of past leadership, current leadership, history, traditions, and size. While the culture is deeply rooted in years of tradition, the organizations climate is a short-term phenomenon created by the vision of the one leading the enterprise.

As a leader, I found it important to have everyone well trained and ready to perform before entering into a crisis or stressful environment. Sometimes the best-trained individuals when placed in a stressful situation --might not perform well due to the pressure of the circumstances. When this occurs, you find others looking to you (the leader) to do something. As the leader, you need to make decisions on the spot. It is necessary to be flexible and adaptive to any situation and always have a back-up plan ready to execute. Conversely, often individuals who you felt were not prepared or not sure, how they might react to a crisis will surprise you and perform better than you expected. Teachable moments can (and do) occur at any time or any place.

Leaders usually have had opportunities during their twenties and thirties to lead to some degree, to take risks, and to learn from both triumphs and disasters. Such learning lessons are essential in developing a wide range of leadership skills and perspectives. These early teachable moments where both the difficulty of leadership and its potential for producing change are first introduced—with the associative responsibility and accountability—are often very sobering events for men and women. Remember, it takes courage to become a leader. Leading by example has never been more important – than is it today. And courage will get you through today and all your tomorrows.

Todd Livick, a retired Lt. Colonel, U.S. Army and my former boss made a statement one day, which I think, sums up the importance of understanding what is important in the workplace. We were working on a project and one of the elements of the project did not go according to the plan we had implemented. As we were critiquing the situation to determine what went wrong – he looked at me and said, *"Life, Limb or vision."* I looked at him and said, *"What?"* He said, *"Today, no one lost their life, an arm or leg or an eye."* He had put it into proper perspective. Corporate America traditionally does not deal with "life or death" situations although many in leadership positions will place an extreme amount of pressure or focus on a situation and "think" it is such a situation when it really isn't. Putting life and work in the proper perspective will allow a leader to live a more balanced life. At the end of the day, life is about choices and consequences.

* * *

While co-chairing the fund-raising and building the USS OKLAHOMA (BB-37) Memorial located on Ford Island, Pearl Harbor, Hawaii. I had the opportunity to work with over 75 former crewmembers from the "Greatest Generation".

One OKLAHOMA sailor who was aboard the ship Sunday, December 7, 1941 had an interesting story to relate. The sailor, Ensign Ed Vezey, and his roommate were up at 0730 talking in their stateroom about what they were going to do on that day…go to the beach, stay in bed, etc. The day was theirs to plan but what happened on that day changed them forever. At 0758, the Office-of-the-Deck (OOD) sounded "General Quarters" which meant everyone would head to their respective battle stations. Vezey's battle station was back aft on the ship and his roommate was the #3 gun turret. They quickly pulled on their trousers, shoes and headed out of their stateroom. Vezey turned right and his roommate turned left. It was the last time they would ever see each other. His roommate, as the ship was going to capsize and the order was given to abandon ship, remained in his gun turret, holding a flashlight so his gun crew could see to escape—unable to make it out in time, he sacrificed his life so that his men could live. For his heroic action that day, Ensign Francis C. Flaherty would receive the Congressional Medal of Honor. One of two men stationed aboard the OKLAHOMA who would be so honored.

Each man had a choice that day and as a consequence one lived and one died. As leaders of people and organizations, each of us have decisions to make every day but our decisions are most often never life or death. But men and women who wear the cloth of our Nation have and do have to make those types of decisions.

History is replete with famous men and women. Many who have left a legacy of kernels of wisdom, comments, statements and observations on life. Reading them often makes one pause for thought about just how apt they really are—for all times and all ages. Following are some of my favorites:

"Great men are meteors designed to burn so that earth may be lighted."

— _Napoleon Bonaparte_

"Leadership and learning are indispensable to each other."

— _John F. Kennedy_
35th President of the United States

"You don't have to hold a position in order to be a leader."

— _Anthony J. DeAngelo_

"Leadership is practiced not so much in words as in attitude and in actions."

— *Harold S. Geneen*

"The quality of a leader is reflected in the standards they set for themselves."

— *Ray Kroc*
McDonald's founder and owner of San Diego Padres

"Leaders aren't born, they are made. And they are made just like anything else, through hard work. And that's the price we'll have to pay to achieve that goal, or any goal."

— *Vincent "Vince" Lombardi*
Former head coach of two-time NFL Champions Green Bay Packers

"The ultimate leader is one who is willing to develop people to the point that they surpass him or her in knowledge and ability."

— *Fred A. Manske, Jr.*

"A leader leads by example, whether he intends to or not."

— *Author Unknown*

"The time is always right to do what is right."

— *Rev. Martin Luther King, Jr.*

"In a place where there is leader, do not seek to become a leader. In a place where there is no leader, strive to become a leader."

— *The Talmud*

"Power tends to corrupt, and absolute power corrupts absolutely."

— *Lord Acton*

"Example is not the main thing in influencing others. It is the only thing."

— *Albert Schweitzer*

"Without organization and leadership towards a realistic goal, there is no chance of realizing more than a small percentage of your potential."

— *John Wooden*
Legendary, former UCLA basketball coach and winner of 10 NCAA championships

"There are three things you should do when you make a mistake: 1) admit it, 2) learn from it, 3) don't repeat it."

— *Paul "Bear" Bryant*
Legendary, former University of Alabama head coach

"It is always a combination of factors that add up to the right person. It's his level of natural ability. It's his competitive instincts. It's also the history of that athlete: his ability to learn, retain, and apply what he has learned: and his ability to work under stress with other people. Then you have to be able to project those qualities into the slot or role that athlete would play for your team."

— *Bill Walsh*
Former head coach of three-time NFL Superbowl winning San Francisco 49er's

"On every team, there is a core group that sets the tone for everyone else. If the tone is positive, you have half the battle won. If it is negative, you are beaten before you ever walk on the field."

— *Chuck Noll*
Former head coach of four-time NFL Superbowl winning Pittsburgh Steelers

"Successful generals make plans to fit circumstances, but do not try to create circumstances to fit plans."
— General George S. Patton, Jr.

"Success is never final, failure is never fatal."
— Joe Paterno
Head coach of Penn State University's football team and winner of two NCAA championships
—

"Put your own ego aside. Don't be concerned with people writing about what a great coach you are. Make the team the focus. If the team wins, you have done your job. I did not need any more satisfaction than that."
— Bud Grant
Former head coach of the NFL's Minnesota Vikings & member of Pro football Hall of Fame

"Experience is the name everyone gives to their mistakes."
— Oscar Wilde

"Honesty is the first chapter in the book of wisdom."
— Thomas Jefferson

"We can't all be heroes because somebody has to sit on the curb and clap as they go by."
— Will Rogers

"The light which experience gives is a lantern on the stern, which shines only on the waves behind us."
— Samuel Taylor Coleridge

"Only those who dare to fail greatly can ever achieve greatly."
— Robert F. Kennedy

"Success is to be measured not so much by the position that one has reached in life as by the obstacles which he has overcome."

– *Booker T. Washington*

Chapter 2

David H. Petraeus
General, U.S. Army
By Paula Broadwell

"Treat people as if they were what they ought to be, and you help them to become what they are capable of becoming."

– Goethe

Profile

General David Petraeus

Born in Cornwall-on-Hudson, New York, General David H. Petraeus graduated in the top 5% of his class from the U.S. Military Academy in 1974 with a Bachelors of Science. He earned his Masters and Ph.D. from the Woodrow Wilson School of Public and International Affairs at University of Princeton.

He has held numerous commands including: A Company-2nd Battalion-19 Infantry Regiment, 3rd Battalion-187th Infantry Regiment, 1st Brigade-82nd Airborne, 101st Airborne Division-Air Assault, Multi-National Security Transition

Command – Iraq (MNSTC-I), U.S. Army Combined Arms Center (CAC), Multi-National Force – Iraq (MNF-I), Commander U.S. Central Command, and presently as Commanding General of the International Security Assistance Force, Afghanistan. Petraeus's command of the 101st Airborne Division during V Corps' drive to Baghdad is chronicled in detail by Pulitzer Prize-winning author Rick Atkinson in his book *In the Company of Soldiers*. He led his division through fierce fighting south of Baghdad, in Karbala, Hilla and Najaf. A Newsweek story stated, "It's widely accepted that no force worked harder to win Iraqi hearts and minds than the 101st Air Assault led by Petraeus."

During the formal MNF-I change of command, Secretary of Defense Robert Gates stated that Petraeus "played a historic role" and created the "translation of great strategy into a great success in very difficult circumstances." Secretary Gates also told Petraeus he believed "history will regard you as one of our nation's greatest battle captains." He is the most decorated U.S. Army soldier since Col. David Hackworth. His awards include Defense Distinguished Service Medal (two awards), Army Distinguished Service Medal (two awards), Defense Superior Service Medal (two awards), Legion of Merit (four awards), Bronze Star Medal (with "V" Valor), Defense Meritorious Service Medal and numerous other campaign awards.

Leadership Story

When General David H. Petraeus assumed command of the Iraq war in 2007, he had accepted a challenge few thought even Petraeus, a rising star, could meet, that of turning around the longest and most troubled war in American history. Iraq is only part of the story, however. His influence continued to expand beyond that battlefield proving ground; it shaped issues relating to foreign policy, defense strategy, and military doctrine. Petraeus's leadership and global influence is so highly respected that President Obama asked him to assume command of the International Security Assistance Force, Afghanistan, in June 2010. This required Petraeus to step down from his position as the Commanding General of U.S. Central Command, where he oversaw over 200,000 Soldiers, Sailors, Airmen and civilians in a theater that spans 20 countries and includes two combat zones. Yet in spite of his narrower focus on Afghanistan and its neighbors, he continues to wield considerable influence across the globe. The President's choice of Petraeus for arguably the nation's most pressing foreign policy issue reflected great trust and confidence in Petraeus's ability to help turn the war effort around through his soldier-scholar-diplomat approach to leadership. Whatever the fate of current military operations, Petraeus's influence on the military – on doctrine, leadership development, and the next generation of leaders – will be felt for years to come.

Petraeus first entered the public spotlight when he was recognized for the adaptive leadership he modeled while serving as the Commanding General of the 101st Airborne (Air Assault) Division in the initial invasion of Iraq in 2003. He was lauded as one of the first field leaders to understand the changing threat environment in Iraq and transition from conventional warfare to full spectrum operations, including non-kinetic stabilization and population-centric counterinsurgency activities. Ultimately, his Division's actions served as a model for other units across Iraq. Drawing from these experiences, in 2006 he led the effort from the Army's Schoolhouse at Fort Leavenworth to galvanize many of the military innovations necessary to retool the American military for counterinsurgency warfare, including the rewrite of the Army and Marine Corps' operational counterinsurgency doctrine, (Field Manual 3-24). This manual served as a guide for the 150,000 forces stationed in Iraq as they sought to stabilize the country.

When Petraeus then returned to Iraq in February 2007 to assume command of MNF-I, he was taken aback by the horrific damage caused by sectarian displacement, and the escalation in militia violence and rampant killing. Most of these negative trends were steadily rising (see chart below). America's tolerance for the war was waning. The future seemed austere. In one month, for example, over 50 dead bodies surfaced from sectarian violence. In another month, there were over 60 car bombs, many of which were detonated in busy market centers – inflicting maximum civilian casualties. The task before him was daunting. Yet within a year after implementing the surge of troops and establishing a theater-wide mandate for population-centric operations (the "Petraeus Doctrine"), Petraeus and the multi-national forces were able to create pockets of stability and reduce the sectarian violence through "persistent presence" and cooperation with exasperated Iraqis who wanted peace. These multiple initiatives converged to create a more peaceful and secure space in which Iraqis could make political progress and stability could give birth to political reconciliation.

How the military prepared Petraeus to resolve difficult missions or situations.

Nature and nurture both played roles in Petraeus's development. He was the son of a results-oriented Dutch sea captain who imbued him with athleticism, a fierce work ethic, and ambitious drive. Petraeus learned to embrace a love of reading and academia from his mother, a well-educated librarian. He went on to graduate in the top of his West Point class and was honor graduate in his Ranger School class and Infantry Officer Basic Course.

Identified as a rising star as a junior officer, Petraeus was often selected for the best jobs along the conventional Infantryman's path. Chosen to attend graduate school at Princeton and teach at the U.S. Military Academy, Petraeus judges both experiences as formative events in his life and turning points where he "raised his nose from the grindstone," and gained a broader perspective on the non-military instruments of national power. That truly began his "soldier-scholar" journey.

Petraeus's exposure to real-world operations heavily influenced his leadership developmental path. Three short but key deployments to regional conflicts and crisis were central to shaping his approach to post-invasion operations in Iraq.

The first tour, in Central America in 1987, complemented the counterinsurgency research upon which Petraeus had embarked for his Princeton dissertation – a study about the American military and lessons of Vietnam. While on loan from teaching at West Point, then-Major Petraeus traveled on temporary duty to U.S. Southern Command and experienced a theater involved in numerous small wars, some of which shared characteristics to operations in Vietnam. The opportunity to participate in the planning and execution of counterinsurgency and security force assistance operations in El Salvador, Honduras, and Nicaragua reinforced for him that conflicts involving war fought among the people, were the new military "paradigm."

The second tour was to Haiti in 1995. Haiti had experienced a coup and the country had devolved into violent and sanctioned repression. Following the U.S. military's response to the violence, the U.N. Mission in Haiti assumed command and control of stability operations. Selected to participate in stability operations and peacekeeping assignments, then-Colonel Petraeus worked as the United Nations U3/Operations officer. The selection was not completely fortuitous; prior to the deployment to Haiti, Petraeus had been serving his War College year at Georgetown. There, he had the opportunity to contribute to the development of Presidential Decision Directive-56, which laid a critical foundation for complex interagency operations. The U.N. mission provided him with the opportunity to implement the directive. His was a small contribution, but it provided great preparation for his future work on the Joint Interagency Task Force in Bosnia and later in Iraq and CENTCOM.

Third, when deployed to Bosnia-Herzegovina in 2001-02 to serve as both the Assistant Chief of Staff for Operations of the NATO Stabilization Force and Deputy Commander of a post-9/11 entity, the Joint Interagency Task Force for Combating Terrorism, Petraeus crossed a figurative bridge into the subversive worlds of transnational terrorists and war criminals. It was clear after 9/11 that non-state actors presented a rising and direct threat to U.S. national security at home and abroad. Their decentralized structures, informal and formal logistics networks, and ability to merge with and hide among civilian populations made them extremely difficult targets. Learning these lessons in Bosnia in 2002 provided Petraeus a perspective on the normative and essential role that joint interagency and international intelligence and security efforts must play in responding to such non-state threats.

These three field deployments exposed Petraeus to the full spectrum of "operations other than war" and the demand for a collective interagency response. They complemented the soldier-scholar's study of international relations and his experience from assignments with the conventional infantry and helped prepare him for the difficult leadership challenges he faced in Iraq, at CENTCOM and now faces in Afghanistan.

Petraeus conveys a consistent message regarding the challenges of dealing with those difficult leadership decisions. "In my view, a strategic leader of any organization or group has a solemn obligation to make sound and ethical decisions, and to do so based on a continuous cycle of learning. That obligation necessarily charges leaders with four critical tasks: get the big ideas right, communicate the big ideas, oversee their implementation, and institutionalize the changes through the capture of best practices." These leadership mantras have served as simple but valuable guides for Petraeus, whether he was serving at the operational level on the battlefield or involved in the geopolitical landscape. Petraeus explains what each task entails.

The first and most difficult task of strategic leadership is master the "the task of getting the big ideas right." Developing the right intellectual constructs to guide the organization's approach is critical. This requires the organization's senior leaders to think creatively and critically about complex challenges and to embrace new concepts in addition to constantly testing one's assumptions and basic thinking." Petraeus states that big ideas come from a "focused process in which strategic leaders and their key advisors collaboratively develop those ideas over time, analyzing, refining, evaluating, and challenging" their concepts to converge on the right ones. Though Petraeus drew on his experiences in Central America, Haiti, and Bosnia, he knew there was no single model that would work well in Iraq. "Big ideas don't fall out of a tree and hit you in the head like Newton's apple; rather, they tend to start as kernels of little ideas – and they are then gradually developed, augmented, and refined through the process of analysis, study, and discussion." The big ideas– such as securing and living amongst the population and promoting Iraqi reconciliation - were crucial for stabilizing Iraq, just as getting the big ideas right is critical for any large organizational undertaking. "In fact," says Petraeus, "if one doesn't succeed in getting the big ideas right in an effort like Iraq, operational plans will be built on shaky or even flawed foundations. And, in that case, no amount of additional troops or other resources will produce success." Complementary to getting the big idea right, leaders must create a "culture of learning" to foster innovative thinking needed to meet this objective.

While getting the big ideas right is critical, simply developing them is not enough, according to Petraeus. The next crucial task of a strategic leader is to communicate those ideas. Communication helps leaders to educate others and ideally motivates those individuals to embrace the big ideas. To be most effective, communication should flow in multiple directions. For those in uniform, "it should flow upward through the chain of command, outward through coalition partners, interagency elements, and the press, and downward through our units and staffs." The most important of these, in Petraeus's mind, is downward: communicating the big ideas throughout the breadth and depth of one's organization. "That's what matters most, as it is the leaders and units within the organization that will turn the big ideas into reality on the ground," he states. Effective communication is a matter of identifying and using every one of the means available for strategic leaders to share the message.

In Iraq, communication of the new big ideas began the first day Petraeus took command. Petraeus was adamant about serving as his own "communications officer," rather than relying exclusively on the public affairs team. He made an effort to rapidly incorporate the new ideas into the joint military and civilian campaign plans and communicate them through a host of speeches, command letters, presentations at commanders' conferences, and briefings to superiors and higher headquarters, press conferences and press releases, meetings with high-level visitors, and even Congressional hearings. Weaving key ideas into every possible communication opportunity and forum reinforced the concepts throughout and even beyond his organization. Over time, his "relentless communication" of the big ideas—took hold, and those responsible for executing them – whom Petraeus believes are the most important audience – came to understand what the organization was trying to do and why.

Without proper execution, getting the big ideas right and communicating them effectively are for naught. Thus, strategic leaders should personally oversee the conduct of operations, establish a presence at various points of decision, and observe various activities first hand. In some cases, strategic leaders must conduct or direct operations, and identify and eliminate obstacles to the successful execution.

"Implementing big ideas typically requires empowering people and organizations to execute the ideas at their levels without the need for constant approval. All insurgencies are local – so all counterinsurgency operations must be fine-tuned to local circumstances as well. Consequently, leaders at lower levels have to be empowered to operationalize such big ideas as securing the population, promoting reconciliation, employing money as a weapon system, and so on in ways that work for their local circumstances." This is precisely what Petraeus and his team sought to do in Iraq, empowering brigade and battalion commanders in particular, but also the so-called strategic lieutenants – "strategic" because these young leaders at tactical levels often took actions with strategic consequences. In so doing, he sought to enable those leaders to turn big ideas at his level into real action at their level.

Finally, as mission results materialize, Petraeus admonishes that it is the responsibility of strategic leaders to ensure that best practices are captured, shared, and, where appropriate, institutionalized. The long-term effectiveness of any organization -- whether a military unit, a civilian government agency, or a business -- depends on its ability to identify and institutionalize adaptations that have proven effective and need widespread implementation. Organizations should strive to be "learning organizations," lest adversaries and competitors prove more adaptive.

Petraeus states that his instinct as a commander, when facing a crisis, is to "observe the situation, determine what direction he might give or choose and to provide a good example to his troopers." Petraeus is quick to admonish, however, that a "higher-level commander has to keep in mind that he should avoid getting so decisively engaged in a tactical action that he jeopardizes his ability to perform his operational-level duties." When leaders decide on a course of action, they should provide intent and oversight, but avoid micromanagement while the rest of the team executes. As a commander, Petraeus seeks to maintain broad situational awareness. Petraeus's instinctual behavior is to seek out the point at which he can best observe the situation in which his unit is engaged and orient himself for decision-making. In these situations, what remains constant is the commander's need to lead by example and provide guidance in dynamic situations. What is not constant is the "point of decision." Variability is based on the leader's level of authority and the operational environment, according to Petraeus. "In conventional military operations, this point would be where the kinetic operations are the most significant, such as when the bullets start flying. In irregular warfare, the point of decision becomes less obvious. It might be the negotiations over an Iraqi 'Awakening Movement,' it might be a particular place in a tactical ground operation, it could be a command post at which all the information on a particularly distributed operation is fused." Petraeus, while commander of CENTCOM, reflected that "the key location can be anywhere from Washington, D.C., to some location in the 20-country region." And as commander of ISAF, he is careful to delegate authority to his regional commanders and other key subordinates: "A strategic leader must be careful not to usurp the authority of key subordinate commanders or complicate the efforts of our nation's diplomatic representative; still, he must actively push the envelope enough to keep issues moving and be as effective as is possible." Petraeus acknowledges that in today's information age, and especially in a command that is across the globe from Washington, D.C., a lot of what one does at his level is actually performed via cyberspace, video teleconference, phone calls, etc., so physical location isn't always the most important issue. "In fact," he says, "mental location or intellectual attention can actually be most important in some cases -- not just for me, but for our staff and other staffs, as well. There is only so much intellectual energy, and physical energy to go around. And you have to commit it thoughtfully and help one's bosses, partners, and subordinates focus it properly."

The lessons for the corporate world are obvious. Leadership in the public or private sector requires developing a vision for the big ideas, communicating these ideas to the team, overseeing their implementation and empowering subordinates for action, institutionalizing the best practices, and continuing to adapt. Leaders must set the example and lead from the front. "Take your performance personally; if you are proud to be average, so will your troops," Petraeus coaches his subordinates. Leaders are responsible for setting the tone, being the first with truth, living the organizational values, and creating a culture that rewards initiative and innovation to achieve these goals. Leaders should seek to do this through carefully chosen physical and mental presence.

In addition to learning how to make difficult decisions from Petraeus's example, the corporate world may also adopt some useful insights from an exploration of the characteristic inherent in the Petraeus model. His leadership model embodies the Army's definition of leadership, the process of influencing people by providing purpose, direction, and motivation while operating to accomplish the mission and improving the organizations.

Petraeus considers professional expertise one of the most critical leadership characteristics. Maintaining expertise in one's profession allows a leader to make informed decisions about the big ideas as well as "walk the talk." Without knowing the capabilities or limits of one's organization and people, a leader cannot properly design a vision, communicate goals, or oversee execution. Many examples illustrate this belief. As a brigade commander, then-COL Petraeus used to drill his subordinates through constant trivia questions during staff meetings, "walk and shoot university" field exercises, and any "down time" the unit had while in transit or in a queue. He frequently admonishes subordinates to research and write about their profession, as he has done since a junior officer. He encourages them to ground themselves in the study of military history, and review of lessons learned through group after action reviews and introspection.

A second critical leadership characteristic has to do with a leader's energy. Petraeus believes in leading from the front and setting the example with the goal of motivating people both inside and outside the chain of command to pursue actions, focus thinking, and shape decisions for the greater good of the organization. One of Petraeus's favorite axioms further summarizes his mentality: "In the absence of guidance or orders, figure out what should be done and do it." This "self-starter" attitude complements the sheer energy and determination he exudes as he embraces leadership challenges.

Petraeus also seeks to attract and empower young leaders with similar qualities; in part, because he believes that subordinate leaders are the key to organizational success. Petraeus places great value on teammates who can "think critically, reason and write clearly and concisely, embody a strong work ethic, bring experience and knowledge to inform the mission, and demonstrate interpersonal skills." Most of these characteristics are obvious force multipliers, but his emphasis on interpersonal skills perhaps embodies one of his own unique approaches to leadership and development of subordinates. "The idea of trying to bring out the best in everyone – and in trying to create conditions and a culture that value pursuing excellence are critical." and 'being all you can be' is a very good description of what I've always tried to do." This can be accomplished indirectly by setting the example and directly through mentoring.

Mentoring can have a critical effect on the performance of the mentored as far as improving job performance, socializing career-oriented personnel to organizational norms and leadership positions, preparing future leaders via exposure to higher-level decision-making, and facilitating upward mobility through sponsorship. In those regards, Petraeus benefited immensely from his own mentors. Now, with an open door (and open-email) policy, he actively works to be a mentor and finds unique ways to influence others, including encouraging young leaders to fill challenging leadership billets or study in civilian graduate school or by helping wounded warriors find their pathway to peace.

Petraeus running with a wounded warrior

Regardless of the objective, Petraeus's preferred venue for mentoring is through physical training. Petraeus firmly believes that one's "body is the ultimate weapon system. Take care of it and inspire others to do likewise. The fastest way to generate respect within an organization is to demonstrate to its members that you are in better shape than they are." Petraeus uses the "tool" of physical fitness sessions to promote unit camaraderie, get to know subordinates, and glean information from subordinates. As a Colonel in the 82nd Airborne Division, he used the tool often. At a mentoring session, Petraeus once asked his soldiers to name the number one leadership priority of the brigade. The soldiers gave answers relating to integrity and infantry tactics only to learn that Petraeus's answer was physical fitness. The brigade thought Petraeus was joking until he then lead his soldiers through a highly intensive 75-minute exercise drill every morning. Soon his point became clear: The workouts drove the brigade to greater strength, alertness, and pride in their unit. The same self-discipline, ability to perform under pressure, and pushing oneself outside the comfort zone served as keys to inspire and empower subordinates to "be all they could be." Whether encouraging self-development through education, pursuit of challenging assignments and the concomitant exposure they provide young leaders, or mentoring and inspiring others to truly be all they can be, Petraeus pushes himself as well as his teammates to get more out themselves and their organizations every step of the way.

# # #

Paula Broadwell, Major, U.S. Army Reserve, is the author of, *An Intellectual Biography of General David Petraeus* and works closely with General Petraeus on this authorized biography. She is a Research Associate at the Harvard Center for Public Leadership. As a military reserve officer, she serves as an associate professor through the Army Reserves in the Social Sciences Department at West Point. Prior to her current pursuits, Paula served as the Deputy Director, Jebsen Center for Counter-Terrorism Studies at the Fletcher School, Tufts University. Paula has served in various military intelligence roles on active and reserve Army duty. In her 14 years of military service, she has focused on intelligence and counter terrorism missions with the Defense Intelligence Agency, Special Operations Command, and FBI Joint Terrorism Task Forces in support of Operation Iraqi Freedom and U.S. Northern Command homeland security programs.

Paula is a Ph.D. candidate in the War Studies Department, Kings College, University of London. Paula received an MBA degree from Harvard in international organizational management and behavior economics and an MA and certificate in international security and conflict resolution from the University of Denver's Korbel School of International Studies. Paula is also a graduate of Army Command and General Staff College. She received a BS in systems engineering, graduating with honors, from United States Military Academy.

Chapter 3

Daniel O'Shea

Commander, U.S. Navy Reserve

"It is by no means enough that an officer of the Navy should be a capable mariner, but also a great deal more. He should be as well a gentleman of liberal education, refined manners, punctilious courtesy and the nicest sense of personal honor."
— *John Paul Jones, 1775, Captain, Continental Navy*

Profile

Commander Dan O'Shea

Daniel O'Shea - CEO/President – Daniel Risk Mitigation. Mr. O'Shea is Founder and President of Daniel Risk Mitigation (Daniel Risk), a security risk consultancy. An asymmetric warfare specialist with extensive overseas and combat experience, O'Shea is a recognized subject matter expert in terrorism, travel safety and kidnapping mitigation strategies.

O'Shea established and served as the Coordinator of the Hostage Working Group (HWG), at the U.S. Embassy in Baghdad Iraq until April 2006. HWG was the U.S. Mission's primary planning facilitator, intelligence fusion node, and coordinating element for all hostage-taking incidents in Iraq. He arrived at the height of the hostage-taking campaign targeting foreigners that averaged more than 40 per month; by the end of his service, foreign kidnappings in Iraq were in single digits with only one foreigner reported taken, in each of the last two months of his tour.

O'Shea is a qualified Navy SEAL officer and Commander (O-5) in the U.S. Navy Reserve. Following the attacks of September 11, O'Shea was voluntarily recalled to active duty and served as a special operations liaison and staff planning officer assigned to the U.S. Central Command (USCENTCOM) headquarters during the wartime planning and execution of Operation Enduring Freedom (OEF) and Operation Iraqi Freedom (OIF).

Dan O'Shea is an Associate Fellow and lecturer at the Joint Special Operations University. A published writer and frequent interview subject for CNN, the BBC, Wall Street Journal, New York Times and numerous other publications. He is a consulting producer for a Discovery Channel series on the global hostage-taking crisis to air in 2011.

He received the Navy League's 2007 MERITORIOUS CITATION the organization's highest award given to individuals who have made significant contributions to the improvement of national security. O'Shea was awarded a Joint Special Operations University Associate Fellowship to publish *Combating Hostage Terrorism* in 2010.

Leadership Story

As a newly sworn in Midshipman on Induction Day at Annapolis, my education in "leadership" began immediately. A morning that started in khakis and Oxford button-down was exchanged for a navy issue sailor "cracker "jack-style" uniform and my hair shorn to a buzz cut. Still confused and adjusting to my sudden transition from the civilian to the military world, I was assembled with the rest of 27th Platoon, India Company in a large classroom auditorium. Standing before the most recently inducted members of the U.S. Navy, was a senior and First Class Midshipmen or "Firstie." He was smartly dressed in the standard

Academy uniform of the day. All black, pressed slacks with a form fitting, button-down open collar dress shirt. On his collar were gold insignia with a five-bar device signifying the rank of Midshipman Commander. Written on the black chalkboard behind the Brigade Honor Chairman was the Naval Academy's Honor Concept: *"Midshipmen will not lie, cheat or steal..."*

He spoke about the Naval Academy's Honor Concept evolution, which was originally modeled on West Point's strict Honor Code. Spearheaded in 1952 by Midshipmen First Class H. Ross Perot, Perot stated, "Honor, personal integrity, and loyalty to the service, its customs and its traditions, are fundamental characteristics essential to a successful Naval Officer." The impetus was to transition from a strict code based on fear to one based on the desire do the right thing the Chairman explained before posing the question:

> *"What serves the nation better, officers who blindly follow a code or those who chose the harder right in a free decision?"*

He continued, "Military members must recognize the need to follow orders, but it is also our responsibility to train officers capable of making sound decisions in the absence of orders or specific guidance. You won't be able to refer to a rulebook when flying an F-14 Tomcat or leading Marines into battle. You will have to trust your judgment to make correct decisions and take personal responsibility for your actions. You won't always have full details in advance, but you will be expected to perform and execute your mission."

He then picked up the pamphlet we all received as we entered the room, and read aloud, "In 1898 when the Spanish and American War broke out, President McKinley needed to get a message to Garcia, the leader of the Cuban rebels to immediately secure their support. The problem was how. Garcia and his guerrillas were hiding in the mountainous hinterland of the island. With no telegraph or mail delivery and no means to reach him. Someone said to the President, 'There's a fellow by the name of Rowan who will find Garcia for you, if anybody can.'

Rowan was sent for and given a letter to be delivered to Garcia. Rowan took the letter and did not ask, 'where is he at?' nor did he ask "how" to deliver the message, because he understood the implied. It would be entirely up to his individual initiative, guile and resolve to complete the mission. Rowan took the letter, sealed it up in an oil-skin pouch, strapped it over his heart, in four days landed by night off the coast of Cuba from an open boat, disappeared into the jungle, and in three weeks came out on the other side of the island, having traversed a hostile country on foot, and having delivered his letter to Garcia.

At this point, the Honor Chairman looked up, "Your first reading assignment at the Naval Academy is, 'Message to Garcia'; it is also the first leadership lesson you will need to learn in order to graduate from the Academy and be successful in your career. That lesson is self-reliance and failure is not an option attitude no matter what obstacles are presented." Rowan completed his mission despite overwhelming odds by relying completely on self-initiative and instinct after accepting the challenge. Rowan was an 1881 West Point graduate whose "sense of personal honor" compelled him to accept a seemingly impossible assignment without protest or question. Thousands of West Point and Annapolis graduates before and after Rowan's heroic service have been put in similar situations and answered the call to duty without hesitation.

* * *

On July 5, 2005 when a "Troops in Contact" (TIC) call came into the Tactical Operations Center from a four-man Navy SEAL reconnaissance element under fire, Lieutenant Commander (LCDR) Erik Kristensen, a 1995 Annapolis grad and Task Unit Commander for a Naval Special Warfare Task Force (NSWTU), responded immediately and assembled a Quick Reaction Force (QRF). LCDR Kristensen was on the helicopter that was shot down during the attempted rescue mission in the rugged mountainous area in northeastern Afghanistan on the Pakistan border. Like the 15 other SEALs and Army air crew also on board, LCDR Kristensen "gave the last full measure of devotion" for his brothers in arms and "Operation Enduring Freedom." Their heroic sacrifice was later recounted in the bestselling novel "Lone Survivor" by Marcus Lutrell, the only member to come back alive. LCDR Kristensen and the others, died living by a warrior code and time-honored vow that a SEAL, dead or alive has never been left behind on a field of battle. LCDR Kristensen and the others were all recovered and buried with full military honors.

"Honor as a way of life" is not a military nicety but a mission requirement. The Army-Navy rivalry or debating the merits or faults of an Honor "Code" verses a "Concept" is not the important take-away fundamental of a Service Academy education. The Academies and all commissioning sources strive to inculcate within an individual the personal sense of honor to accept a mission, even at the risk of life and limb, as a moral duty and fundamental belief that failure is not an option. Without this sense of duty, patrols would never leave the safety of a forward operating base (FOB); helicopter pilots would not fly into hot landing zones to medevac wounded soldiers or deliver a rescue QRF into the desperate situation that confronted recently promoted Army Captain (CPT) Nate Self (West Point '98) and his Ranger element.

Early morning March 4, 2002 on Takur Ghar Mountain, Afghanistan in the opening moments of Operation Anaconda, the call came for follow-on forces to rescue an unnamed Navy SEAL who was missing in action. Without hesitation, CPT Self and his men honored their Ranger Creed that *"Surrender is not a Ranger word. I will never leave a fallen comrade to fall into the hands of the enemy..."* and inserted into a firestorm.

The battle on what became known as Robert's Ridge (named for Neil Roberts the missing SEAL) lasted hours and would be the highest-altitude combat action ever fought by American forces in history. CAPT Self's soldiers completed the "Ranger Objective" but at a tremendous cost – the lives of seven Americans – the earliest casualties of the War on Terror. Specialist Oscar Escano, a surviving member of CPT Self's Ranger QRF recounted that the tenets of the Creed are *"more than just a slogan...Rangers live by this... It is honor and respect for your comrade."* and about keeping one's word. As Nate Self recounted in an NBC Dateline interview more than three years after the incident, *"I want the legacy to be continuing the spirit of the American soldier..."* Army *Rangers*, Navy *SEALs*, Marine *Recon*, Air Force *Pararescuemen* and many others in our military today who will keep a promise even if it means making the ultimate sacrifice for a brother-in-arms or cause they believe in.

Since 9/11, seventy-five West Point graduates have made the ultimate sacrifice in the wars in Iraq and Afghanistan; nine in the class of 2004 alone, all continuing the Long Gray Line and tradition of living and dying for *Duty, Honor, Country*. These are not just West Point or Army values alone but resonate with every veteran regardless of service just as *"Non sibi sed Patriae"* Not for Self but for Country" is not the exclusive domain of the armed forces. Service above self happens every day on a battlefield but also within hospitals, at homeless shelters and in service organizations like the Rotary International.

After I graduated and served a tour in the elite Navy SEAL Teams, I lived the Navy core values: *Honor, Courage & Commitment* every day leading some of most capable warriors in the U.S. military. After I left the service for a civilian career, I discovered Navy values were as universal and timeless as the lessons of 'Message to Garcia' that self-reliance and initiative would allow one to overcome any challenge and accomplish any task.

Following the attacks of 9/11, like thousands of other Americans, I volunteered to serve in uniform again. As my two-year mobilized recall was drawing to a close, in July 2004, I accepted one more assignment for a three-month (90-day) tour in Baghdad as the Officer in Charge of the U.S. Central Command Inter-Agency (IA) cell at the American Embassy and headquarters of Multi-National Forces-Iraq (MNF-I) in Baghdad. It was only days after the Civil Provisional Authority (CPA) leadership of the international Coalition had been turned over to the U.S. Ambassador and Department of State. It was also at the height of the international hostage-taking crisis that was plaguing Iraq with routine beheadings and daily reports of kidnappings coming in every day on the news wire.

The first day on the job, at my first Embassy meeting in Saddam's former Republican Palace, I sat in as Tom Duffy, a career Foreign Service officer and former naval officer read off the daily list of action items for the department. He was passing off items to the various staff assembled when he came to the following: "Two Bulgarian truck drivers were kidnapped in Mosul ten days ago and some guy named Zarqawi is threatening to cut their heads off unless Bulgaria pulls out of the Coalition. President Bush spoke with the President of Bulgaria yesterday and promised that the U.S. would do everything in its power to save these two individuals." Duffy continued, "Well the request was passed over to Foggy Bottom and SECSTATE Powell has directed us to support the mission. Now two envoys from Bulgaria are flying into BIAP today at 1400 and we need to find someone to brief them and tell them everything we know about the case and how their people can be rescued." He then looked directly at me and stated, "Dan, you're a Navy SEAL, go call your friends."

I didn't flinch; I had been preparing for a "Message to Garcia" moment my entire life. I was not deterred when I quickly realized that an organization to handle an international kidnapping crisis did not exist; I stood the organization up myself. Within ten days of my arrival into Baghdad, a Hostage Working Group (HWG) was established at the U.S. Embassy comprised of the appropriate components from military special operations, intelligence analysts, Navy Criminal Investigative Service (NCIS), and FBI Special Agents, Coalition partners and Iraqi police investigators. HWG became the U.S. Mission's primary planning facilitator, intelligence fusion node, and coordinating element for all hostage-taking incidents in Iraq.

In 2004, the Iraqi-wide hostage-taking campaign targeting foreigners averaged more than 40 per month. By April 2006 at the end of my tour, foreign kidnappings in Iraq were in single digits with only one foreigner reported taken, in each of the last two months of my tour. As my last C-130 military flight out of Baghdad International Airport in April 2006 departed Iraqi airspace, the lasting success of the HWG was not readily apparent but the positive trend continued. Two years later, only 12 foreigners were reported taken hostage in Iraq in all of 2008.

In the years since that eventful tour, I reflected often on the personal leadership lessons learned and often asked the larger questions: *Why I was chosen and how did my background, training, and experiences to date prepare me for the most challenging assignment of my life? When the situation seemed most dire at the onset, what leadership mindset and execution strategy allows a failing situation to be reversed 180 degrees?* My rhetorical leadership *truisms* and responses throughout will provide my answers to this and other queries in the timeless debate about the leadership fundamentals.

* * *

SEAL Team THREE Echo Platoon on Combat Search and Rescue (CSAR) standby

My personal decision-making thought process when faced with a difficult challenge is summarized in a leadership philosophy that encompassed my Annapolis, SEAL Team and Ranger school experiences. It was written shortly after I completed my platoon commander tour in the Navy and during a master's program in Executive Leadership at the University of San Diego. Succinctly written, it represented the sum total of my formal leadership education, first-hand experiences leading elite military units and many lessons (and mistakes) learned along the way. As I honed my "troop leading procedures" and warrior leadership ethos I codified a "Warrior's Creed" that formed the basis of a universal team-building, decision-making operating model. Its application is not limited to the military alone and would apply to anyone facing a "difficult leadership decision." It captures a course of action for any leader looking to build a team, inspire them and lead them to a solution. Modeled on the U.S. Army Ranger School Creed, a code that present day soldiers live and die by in Iraq and Afghanistan as they defend our way of life. It pays humble respect to their legacy and Ranger fraternity that I am proud to claim membership in.

WARRIOR CREED

Who am I? I am a WARRIOR. I always *lead my team by example from the front* and I never ask someone to do something that *I would not be willing to do myself.* Before either my team or I embark on any task, *we first get clear on our mission*. I then create a plan of action with each teammate working together *to accomplish the mission.* I am more focused on *results than the methods* necessary to achieve those goals. I live by the motto, *mission first, and people always.*

Acknowledging that I am an elite member of a team of leaders, I have a special sense of duty to society. We are a force for good and we fight for what's right. I am proud of my team and our significant contributions to society. For me, it is not about the bottom line but being able to look at myself squarely in the mirror at the end of each day.

Recognizing that I choose my station in life, I am a proud volunteer. No matter what my role is on my team, I am first a team player. I will always be courteous and treat my teammates and others with dignity and respect. I am proud of my team and I will never embarrass them or let them down. I will do whatever it takes to help accomplish the mission *without seeking personal glory*.

Readily do I accept all tasks as an opportunity to excel and to raise the standard one notch higher. I *expect more out of myself* than others could ever expect because the body will achieve what the mind can conceive. The only limits to what I can do are self-imposed. I will give 100% and then some. No matter what I've done or accomplished, I will always have something left within me. *Warriors Lead the Way!*

I will always strive to win because *I train better* and *fight harder*. I thrive on challenge, accepting every obstacle in my life as an opportunity to raise the standard. Mistakes are a temporary setback and an opportunity for learning and self-improvement. The greater the challenge, the greater the reward. For me, *the only easy day was yesterday.*

One for all, all for one is the core belief I have in my team. I am loyal to my company and to each teammate who is committed to living the company's values. We trust each other with our safety, resources and reputation because we know that each teammate will do their utmost to exemplify the vision and values of our team.

Realizing that the greatest battle I face is the battle within... against self-doubt, or the fear of failure. Yet failure occurs only when I don't learn from my mistakes. I am constantly learning and moving forward in my progress toward the goal of becoming the warrior. In overcoming all the challenges in my life, be it in my work or personal relationships, *I will either find a way or make a way because failure is not an option...*

* * *

Corporate leaders do not need to experience combat or survive the rigors of Navy SEAL training or U.S. Army Ranger School to have a warrior leadership perspective or philosophy. Leaders of character, integrity and selfless service to others are not found solely from the military ranks, but come from every walk of life. Leadership fundamentals expressed in the Warrior Creed are basic dictums, common sense principles and should be recognizable by any individual in a position of influence or management role. Leading by example, soliciting input, gaining consensus with others and articulating the desired outcomes are team-building basics. Taking responsibility, accepting risk, demonstrating loyalty, treating others with respect are operating values of any high functioning team. Being a warrior leader is more about "leading" than warfare.

Leaders set the expectation and vision, charting the course for his or her followers. Foremost a leader understands what the mission is and what will be required to accomplish the objective, targets or meet the benchmarks. State up front what your mission and priorities are. The original draft of the Hostage Working Group charter was stated bottom line up front.

> <u>Our MISSION is to facilitate the recovery of hostages</u>. We advise and make recommendations to the U.S. Ambassador on actions to deter, prevent, and be prepared to respond to hostage-taking incidents. To be a force multiplier by integrating all elements of national and regional power, diplomacy, intelligence, law enforcement, and military forces to bear as hostage situations develop in the Iraqi Theater of Operations (ITO). HWG Priorities are:
>
> 1) Safe release of hostages
> 2) Prevention of future incidents
> 3) Bring hostage takers (HTs) to justice

Be clear on the mission and guidance you give your team. It doesn't have to be a flowery mission statement that no one can recite from memory. It should be a mantra. A simple one-line phrase that will resonate with everyone is the goal. "FIND A WAY... OR MAKE ONE" represented more than a motto for the Hostage Working Group – it was the defining operating principle in everything we did to establish and run the organization.

* * *

The month I arrived in Baghdad, July 2004, there were 31 international kidnappings of non-Iraqi hostages, in August there were 46, in September the victim count increased to 56. The situation seemed hopeless but that changed with the difference warrior leadership makes. It is fundamental that leaders believe they can make a difference and when a cause seems lost, they become the catalyst for that change. Throughout my training, when a situation turned for the worse, SEAL or Ranger instructors would constantly harp, "it's a leadership problem sir," and expect you to solve the dilemma. "Leadership solves problems" still echoes in my mind as a fundamental truism. Leaders are paid to make decisions and expected to make the tough calls in order to turn deteriorating situations around. There is no problem-set too large or crisis to complex that the right attitude and leadership can't solve. History provides plenty of precedence and role models.

The Iraqi kidnapping crisis was a metaphor for everything that was going wrong in Iraq during the insurgency that ravaged the country from 2004 to 2006. It prompted pundits to write off Iraq as an unmitigated failure. A change in leadership and approach marked the arrival of General David Petraeus and his counter-insurgency (COIN) "Surge" campaign. Petraeus and his key staff argued for and executed a revised U.S. Army and U.S. Marine Corps COIN strategy that called for "protection of the civilian populace as the center of gravity" to turn the tide in the insurgency campaign for the hearts and minds for the Iraqi population. The legacy of that decision proved that the right leader, strategy and team can re-write history.

Appropriately, the Hostage Working Group (HWG) adopted "find a way or make one" as its operating philosophy. It was the personal motto of Hannibal, the Carthaginian General who led his army and 40 war elephants over the Alps to face off against Rome, his sworn enemy. Like its philosophical role model - HWG succeeded despite tremendous odds. Hannibal's enemy was Rome; HWG's were the insurgency-led kidnapping gangs. How each organization accomplished its mission was different but there were shared perspectives, principles and philosophies that are timeless and universal. Hannibal's army overcame the seemingly insurmountable snowcapped mountain range and the odds because he followed fundamental leadership maxims. Adopting leadership principles embodied by Hannibal allows me to answer the question about the *three (3) most important leadership characteristics of a successful leader.*

Characteristic of all charismatic field marshals, Hannibal accomplished his mission by sheer force of will and an unfailing belief in self (personal ability), service (defense of his nation), and his soldiers (his people, whose burdens he shared as an equal). As a young boy, Hannibal accompanied his father Hamilcar, the commanding general during the Carthaginian's failed first Punic War campaign against Rome. After Carthage was forced to sue for peace, Hannibal witnessed firsthand the loss of Carthage possessions and preeminence in the Mediterranean and the seed of revenge was planted. Hamilcar had Hannibal swear an oath to defend Carthage and declare Rome his mortal enemy. Hannibal crossed the Alps with an army of 50,000 troops and 40 war elephants through narrow snow-choked passes in the Pyrenees – more than 7,000 feet in elevation, to invade Rome. For fifteen years, he defeated every Roman army he faced in Italy by living off the land, spoils of war and surviving by tactical intelligence. It was said, *"He never required others to do what he could not and would not do himself."* Hannibal's innate leadership ability, total commitment to country and cause above self, and his ability to fuse that same passion in his men were the keys to his success against overwhelming odds.

Like Hannibal's vow to his father to defend Carthage, I had taken an oath that every commissioned officer takes to defend America against all enemies, foreign and domestic. That enemy was an Iraqi insurgency that utilized kidnapping as an asymmetric warfare force multiplier to fund terrorist attacks against Coalition soldiers and Iraqi civilians alike. An oath signifies a public statement of personal commitment and obligation to a cause regardless of what it may cost. No matter the challenge, an officer takes personal responsibility, and knows he will be held accountable for his actions. Dealing with Iraq's hostage crisis became my mission, to which I dedicated my personal reputation, devoted my service and developed a team of committed adherents.

The Hostage Working Group (HWG) evolved out of an initial effort to address an international kidnapping case that resulted in the murder of two innocent truck drivers who were simply supporting their families back home in Bulgaria. Their deaths, like so many others on 9/11 were the driving motivator for me to return to military service and why I volunteered to extend my service with the HWG. The driving priorities of our organization were simple:

1) Rescue/recovery of all hostages,
2) Prevention of future kidnapping
3) Bring those responsible to justice

We did not discriminate between cases--treating international and Iraqi cases with the same sense of urgency that we did American citizens or AMCITs. This approach was not initially embraced by everyone within the U.S. government but quickly earned a reputation within the multinational Coalition and local community that HWG was here to help bring loved ones home to their family. Hundreds of Intel analysts, law enforcement officers, diplomats, and military veterans, from many nations, dedicated countless hours, performed beyond their assigned duties to support our efforts and helped us turn the tide against the kidnapping scourge. *Service above self, mission first and people always*, were the underlying motivators for membership in the HWG and why we never lacked for volunteers.

* * *

Individual in positions of power and influence who are responsible to society and hold a special covenant to the greater good of the community over than their own wellbeing or interests are what separate divine monarchs from despotic kings, statesmen from politicians, and leaders from managers. While dictators' demagogue, plunder and profit for self-interests, visionaries inspire, lead, and serve a cause greater than self. An unfailing belief in one's own abilities, service to a noble cause and people who believe in your leadership is an unbeatable combination. Chairman of the Joint Chiefs, Admiral Michael Mullen at the October 31, 2008, Central Command (CENTCOM) Change of Command, speaking of the role played by General David Petraeus, "Fired the minds of generations to understand the true purpose of power as a force for good..."

I believe leaders are a developed quality, whose innate charismatic skills are honed and sharpened by the sum total of their education, training, trials-by-fire, mistakes and learning moments. Many leaders believe they are called to lead and have a sense of destiny about the "command" path, which they have intentionally chosen. Usually the road less travelled by others, because leading inherently means accepting more responsibility and risk.

I had always assumed that my path from Annapolis to Basic Underwater Demolition/SEAL (BUD/S) training and later Army Ranger School was in preparation to lead a team of Navy SEALs on covert combat missions but real world operations were in short supply in the 1990s. I originally left the Navy after my platoon commander tour and only returned to service after the attacks of 9/11. I spent two years as a special operations planner and staff officer at U.S. Central Command (CENTCOM) higher headquarters (HQ) far away from the sound of guns mostly in Tampa, Florida and Qatar at the forward CENTCOM HQ. My last set of military orders was a 90-day assignment to serve at the U.S. Embassy and Multi-National Forces- Iraq command in Baghdad. A random tasking my first day on the job changed everything and became the assignment I had been preparing for my entire career and I ended up staying nearly two years to finish the mission.

From its inception, the HWG espoused the "failure is not an option" ethos of the unconventional, elite special operations forces or "SOF". Traditional SOF consists of U.S. Army Special Forces, Rangers, and U.S. Navy SEALs. Due to the collective SOF community's reputation as having the most physically and mentally challenging selection process, be it BUD/S, Ranger school or the Special Forces Qualification or "Q" Course, successful graduates usually consist of the top performers of each respective service. The 70 to 80% attrition rates alone means only the most committed in body, mind and motivation survive the indoctrination process. When a nation's survival depends upon a select few at the tip of the spear, the process is meant to be Darwinian and has historical precedent. *Yet where and how does a nation develop her youth to become her staunchest defenders and leaders willing to make the ultimate sacrifice to preserve a nation's sovereignty?*

"We must remember that one man is much the same as another, and that he is best who is trained in the severest school."

– *Thucydides, "History of the Peloponnesian War"* (431-404 B.C.)

Nearly every society in history has had an elite training academy for the warrior class upon which a military builds its ranks and leadership infrastructure upon and nationalistic core to protect society, preserve her culture and promote her values. The end-state product is a warrior who routinely seeks out and accepts the most demanding (and dangerous) assignments as a means to validate his quest in life to be the very best in his profession of arms. This "mission-quest" for SOF operators shares a universal warrior lineage that traces its origins to the Greek ideal of *"Arête"* – the pursuit of excellence and living up to one's full potential. In the ancient Greece city-state of Sparta, it meant courage and strength in the face of adversity or battle. For young male Spartans, the path to arête began at the *"agōgē,"* a rigorous education and arduous military training commune. Competing in daily athletic competitions and military battle drills, the regime cultivated loyalty to and dependence upon one's peers, allegiance to the state above personal interests and produced individuals who were indifferent to suffering or pain. The result produced physically and morally superior males and the elite of Spartan's warrior cult society. Today's supremacy of Western ideals (rule of law, separation of Church and State, individual rights, etc.) and democratic principles over autocratic rule and state repression owes its success to 300 chosen Spartan Hoplite warriors who defended the pass at Thermopylae against a Persian horde estimated at more than 300,000 in 480 BC. The Persians were led by Xerxes, a self-declared Zoroastrian demi-god monarch, who intended to add the Peloponnesian archipelago to his list of conquered territories forced to submit to his divine rule. 1,000 to 1 odds would normally overwhelm any defensive advantage, but the Spartans held out for three days. It would prove to be a Pyrrhic victory for Xerxes as Athens was able to evacuate and survive. The democratic Greek city-state model that flourished and evolved into today's nation state was not pre-ordained. It was only due to the sacrifice of these Spartans who held off a vastly greater force allowing the other

Greek states crucial time to gather military might, prepare their defense and ultimately build a fleet that won the naval battle of Salamis and the strategic victory against the Persians on the plains of Plataea a year later. The Battle of Thermopylae remains a case study of the advantages of superior training, equipment and individual soldiers as force multipliers and symbol of steadfast courage against impossible odds.

> *"The bravest are surely those who have the clearest vision of what is before them, glory and danger alike, and yet notwithstanding, go out to meet it."*
> — *Thucydides.*

The modern day Spartan Hoplite is today's SOF warrior. On constant deployment since 9/11, the elite of our nation's military represents the tip of the spear that engages our enemy in close quarters combat, and sometimes hand-to-hand not unlike their historical Greek hoplite, Roman legionnaire or Samurai predecessors. SOF operator's account for less than 1% of the total inventory of American military forces yet have disproportionately shouldered our nation's post 9/11 burdens and taken the fight directly to al Qaeda, and the Taliban. Two out of the five Medals of Honor, our nation's highest award for valor have been awarded to the SOF community since 9/11 – Navy SEALs Lieutenant Michael Murphy and Petty Officer Michael Mansoor. SEALs have earned six out of seven Navy Crosses awarded to Navy personnel and both Air Force Crosses were given to Air Force special operations personnel. Valorous awards for Army Special Forces and Rangers number in the hundreds. Many of our SOF peers have made the ultimate sacrifice. Like the original 300 Spartans, we are all are called to accept any sacrifice of life and limb to defend our country and way of life. Our finest intrinsically understand that the West is fighting a menace from the east that has risen again in the form of Islamic extremism that seeks to reestablish the Caliphate and enforce Sharia (religious) law. Today's Navy SEAL, Air Force Para-rescue/Combat Controller, Army Green Beret and Ranger lives by the spirit of a Spartan warrior proverb *"This is my Shield. I bear it before me in battle, but it is not mine alone. It protects my brother on my left; it protects my city. I will never let them out of its shadow, nor my city out of its shelter..."*

When I arrived in the summer of 2004, there was no U.S. government hostage response manual to reference so much of the initial effort was trial and error. I was personally tasked by the Deputy Chief of Mission, Ambassador James Jefferys to formalize the U.S. response to the evolving (and growing) kidnapping crisis and thus the Hostage Working Group was established. What started as an ad hoc response to an urgent crisis evolved into a complex organizational challenge, one that included navigating through a non-pyramidal structure and a web of reporting chains of command that went all the way back to Central Command in Tampa, the U.S. State Department in Washington D.C. and multiple intelligence organizations. Our organization reported directly to the U.S. Ambassador but ultimately we served many masters and supported many entities.

The HWG had no budget or formal authority and relied instead upon a wide network of Coalition liaison officers, diplomats, Iraqi police officers, Intel analysts, private contractors, media security advisors, journalists, Iraqi citizens, conventional and special operations military, and countless others to share information, pass warnings, follow every lead or go into harm's way to action gathered intelligence. Each relationship developed over time and was nurtured by building trust and everyone's willingness to do one thing – save lives. Unfortunately, not everyone within the organization operated by such simple maxims. Politics, egos, risk aversion and inter-agency rivalries hampered the efforts of the Hostage Working Group. Bureaucracy and indifference impeded the efforts of many dedicated professionals, even when lives were at stake.

When these situations were presented, we relied on our motto, *find a way or make one* and learned to navigate the inter-agency minefields. Even when "partners" within the U.S. government (USG) architecture attempted to minimize the collective influence or assert partisan agendas we stuck to our original intent. By embracing simple priorities and definable goals of: #1 Rescue & Recovery of Hostages, #2 Prevent future Kidnappings and #3 Bring Kidnappers to Justice; the HWG became a model for inter-agency integration and collaboration. This did not happen without considerable challenges and internal turf battles over traditional rice bowls (a term in the military meaning a jealously protected program, project, department, or budget; in other words … a fiefdom).

In the initial days of establishing a cross-functional, multi-agency organization, post 9/11 information-sharing challenges were present in Iraq. The traditional organization within the United States government responsible for investigating kidnapping incidents is the Federal Bureau of Investigation or FBI. The FBI focus was American kidnappings and Special Agents were required to follow established protocols and procedures. The FBI's initial stance was to monitor and advise but limited their direct participation. At the onset of the kidnapping crisis, overwhelmingly the victims were internationals and Iraqis themselves. As the U.S. Ambassador's diplomatic action arm for all kidnapping incidents, the HWG was meeting with embassy officials from across the Coalition on a weekly and many times, a daily basis.

Entreaties to the investigation expertise of the Bureau many times went unfulfilled due to a "corporate" policy by the FBI that did not consider these non-AMCIT (non-American citizen) kidnappings a priority in the summer of 2004. Exacerbating the situation, the military leadership of Multi-National Forces-Iraq (MNF-I) was focused primarily only on Coalition partners and traditional American allies like the United Kingdom, Australians, Italians and Canadians. Most kidnappings received a limited U.S. response.

A new case every day in July, the first month of HWG's establishment, quickly demonstrated to us that hostage-taking incidents were having a catastrophic effect on the entire international community. High profile cases became part of the regular reporting from Iraq and made daily international news. Gruesome executions broadcast worldwide as breaking headlines from the war. It provided the world with a compelling glimpse of this new Jihadist-style tactic. Decapitations of Westerners in orange jumpsuits created visceral images that repulsed the mainstream consciousness. The extremists responsible for these incidents achieved their strategic communication objective—to spread shock and fear. Radical Sunni terrorist factions led by Al Qaeda in Iraq, used kidnapping executions to send this message of terror to soldiers, civilians, aid workers, journalists, contractors, missionaries, Westerner and Iraqi alike. Kidnapping ransoms in the millions were financing attacks on soldiers and civilians alike. No one was safe from this horror.

One particular incident in the early stages of forming the HWG provided an invaluable lesson in learning from early mistakes and how non-traditional methods are sometimes required to find solutions. Building consensus within a diverse group or organization is challenging, especially in the middle of a crisis when the stakes are high and lives are at risk. August 13th, an American freelance journalist and documentary filmmaker, Micah Garen was kidnapped and held hostage in Nasiriyah in Southern Iraq. I was alerted by the U.S. Embassy press office and moments later, was on the phone with his French girlfriend, Marie-Helene Carleton who had only recently departed Iraq the week prior. After confirming basis details I e-mailed a Kidnapping Report Checklist to Marie Helene to fill-out the critical details that we would need to start our investigation into the kidnapping. She requested assistance on how to deal with the media and I promised the FBI would contact her immediately. Hanging up, I alerted the FBI liaison to the HWG, relaying the information and passing Carleton's number to call in order to provide requested support. After alerting the U.S. Ambassador that our first American had been taken hostage, I recalled the HWG team to the MNF-I Strategic Operations Center to begin our course of action planning. We had been through this drill on numerous international cases, the mechanisms were in place and coordination with military and Coalition units began immediately. Even the French mission provided invaluable assistance refusing to deny initial reports that Micah Garen was a French national as Micah and Marie-Helene wisely traveled as a "French" couple using her passport to check into hotels to minimize rising anti-American sentiment in the region.

Hours later, after midnight, when I returned to the FBI compound I was ordered to report to the senior FBI agent in Iraq, the On-Scene Commander or OSC. Any expectation of gratitude for spearheading the effort was quickly dispelled as I was chastised for "injecting myself into an official investigation of an AMCIT kidnapping." The OSC was adamant that I recuse myself from further involvement in the case and let the professionals from the FBI handle the investigation. I bowed out of the office with a "yes, sir" feeling deflated and humbled. Yet my feeling of "no good deed goes unpunished" evaporated moments after leaving the room. I received a frantic call from Marie-Helene that no one had called her to advise how to handle, Micah's kidnapping. Media vans and reporters were stationed outside her apartment in New York City and she pleaded with me, *"What am I supposed to tell them?"* *"No one from the FBI called you?"* I responded. *"No, no one has called,"* she replied. I was incredulous as it had been more than eight hours since our original conversation earlier in the day. I promised Marie-Helene I would handle the situation with the FBI but apologized profusely that in the future, I could no longer intervene directly on Micah's kidnapping.

Now with my "Irish" in simmering boil, I immediately confronted our FBI liaison officer who was watching satellite television in the lounge area of the FBI compound. Storming in the room, I barked, *"Why the hell didn't you call Garen's girlfriend in New York?"* The Agent jumped to his feet claiming that he was not authorized to reach out to her as the call originated from New York City (NYC) and therefore, the NYC FBI Field Office had to make the call. Asking the obvious question as an "untrained" investigator, *"You mean to tell me that the FBI Agent in Iraq who has the lead for the Micah Garen kidnapping is not authorized to contact the last known individual who saw him alive?"* The agent could only mumble a response that it was FBI protocol. *"Well your On Scene Commander just chewed my ass for calling Marie Helene in the first place, which resulted in the only intelligence gathered to date. She just called me in tears claiming no one from the FBI has called her and that the media is parked in front of her apartment wanting a response. So get on the phone and have someone from the FBI do their damn job!"*

It was the first of many eye-opening exchanges and lessons in working with different cultures within the same community, in this case, the USG who have entirely different operating procedures and priorities. It was only the first of many confrontations with the FBI leadership over the Garen kidnapping case that culminated in my dismissal from the FBI compound as their military guest. Yet the Hostage Working Group survived and the FBI remained a vital if tentative partner over the entire two-year relationship. The key was finding "trusted agents" within the FBI hierarchy who we could work *by, with and through* to accomplish our objectives. We broke many eggs to make the omelet but as Colonel Mathew Bogdanos U.S. Marine Corps who sent me on the original orders commented in the early days of forming the HWG – "Dan, if you aren't pissing people off, you probably aren't doing the job I sent you to do..."

Ultimately, Micah Garen was safely recovered and reunited with his girlfriend and family back home in America. Working closely with my FBI counterpart, the Embassy's Regional Security Officer and Coalition military, we facilitated Garen's return to friendly forces. It was an all-hands effort and I personally delivered the Letter of Commendation from the U.S. Ambassador to the FBI liaison to the Hostage Working Group.

Rear Admiral Slavonic and Micah Garen at the MNF-I press conference announcing Micah's release from the Mahdi Militia, August 22, 2004

A leader has to have the courage of his convictions and be willing to deal with the fallout when doing the right thing isn't always the expedient or easy thing to do. The hard right over the easy wrong will always be a competing interest. Dealing with a crisis is bound to test relationships and will cause conflict. Infighting will occur and maintaining relationships can be a delicate balance. Resolution and solutions are more important than winning arguments or scoring points. The Chinese symbol for crisis is composed of two characters – *wie* – meaning danger plus – *ji* – opportunity. Getting past peril and tactical flashpoints requires strategic focus on the big picture in order to navigate the minefield to safety. At all times, rising above the fray is a critical skill for leaders to manage turning deteriorating situations around.

Award ceremony at U.S. Embassy Baghdad – Letter of Commendation from U.S. Ambassador Negroponte to FBI Liaison to the Hostage Working Group

* * *

The mission of the Naval Academy is to produce physically, mentally and morally superior leaders who will defend the nation and serve in the highest offices in the land...

The moral, mental and physical development for young leaders at the military service academies begins with a simple "mission statement" that articulates the desired end-state. The Academies expect a lot from their graduates and state up front what their expectations are. This concept is not sole province of the service. It applies in any environment – academia, public service or private industry. Every prominent university and corporation has a mission statement and list of organizational values that pronounce their operational philosophy. Yet an optimistic vision and lofty ideals etched in a plaque on the wall rarely register more than a glance if your people don't live by the announced company creed. The rubber meets the road when achieving the mission requires living by the stated code of conduct and ethics—that is where your core philosophy is revealed and resonates. Annapolis graduates will be expected one day to captain Navy warships, command aircraft squadrons, and sometimes lead Marines into combat within months of leaving the Academy.

I may have arrived at Annapolis in the summer of 1987 with the intent to become a Marine or fly Navy jets off an aircraft carrier but the bigger purpose for my attending wasn't revealed until much later. My journey to the halls of Saddam Hussein's former Republican Palace and seat of the American power in Iraq began like all others, taking that first step. The traditional military method is *crawl, walk, run* where proving you can survive is usually the first challenge to overcome. My first year in the Navy was more about simply surviving the rigors of plebe year, passing my mathematics and engineering courses and memorizing my "rates" or knowledge to commit to memory. One of those rates was the official Naval Academy mission statement:

> *"To develop midshipmen morally, mentally and physically and to imbue them with the highest ideals of duty, honor and loyalty in order to provide graduates who are dedicated to a career of Naval service and have potential for future development in mind and character to assume the highest responsibilities of command, citizenship and government."*

Although I committed this to memory, I didn't envision that one day that I'd be serving in Iraq reporting directly to the U.S. Ambassador and the General officers running a war, but the die had been cast on the first day when I took my oath of office.

"I solemnly swear that I will support and defend the Constitution of the United States against all enemies, foreign and domestic; that I will bear true faith and allegiance to the same that I take this obligation freely, without any mental reservation or purpose of evasion; and that I will well and faithfully discharge the duties of the office on which I am about to enter, so help me God."

A mission statement and oath of why you were chosen and what is expected of you can be summarized into a three word motto like West Point's *Duty, Honor, Country…* a mantra that resonates with every serviceman or woman, officer or enlisted, regardless of branch – Army, Navy, Air Force, Marine Corps and Coast Guard.

I may have not known where my navy career was going to take me but the underlying principle of what would be required of me was never in doubt. From that first reading lesson – *Message to Garcia,* you are expected to assume responsibility, solve problems, overcome challenges, and lead others. The Academies don't predict which graduates will rise to the rank of Admiral or General but their graduates dominate the ranks of flag and general officers. West Point, Annapolis, Air Force and the Coast Guard Academy alumni presently command more than sixty percent of the forty four-star billets despite producing only ten percent of each service's annual commissioning class. In 2010, the Chairman of the Joint Chiefs of Staff, U.S. Special Operations Command (SOCOM), Command Central Command (CENTCOM), Commander Multi-National Forces- Iraq (MNF-I) and Commander International Security Forces (ISAF)/U.S. Forces- Afghanistan (USFOR-A), arguably the most critical four-star positions in the post 9/11 world, were all held by distinguished Academy graduates. The ultimate purpose of our nation's military academies is to produce wartime combatant commanders and combat leaders willing to go into harm's way to defend our values, democratic principles and American way of life.

Annapolis was my *'agōgē'* indoctrination; BUD/S and Army Ranger School were the finishing schools where excellence in the art of warfare and small unit leadership was the required end-state. *Arête* – the pursuit of personal excellence and living up to one's full potential was a rite of passage for membership. Individuals who chose the elite Special

Operations Forces or "SOF" units are a breed apart and a "distinctive" class within the warrior society. We learn fundamental SOF truths and leadership maxims that your people are more important than hardware, quality is better than quantity, and "operators" cannot be mass-produced nor created overnight. Building someone "special" requires a dedicated and disciplined individual, uniquely selected and trained, with the fire in the gut to succeed at all costs. The end-state is a community of highly skilled individuals who demand personal excellence, expects it from his teammates and together they don't know the meaning of the word quit or failure.

Developing young leaders takes considerable time, commitment, mentorship and investment but will pay tenfold dividends when done right. Lead from the front and set the example for others to emulate. Allow for mistakes, both individual and collective. Lessons learned are invaluable tools and can be leadership moments for mentoring. Praise in public and counsel in private. Put faith in your people and they will return in kind. Have a vision of the desired result you are looking for and set high standards. Leaders are responsible for "Commander's Intent" and defining the left and right limits of the landscape. Paint the picture of what success looks like yet realize the canvas is always a work in progress with peaks and valleys, victories and setbacks in the journey. When objectives are met, set the bar higher. Caution against ego and remember--success has a thousand fathers while failure is an orphan. Leadership is about setting goals, overcoming challenges and leading the way.

For all leaders, the greatest battles are internal, balancing competing interests, demanding responsibilities and what is best for the overall organization and team. Warrior leadership is about confronting challenges head on, realizing every challenge or crisis is an opportunity to test oneself, his team and raise the collective bar. A warrior lives by a code, he believes in himself, his service and his people and most importantly—that they *will find a way or make a way because failure is not an option*...

Chapter 4

Thomas F. Faught
Marine, Former Assistant Secretary of the Navy

"Never tell people how to do things. Tell them what to do and they will surprise you with their ingenuity."
— *General George S. Patton, Jr.*

Profile

Thomas F. Faught, author of *"So You Want To Be A CEO...* (Fortis Publishing, 2010), brings to the guidance expressed in this book considerable global senior management experience as well as an executive background in working with both U.S. and global government organizations. He was the President and Chief Executive Officer of Dravo Corp., a major, NYSE-listed manufacturing, engineering and construction corporation, for which he was acknowledged in the 1980s as among "The Nation's Outstanding CEOs." He served as Assistant Secretary of the Navy during President Reagan's Administration, has acted as strategic advisor to several leaders in global corporations, government agencies, and military organizations, and currently is the Adjunct Professor for Business Strategy in Carnegie Mellon University's David A. Tepper Graduate School of Business' MBA program. He also served as a global management consultant for several years, working and living in Europe and engaged in Asia, Latin America, the Middle East, Africa and the Pacific Rim as well as in the United States and Canada. He is a Marine, having served as both an enlisted infantryman as well as an officer. He holds an MBA degree from Harvard and a BS degree from Oregon State College.

Leadership Story

In one way, it is extremely easy to define "leadership" and to describe its characteristics. A leader possesses more passion, dedication, singleness-of-purpose, self-confidence and a greater, more focused work ethic than anyone around him or her. They are quick and agile in looking into the future, identify and evaluate options and deciding where and how to achieve their decided objectives that anyone else.

They also, through maturity and experience, realize that they must dedicate their efforts and energies to inspiring rather than merely managing. They are people who are 360^0 in their thinking and 110% in the time and concentration given their jobs. Their total life is committed to this responsibility and opportunity, and they never take actions or make decisions without first identifying and assessing all possible unintended consequences of such actions or decisions.

I believe it goes without saying that the person who aspires to leadership must be an Individual – a "Self Starter"- (in every sense of these words) and possess reasonable intelligence, curiosity and imagination, and do not even consider a "box" in his or her thinking. As General Mattis exclaims, they must think and operate outside the perimeter. They consider such bureaucratic aspects as "policies," "practices," "techniques," procedures," "doctrine," "processes," and as protective devices as make-work projects of the limited, poorly informed and non- inquiring mind. These vague, precedent setting obstacles are to be ignored whenever and wherever possible, forcing increases in fresh, uncorrosive thinking.

Also, there must always be a quantifiable "product" or "deliverable" resulting from the time, attention and resources given deliberations, actions and decisions. A "Team" approach is considered by the leader as secondary or tertiary as compared to an individually assigned effort, and any "Team" actions must be focused in these same terms, both having definite "Start" and "End" points. Otherwise, people banded together in teams have a tendency to operate in time consuming, ever decreasing circles, concentrating on analyses, discussions and deliberation rather than on accomplishing a piece of work to the highest possible level. Acknowledgement of successful work also should emphasize an Individual's success rather than being diluted through "Team" acclaim. "Team work" usually falls to results of the least common denominator, giving greater attention to protection rather than advancement.

The People Challenge: Selecting, Developing, Evaluating and Leading

The people equation will be among your greatest challenges as you progress in your professional career. Herein are some thoughts on this issue and proposed guidelines in meeting this challenge. All of us have participated in selecting people. Since our youth, we all have engaged in this process.

Most of us also have experienced at one time or another being the person who has been selected, or rejected. Depending on circumstances, in some of these early experiences we have questioned the decisions, and have gained or lost respect for the individual making them. This aspect of respect is an important factor in the people equation.

A significant aspect of the selection process is our own experience. Reflecting on this, we were favorably or unfavorably affected – and remember most vividly, in most cases – during our middle school and secondary school days. In many instances we can even remember the names of the instructors who determined who would be chosen as team participants responsible for developing a project or playing on a school sports team. We also, those who were so selected, recall the frustration experienced when on a Sunday evening we learned that the quality – and grade – of a project and presentation due Monday morning fell to us because some team member, chosen by a given instructor, failed to do his or her part. We soon determined, even at this relatively young age, despite alleged friendships or the proximity of our study desks, if success was to be achieved, our selection of team members, or the drive to become participants of a certain group, depended on their commitment to work hard and on their "brain power" and focus to contribute. "Popularity" soon went down the tube insofar as useful productivity was concerned.

These conclusions, in large, part, permitted you to excel in the final years of your secondary education, your college years and in your work experience to date. With continued objectivity, focused effort and refinement of thought in the people selection process, this background will significantly affect your career advancement and your success in achieving your leadership career goal.

A discussion of the people challenge is difficult without touching on related matters such as career planning, organization and relationships – and the value of a "Team" versus "Individual" approach to work. Admittedly, career planning has been largely addressed, and organization will be subsequently addressed. Suffice for now is to emphasize that, from this point forward, your principal task in achieving career advancement is how well you handle people. True, your functional and technical knowledge and expertise are important and must be kept current. However, these assets pale in importance compared to you skill in dealing with people, particularly the employees of your organization.

Sensitivity is important. As you proceed on your career path, you frequently will be inheriting a group of people with whom you have had no prior relationship. You must be aware that, given your entry as the "boss," some of these people, being disappointed in not being recognized for promotion, will be challenging, surly, and possibly downright angry; some to the point of quitting or resigning. These advances, continually facing new personnel challenges, will represent your litmus test as far as senior management is concerned. You can't fire everyone and start over. You must be capable of exercising considerable sensitivity in these situations, and yet move with alacrity in getting the job done.

Selecting and Developing People (successful leaders excel at this)

A key to the "people selection" process is to understand the individuals' interest and objectives, and how well they correspond to the job for which they are being considered. Frequently, these people's thoughts are superficial; they don't have a definitive idea of either interests or goals. Often the "test" is by the process of elimination, that is, in determining things in which they are not interested and objectives they don't have. You are not a psychologist. However, if you don't take time at the outset to equate one's interests with the challenges of the job, the chances are that you will be searching for a replacement soon for this person, and the work is not being done.

Your people challenges is somewhat analogous to a vast lake which feeds gradually into a large, shallow river which, with an increasing current becomes narrower and more rapid until its waters pound against a dam; pounding with the force which results in a portion of this concentrated stream creating power or electric energy – equaling the success of the organization.

Initially, in your quest you will find yourself in this vast lake of people, some of whom, knowingly or unknowingly, are "in the swim" merely for the hour-to-hour or day-to-day compensation. For these people, and this often is regardless of family background or level of education, "the swim" represents only a job in which they spend their time, satisfied with attempting to do what they are told. At this nascent stage, it is easy for you, in the selection process, to eliminate these people from those contributing, or at least making a constructive effort to contribute. I'm certain you have witnessed the results if not having participated in such initial screening phase in the work experience you have had to date.

However, a crucial step now is to determine from among the individuals who have passed this first screen, those who appear to possess the potential, with development, to make further contributions – how much, and what do they need to succeed? One selection criterion is that it is prudent to associate with individuals who are your equal – or, preferably, your better – in intelligence, judgment, values and commitment. Your challenge in the "people quest" is a good place to reaffirm this position.

Selection Criteria

You and your working colleagues now are out of the aforementioned "lake," and have entered the increasingly swift, focused career advancement "stream" (always remember that some of these colleagues are your career competitors). At this point, you may or may not have had supervisory responsibilities. Nevertheless, you will want to continue identifying people who have the interest and talent for making greater contributions and for assuming increasingly important management duties. You should become acquainted as soon as practicable with these people. Regardless of background, these people have potential. Your task is to identify those having the greatest potential for development.

"What makes an individual tick" is a difficult thing to identify. We all want "more," but what of and how much is not easy to determine – even for ourselves. However, it is possible – indeed, for you, mandatory – to determine criteria against which to evaluate an individual's potential through observations made during your working relationship. These criteria include the following (one might wish to quantify the relative importance of these criteria):

- <u>A Keen Interest in What Makes the Business Succeed</u> – How much time does he or she spend at their desk and in the office, as compared to the amount of time they are out in the plant, laboratory or marketplace where things are happening and on which the business depends? The only way an employee will understand the strengths or weakness of a business is to experience the work first hand – to see and feel it, and have the background to ask useful questions.

- <u>Sound Judgment</u> – Gaining an impression of the individual's judgment and analytical ability, which should enable him or her to identify and focus on the more important issues, the actual causes of an event, and determine the "Whys." This also includes 360° thinking and the calmness of taking time-even under pressure-to consider the possible unintended consequences of decisions or actions, and to provide for their resolutions.

- <u>Sagacious Rather than Astute</u> – Not to get wrapped up in hair-splitting etymology, I would strongly advise that your executive assessment criteria seek sagacity rather than astuteness. While both characteristics denote shrewdness, the latter often centers on keen perceptions and discernment <u>in which personal benefit are planned or are to be derived</u>. Yes, we want sound judgment and wisdom, but such must be directed toward the good of the organization, not to the advantage of the individual. This is a very important distinction particularly concerning executives in vitally significant positions.

- Self-Expression Capability – Alert, well spoken. The ability to speak and write convincingly, concisely and to the point, avoiding an enigmatic and/or sententious style which often indicates a failure to understand and deal clearly with a subject.

- A Positive Attitude; Flexible – One that deals objectively with the "plus" side of issues, but recognizes and is prepared to address problems that often are involved in such issues. Constantly seeks alternative or optional solutions, never admitting that something is "impossible." Works best in a non-structured, relatively laissez-faire environment. Clearly, an "out-of-the-box," non-regimented thinker; not adverse to practical risks.

- Dedicated to the Work – Diligent. Hard working. This is demonstrated by total absorption in the work, punctuality, the commitment to timelines, time being spent is secondary to the successful and timely completion of the assignment.

- Goal-Oriented – Knows what he or she seeks, and is objective in assessing their worth and the value of their contribution. Aware of personal strengths and weaknesses and active pursue resolutions to the latter. Strives constantly for self-improvement. Anticipates guidance and is not timid about seeking recognition – greater responsibility, visibility and reward. "Sets themself apart"; usually is far "ahead of the curve" in developing analysis and conclusions.

- Time Conscious – Evidences a keen sense of time, both their own and that of others. Thinks before speaking, centering on significant aspects of a problem or solution. Demonstrates a talent (Judgment) for identifying the "Pros" and "Cons" of issues. Listens.

- Respectful of Others – Demonstrates honest, open respect for others and for himself. Cordial, courteous and relaxed in dealings with others. Acknowledges the value of others' opinions. Avoids patronizing behavior, even the remote appearance of such.

- <u>An Affable Personality</u> – Pleasant "to be around." Exhibits an interest and an ability to work with others. A cheerful and calming influence. Frank defends his or her positions well, yet in a quiet manner.
- <u>Appearance</u> – His or her self-respect and their respect for their working environment are reflected in their appropriate dress and professional bearing.

All the above are critical points that many successful leaders share. They are worthy of your attention.

* * *

There are many perspectives and philosophies on leadership. And there are countless tips, strategies and lessons that purport to teach how to become better leaders. What I've shared above is really a simple approach to the fundamentals for an individual to follow that in doing so, establishes a framework from which, strong leaders develop.

Chapter 5

Douglas L. McClain
Rear Admiral, U.S. Navy

"The greatest leader in the world could never win a campaign unless he understood the men he had to lead."
— *General Omar N. Bradley*

Profile

Rear Admiral Doug McClain

Raised in Oklahoma City, Oklahoma, Rear Admiral Douglas L. McClain was a 1975 graduate of Putnam City High School and attended the University of Colorado, helping the Buffaloes to a berth in the 1977 Orange Bowl before transferring to the University of Oklahoma. He graduated in 1979 with a Bachelor of Business Administration degree and earned his commission through the Oklahoma University Naval Reserve Training Program (NROTC). He instructed the freshman NROTC class until 1980 assigned to the staff of the Oklahoma NROTC Unit while awaiting flight school. He received his Navy Wings of Gold from VT-22 in Kingsville, Texas, in August 1981.

McClain's command tours include the Stingers of Strike Fighter Squadron (VFA)

113, the Rough Raiders of VFA-125 (Fleet Readiness Squadron) and commanded the Navy's only forward deployed air wing, Carrier Air Wing 5 (CVW-5) based in Atsugi, Japan. McClain reported to USSTRATCOM from Commander, Battle Force U.S. 7th Fleet (CTF-70 and Carrier Strike Group 5/ USS KITTY HAWK (CV-63) Strike Group), commanding all Carrier Strike Forces and Surface Combatant operations over the 150 million square miles of the U.S. Seventh Fleet. He has flown in support of Operations *Desert Storm*, *Desert Strike* and *Southern Watch*.

McClain with daughter Megan, home from "Desert Storm"

Significant assignments include tours with the Eagles of Attack Squadron (VA) 115 (1982-1985) onboard USS MIDWAY (CV-41), The Golden Phoenix of VA-128 as an instructor pilot and head of Carrier Qualifications (1985-1987), The U.S. Navy Flight Demonstration Squadron (Blue Angels), (1987-1990), The Green Lizards of VA-95 (1991-1993), was the Chief of Policy for the Joint Chiefs of Staff J-5 Directorate (2001-2003) where his division led the efforts in writing the 2002 Unified Command Plan (UCP), standing up U.S. Northern Command and the merging of U.S. Space and U.S. Strategic Commands. Following his Joint Staff assignment, he was assigned to the staff of Commander, U.S. Pacific Fleet where he was the deputy chief of staff for Operations, Plans and Policy and Training (N3/5/7) (2003-2005) while simultaneously holding the position of director of operations (J-3) for Joint Task Force 519 (JTF-519), which is responsible for contingency operations in the Pacific.

McClain with his son Jared

In 1993, McClain attended the United States Naval War College earning a Master of Science degree in National Security and Strategic Studies and was awarded the President's Honor Graduate award.

His awards include the Defense Superior Service Medal, Legion of Merit Medal (four), Meritorious Service Medal, Air Medal, Joint Service Commendation Medal (two), Navy and Marine Corps Commendation Medal (three), the Navy and Marine Corps Achievement Medal (two) and various unit and campaign awards. He has also received honors as the Tailhooker of the Year in 1984, Landing Signals Officer of the Year in 1985 and Instructor Pilot of the Year in 1986.

He has logged more than 6,500 hours in jet aircraft including 2,000 hours in the A-6 Intruder and more than 4,000 hours in F/A-18 Hornet and Super Hornet aircraft. He has more than 1,500 landings on 12 different aircraft carriers including over 500 night landings.

Rear Admiral McClain is departing as the director of Global Operations (J3), United States Strategic Command. He serves as the principal advisor to the Commander, USSTRATCOM on all operational matters, providing strategic guidance to planning and execution of Strategic Command's Global Missions, to include providing coordinated space, information capabilities, network operations and global strike in support of deterrent and decisive national security objectives.

Leadership Story

When asked if I would write a few words on what corporate America might glean from U.S. military leadership, I thought my way through something that represented an outline of a book series. Though it is difficult to capture 30 years of experience in a single chapter, I settled on one thought. Leadership begins with *fundamentals* and my view of breaking down leadership to football fundamentals--"blocking and tackling"--is what guides me today.

In thinking of the differences between corporate leadership and the military, some may believe it is our authority to issue lawful orders that makes the difference. It is in fact much larger than that. We have the benefit of having men and women in our military that view their volunteer service as a "higher calling" and our troops for the most part, understand "why" they serve. We view our sacrifices as benefiting a "greater good" and have sworn an oath to defend the U.S. Constitution and our way of life. Hard to argue with 235 years of holding to our American values as motivation enough. Beyond the ideology of our commitment, when on the battlefield, the reasons we fight are much more personal. Regardless, our military is a very professionally led organization and there are great leaders at every level, doing great things everywhere I turn. The weight of our great Nation is being carried on the backs of our youngest troops today and I have been blessed by being able to lead the finest warriors to ever sail in harm's way.

As military and specifically naval leaders, we are entrusted with America's sons and daughters; taking them to sea with two goals, mission success and to bring everyone home, 180 plus days later. The elements of being on the seas, the unforgiving nature of a single human mistake, the extreme conditions, the mission dangers that test a Sailor's endurance at every turn, combined with unseen threats from a lurking enemy, are the risks we face every day at-sea. It is a testament to our Navy's professionalism and training that we are able to deploy 50,000 Sailors afloat every day of the year and we are committed as leaders, to bring everyone home safely. We WILL complete the mission but unfortunately, not every deployment is successful in bringing everyone home. It takes great leadership and leaders who are involved at every level to fulfill this commitment. It is how we do business in today's Navy.

On the flight deck, McClain reviews aircraft a pre-flight inspection card with Chief Aviation Structural Mechanic Cheryl Miller

Every day that I am blessed to put on our Nation's cloth and trusted to lead our finest, I count on my years of experience, some coming from the "school of hard knocks" and some of it from understanding and practicing the fundamentals that are the very essence of leadership.

Our environment and our experiences shape us all. I came into the Navy in the late 1970's and was led by leaders who came from the Vietnam Era. Those "hard lightin', hard fightin', knife in the teeth" aviators taught me from day one that you have two challenges to becoming an accomplished Naval Aviator. You have to have credibility in the air and on the flight deck. They are not exclusive but they are not the same. Nothing can replace the "forging" that takes place in the intense environments we operate in but it is essential if you are going to lead effectively at the "next level".

When I joined the fleet, my first flight was in the Philippine Sea — blue-water, with no divert airfields available. You either landed your jet back aboard the "boat" or very few options remained; none of them good. We knew why we were at sea and clearly understood our mission; freedom of the seas, projecting power in support of national objectives and with that came being prepared to challenge the Soviet Union at every turn. The U.S. was deep into the Cold War, the draft was over, the Navy was coming off some turbulent times with drugs and race issues, but we all wanted first and foremost, to be at-sea.

My first fleet assignment was with Attack Squadron 115 (VA-115) and my first air wing, Carrier Air Wing FIVE (CAG 5), knew how to fight as a team. My first ship, USS MIDWAY (CV-41), was the oldest ship in the Navy and we enjoyed the luxury of being forward deployed, where we were ready for any contingency. MIDWAY had only two catapults and three arresting wires and CAG 5 was still flying F-4N Phantoms, E-2B Hawkeyes, A-7E Corsairs and our venerable A-6E and KA-6D Intruders. CAG 5 was always together, unlike the air wings in the U.S., we literally lived together at Naval Air Facility Atsugi, Japan. We were part of the OFRP (Overseas Family Residency Program) or as we affectionately referred to it, *The American Foreign Legion*. We knew our sister squadron's strengths and weaknesses and CAG 5 was tasked with protecting the Western Pacific as the striking arm of U.S. SEVENTH FLEET. We were at-sea an average of 300 days per year and our training was mostly done from the ship in cyclic flight operations or down flying out of Naval Air Station Cubi Point in the Philippines Islands. Numerous west coast battle groups deployed to our home waters and each time we would launch a 1000 nautical mile "Welcome to WESTPAC" simulated strike on the "tourists" as a scene-setter for what they were going to be part of operating with MIDWAY under the command of Carrier Group FIVE. No ship/air wing team could match us with sorties flown or speed of launch and recovery, despite the *limitations* of our "small" 60,000-ton "MIDWAY Magic" (as we affectionately called her). This was the Navy I grew up in--survival-of-the-fittest and looking back; it was the defining tour of my career.

Every Naval Aviator, throughout the nearly 100 year history of Naval Aviation, has come to the Fleet with the requirement to test and hone his/her leadership skills, first in the air, learning to fight and win in any and all weather conditions and second, leading on the ship, in our squadrons. Because we are Naval Officers first, we are also assigned one of several squadron duties or "ground jobs" as we call them. My first ground job was in the maintenance department of VA-115 as the Line Division Officer. The Line Division in a Navy squadron is comprised of two branches. One is a combination of members from every technical rating in the squadron called *The Troubleshooters*. These men came from the Electrical, Avionics, Life Support, Fire Control, Hydraulics, Air Frames and Power Plant shops. They were independent technicians when put together on the flight deck, comprised the "experience" base for getting the jets off the flight deck and were tasked with incredible pressure to get them "turned around" or repaired and ready to fly in less than an hour. The other was *The Line Branch*. These Line Branch Sailors are 18 to 22 years of age, first tour "boot camps", but are the backbone of any Navy carrier squadron. Line Division Sailors are on the flight deck 12-16 hours a day in temperatures that range from 20 degrees below zero in the North Pacific Ocean to 150 degrees in the North Arabian Gulf taking care of their assigned aircraft. They eat and sleep in their shop and when they did get a hot meal, it was on a "no fly" day. They are the true heroes of the air wing, responsible for being on their jets at all times, preparing them in advance of their aircrew arriving. They assist their aircrew in starting, performing final check and then handing their aircraft off to the flight deck directors who taxi them to the "cat", all the while, carrying 100 lbs. of aircraft tie-down chains over their shoulders up and down the flight deck, following their jet everywhere it goes should there be an immediate need to tie her down. This "disparate" group of our youngest Sailors provided me countless opportunities to lead but I was not alone. My mentor was a crusty stalwart called The Flight Deck Chief (FDC), who orchestrated every 'on deck' maintenance effort on behalf of the squadron. Leading the youngest and least experienced Sailors on the ship was challenging enough but combined with putting them into the most dangerous and unforgiving environment in the world, on the deck of an operating U.S. aircraft carrier, made me (as a young lieutenant) grow up very fast. I had the most gifted and talented FDC I have ever known, but under him, my next tier of leaders, the Line supervisors, were not the hard charging petty officers I needed to survive. It soon became apparent that I was going to make changes or fail at my first fleet ground job.

Inside our 35-man "Line Shack" was a young Sailor who immediately caught my attention. He was several years older than the other sailors and clearly, he had experienced life's challenges before he ever got close to a Navy uniform. His name was Airman Apprentice Luscious Oldham. Airman Oldham was the kind of Sailor every division officer would kill to have. He worked longer and harder than any three men and when it came time to depend on someone, Oldham was always the one that "just went and did the job", without a word spoken. Despite knowing his place in the pecking order of the Line, Oldham took up, on his own, the task of training the "boot" plane captain trainees. Every one of his *charges* completed qualification long before any of the others and their knowledge of the jet, and how to operate on the flight deck was second to none. He was simply one of the finest men I have ever known. Oldham didn't have great ability to take advancement exams, but he knew his job and I needed a strong figure to lead when the Chief and I were not around. Oldham never hesitated accepting the challenge, despite being outranked by 75 percent of the shop. Oldham came into VA-115 as an E-1 and left four years later as a Second Class Petty Officer (E-5), having been twice meritoriously "Command Advanced". Oldham knew more about "deck-plate" leadership and how to inspire young men to follow than anyone I have ever met. He led by example and his judgment was superb. With Airman Oldham in-charge, we ended discipline problems and he forged his plane captains into the finest fighting team in the air wing while making me look like I knew what I was doing. What this example is meant to show is that the U.S. Navy prides itself at being able to bring inexperienced "kids" from every walk of life and giving them the opportunity to self-actualize beyond where they ever thought their potential was and very quickly forging them into warriors. Oldham went on to lead at the highest enlisted rank and my only regret is that I was not privileged to serve with him again.

The strength of the U.S. Navy comes through its dedicated and motivated Sailors. They are magnificent in crisis and working in a hostile high-risk environment; but if you want a china doll in the cabinet, you aren't going to find them on the flight deck of an aircraft carrier or for that matter, flying off them. They are men and women of profound dedication and pride and my love and admiration for them has only gotten stronger through the years because they will always be there when the going gets tough.

We train our Sailors to act autonomously and with decisive action. We expect, no we demand, that our youngest, act with confidence and we purposely put them into stressful positions very soon after boot camp. There is no time for indecisiveness when faced with the mission we are tasked to perform.

The most effective leaders I have served with have passion to excel. They motivate through energy transfer. They understand the "why" of the mission and are able to effectively communicate it to those below them. Great leaders always "do the right thing". Leaders have integrity first and foremost and they know if you do not, you will never inspire loyalty in your people. Leaders lead from the front of the formation in the air or on the ground. The leaders I seek out, motivate from positive example through our core values of honor, courage and commitment.

Leaders aren't afraid to get their hands dirty and know when it is time to get involved. They anticipate problems and expect those under them to do the same. Communications up and down the chain of command are key to being good leader.

Leading is more than being the person "in-charge". Intimidation is a poor way to lead and a hypocrite can be seen by the troops, a mile away. Credibility is the single greatest trait that a leader can possess. Without continually validating your credibility, you will be ineffective and your credibility is tested hourly in a squadron at sea.

I believe that an effective leader is always fair but does not profess equal treatment. The Navy is a *performance based* business and those that perform, are rewarded better and faster than those that don't. True Naval leaders know their Sailors and Marines are their greatest resource. America's parents entrust their children to us and we owe it to them to train, protect and enrich them, all the while, demanding exceptional performance under fire.

Leaders, on occasion, will not make everyone happy with their decisions. It is the "nature of the beast". The Navy trains our leaders to exercise good judgment, sometimes beyond their years. Hard decisions coming from credible leadership will always be respected.

Trust starts with you — with what's inside you. If you don't trust your own judgment to make timely and correct decisions, how will you ever inspire trust from your people? I frequently use the old adage of "no decision is in fact, a decision" — and often that is the poorest level of leadership — in fact, it constitutes a lack of leadership. It amazes me to witness leaders who fail to make a decision.

Unity of Effort and *teamwork* is not just a cliché', it is in truth — the only way organizations succeed. The military is the consummate team building organization. I have long held that is the reason we draw so many athletes into our ranks, they want to be on a winning team.

Leaders never forget that standing up for your people ensures they are there when the going gets tough. Criticize in private, praises in public and woe-be-it to the man who dresses down "my guys" without first going through me. Every Sailor deserves to know you have their backs and their best interests at heart. Additionally, it doesn't matter how big or small an issue appears to be; if it effects 'good order and discipline' or is a distraction to them, it demands you get involved early.

I believe too that life is made up of a series of defining moments. Some small and relatively insignificant but a few are real "game changers". Being put in an environment where dreams can be fulfilled was a key to my development and a key to motivating and retaining our best and brightest. I didn't grow up with a silver spoon in my mouth but I was given every opportunity to succeed. I was taught from day one that nothing was beyond the realm of the possible when enough work and effort was put forth. My father was my role model and my mother remains the core of my confidence. I grew up in the Bible Belt of Oklahoma, taught right from wrong, attended every church event, and accepted Jesus Christ as my personal Savior, all the while being expected to excel in school. I always have feared failure and it has proven to be a great personal motivator in my life. I was an athlete and athletics taught me to demand more from myself than I ever thought possible. Football was and always will be my game of choice, and nearly all my friends played at some level. Today, I would willingly hire a *"C-Plus jock"* to fly my strike fighters over anyone else as they are generally fearless and are decisive decision makers that have the hand/eye skill to win-at-all-cost in the air.

I was taught growing up, that the only time success comes before work, is in the dictionary and work is the key to success. The Boy Scouts of America played a major role in defining who I am today and the character I ascribe to follow. Scouting gave me the tools to lead at a very early age and becoming an Eagle Scout is still one of my most cherished accomplishments. I grew up with a love for the outdoors and profound respect for animals, where through the years, 1700 lb. *Bucking Bovines* remain a big part of who I am.

I found early on that I could generate action in those I was around simply by energizing any activity with motivation and by diving in head first with all I had to give. I learned early that a solid work ethic occasionally was going to involve pain, which I learned to "expect". I was drawn to the most difficult and dangerous challenges. I grew up knowing exactly what I wanted to do and flying jet aircraft from pitching flight decks was the epitome of success in my mind.

I believe leadership must work hard to create a *culture of success* inside any organization and that the environment you set, will determine your success. As a leader, you must continually seek out opportunities for education and with that comes inspiring your people to do the same. Self-improvement leads to self-actualization and it is paramount to developing the leaders you want to eventually replace you.

Leaders transmit the strategic vision or the "why" to their organization and then continue to live that vision. Without it, you (and they) will fail.

We in the military have the benefit of swearing allegiance to defending our Constitution and that defines a big part of the "why". When I see disgruntled Sailors, I will guarantee he or she doesn't feel part of the team or does not understand the "why". I believe that no one comes to work to be a failure; it is our job to set the stage for success.

Inspiring trust and empowering your people gives an organization the ultimate confidence and I assure you, you will be amazed with the results. This is a key to our success in the Navy. I often ask myself whether or not I can walk away from my job and have my organization continue to function effectively or even do better without me there. We have all seen workaholics that build an empire based on the belief that they are the primary reason their organization succeeds. As soon as they rotate to another assignment, the organization fails.

Create a *culture of excellence*. We in Naval Aviation are often asked why particular squadrons are always successful from year to year, despite a complete turnover in personnel. I believe that the culture of excellence is embedded in that squadron and it continues to manifest long after any individual transfers. It takes amazing effort to get a squadron "combat ready", but one aircraft mishap or loss of a Sailor can shake a squadron for years, especially if it was a non-combat loss.

Set priorities based on critical functions. If every task has the same priority, nothing has priority. When 80 percent is good enough, don't kill your people to get to 100, move onto the next priority and continue to re-evaluate and adjust fire when required. If it was a critical "fix", it will continue to be embraced.

Groom and develop leaders that will be there, with the skills to succeed, when the *going-gets-tough*. Inspire innovation. Innovation is not a proprietary quality but it certainly defines us as Americans and as warriors. Put your people into the position to be innovative and watch your "luck" start to change.

Leading through *risk*, must be developed; and must be thought through far in advance of accepting it. You as a leader have to possess the judgment to make the hard call on acceptable levels of risk and you better know what you are doing when you decide. You cannot expect your people to thrive in intense environments without a complete understanding of the risk you are putting them into. Whether fighting over enemy territory or landing aboard a 40 foot pitching flight deck at night in marginal weather it takes a complete understanding of risk. One of the ways we manage risk is by putting our leaders themselves into the same high risk environments as everyone else and leading the fight. We in the Navy have every level of air wing seniority in the skies; leading from the front of the formation, day and night. It is a part of our culture and forges the credibility of leadership, where the "self-cleaning oven" of Naval Aviation, levels the playing field without bias: *behind the ship*, at night. It makes us the fighting force we are today.

Risk Aversion is a recipe for failure, understanding risk and leading through it with smart, well thought out inclusive processes, will ensure success every time. There is no magic formula to building warriors who lead; but without real world trial-by-fire, we would not be prepared for an enemy's unexpected surprise.

I ascribe to a higher power and would submit that I have never met an atheist who lands a jet aboard a pitching heaving flight deck at night. My personal faith has seen me through countless trials. Additionally, without the love and support of a great Navy family, none of my success would have been possible. My wife has given me the confidence and support to reach goals far beyond what I thought possible. A key to my success has been her amazing ability to run the home corporation, raising our family when I am deployed and supporting me in all things and I give her all the credit in keeping me grounded in reality. Staying rooted in my principles, understanding where my inner strength lies, taking the time to 'give a darn' about my troops and their families has and always will, serve me well.

I encourage my leaders to keep perspective, forcing them to step back and "see the forest", all the while, keeping physically and mentally fit. I don't think the U.S. military has a corner on the leadership market but do believe we are the best in the world because of how we build leaders forged by experience.

Finally, losing a Sailor or Marine entrusted to my care, defines the mantle of leadership. Those of us that have written the letters to our fallen heroes' families, forever second-guess what we could have done differently to prevent their death.

To Corporate America I would leave this thought: Lead like your son or daughter's life depended on your decisions, in ours, it literally does.

God bless all who carry the mantle of responsibility to lead, may we do so with Honor, Courage and Commitment regardless of the cloth we wear.

Chapter 6

Donald J. Wetekam
Lieutenant General, U.S. Air Force (Retired)

"Remember praise is more valuable than blame."
— General George S. Patton, Jr.

Profile

L

Lieutenant General Don Wetekam

Lieutenant General Donald J. Wetekam entered the Air Force in June 1973 after graduating from the U.S. Air Force Academy. A career logistics officer, Wetekam commanded three maintenance squadrons, a logistics group and a logistics center. He served staff tours at both major command and Air Staff levels. He holds a master maintenance badge, a basic parachutist rating, and is the only general officer in Air Force history qualified to wear the explosive ordnance disposal badge.

Upon retirement from the Air Force in 2007, Wetekam joined AAR Corporation, a publicly held aviation services company. Initially serving as a group vice president, he established the maintenance, repair and overhaul functions as a separate business unit growing it to the second largest independent MRO in

North America. He currently serves as Senior Vice President for Government and Defense Business Development.

U.S. Air Force Academy 1973

Leadership Story

Leading in the Military, Leading in Business

Those who have served in the U.S. military would likely agree by near-unanimous consent that military service provides a great leadership learning training ground. In fact, there may not be a better leadership laboratory anywhere in the world.

In my own particular case, 34 years of active duty leadership experience was preceded by a four-year stint at the Air Force Academy. I may be a little biased in this regard, as we all tend to be when it comes to schools we attend, but I believe our nation's service academies provide unparalleled academic education and practical experience in the art and science of leading people. From that first sunny June day when I walked up that ramp to a throng of eager upper classmen ready to "help me" with my transition to military service, to another June day four years later when I accepted my diploma and joyfully threw my hat in the air; I was presented with an opportunity to learn the theory and application of leadership that few others receive.

Those four years of intense academic challenge were followed by more than three decades of hardcore, practical experience that enabled me to apply those lessons in the real world with real people. Thanks to some forgiving bosses, especially early in my career, I was permitted the luxury of making most of the mistakes imaginable and being able to learn some hard lessons without getting myself or anyone else killed. Looking back, there were a couple times when Divine Providence may have had a hand in preventing such an outcome, but I was relatively oblivious at the time. Most of those near-miss experiences centered on my early days in Explosive Ordnance Disposal. Eventually, I made my way into the aircraft maintenance field and its larger parent, logistics. And it was here that I was afforded the opportunity to lead large, complex organizations even at an early age.

So for a variety of reasons, I was able to obtain substantial experience leading large numbers of people from the very start of my Air Force career. Many of the senior military leaders I've known, and I've been privileged to work with some of the best, have developed lists of key attributes they deem important to effective leadership. I will say that many of these lists are quite interesting and enlightening, showing a lot of thought and reflection on the part of those that put them together. In my own case, I've avoided doing likewise not so much because I don't care for the content of the lists, but rather I seem to have a hard time deciding what is important enough to include versus what are only ancillary concepts. Likewise, many of the attributes seem to be common to several of the originators. So while I'm not denigrating registries of leadership characteristics and traits, it's just something that I decided to avoid in my own case. For the purpose of this discussion, I'm going to concentrate on three key aspects of leadership that I learned in the military and that have been reinforced in my follow-on career in commercial industry. They're not specific traits that you find on the typical lists of leadership attributes, but I think they illustrate my approach to leadership and my views on a few of the things effective leaders need to know.

* * *

<u>Leadership and Management</u>

The first aspect really centers on the concept of leadership itself – what is it and how does leadership differ from management. To the latter, I have to reply with an emphatic "there is a big difference." I've listened to many differing views on this, many of them sophisticated in their approach. Most acknowledge a clear distinction. Personally, I like concepts that are straightforward, logical and, most importantly, simple to grasp and remember. Following that construct, I have to go back to a notion heard from a senior Air Force leader over 30 years ago: "You lead people--you manage things." That certainly fits my criteria of being straightforward and easy to remember. More importantly, the logic behind it makes sense on closer examination.

Management is about applying and controlling the use of resources. When I talk about resources, I'm referring to things you can touch such as equipment, facilities, parts, vehicles, energy, and that resource that surpasses all others, money. In recent years, we've come to see information in this light as well. Management tends to be more of a science in my mind rather than an art. There are technical aspects to learning to manage these things and our education system is rife with courses that teach the nuances of getting the most from available resources.

I get very nervous when I hear the term "managing people" in a conversation. It's one of those phrases that I've been conditioned to key on. And if I hear it more than once from the same person, I start to question their strength as a leader. In some cases, it may be a matter of semantics. But over the years, I've met many people who honestly looked at their workforce as just another resource and the term management seems much more prevalent in their vocabulary than leadership. My observation is that they generally fall toward the bottom end of the effectiveness scale when it comes to organizational performance over the long haul.

I'm very much aware that the concept of "human resources" has been in widespread use primarily in business for decades although it seems to be less in favor today than it once was. In my mind, the fact that the phrase seems to be disappearing from the business lexicon is a good thing because the concept of HR tends to imply that people are essentially just another resource to be utilized and manipulated like copy paper, tools, or money. I'm glad to say that the HR term is one that never really caught on with the military. I would like to think that's at least a partial reflection of the fact that there is a clear recognition that people are different and more important than run-of-the-mill resources even in a military that is increasingly dependent on technology.

In contrast, I think that leadership leans more toward the art end of the spectrum rather than the science end. That's not to say there isn't plenty of science involved. I learned a lot over the years by studying various behavioral theorists and I have found that strong leaders routinely do the same. But even there, I think leadership diverges from management in that leaders are focused on taking their team – their people – to a destination. It's about convincing, motivating, building a sense of teamwork and overcoming hurdles while aspiring to a goal.

I've been asked whether leadership is more difficult in the military or private industry and my answer to that is that the difficulty level is essentially the same. Oh, there are differences to be sure. Military members tend as a whole to be a bit more compliant and they can't just quit if they don't like something. But effective military leaders know that it's important for the members of a team to understand the goals and reasons behind the actions. Remember the U.S. military has been an all-volunteer force for nearly 40 years. Orders are still orders, but over the long haul, effective leaders understand the need to build a motivated, informed and focused team. That comes through clear, consistent and protracted communication.

Likewise, I believe the military focuses a bit more on teams and teamwork both in terms of formal training and education as well as in practice. The military's hierarchical structure features the unit and members are trained from the start to value the unit's accomplishments above all else. Personal rewards are more limited since pay is the same for a given rank and there aren't any cash bonuses paid for exceptional performance.

There are other differences besides the more compliant nature of the military and the heavy team focus, but I contend that leadership challenges within the military and commercial sectors are pretty close at the end of the day. It's about the art of taking people somewhere new, of building a vision that captures the imagination, of establishing a sense of teamwork where the strength of the sum is greater than its individual parts. Compare that to management concepts that center on manipulating resources and a clear distinction starts to emerge.

<u>Training for Leadership</u>

With a little better idea of what constitutes leadership, let me turn to the importance of training for leadership. This gets to the issue of whether one thinks leadership is an acquired skill or an inherent one. I think some people have a stronger aptitude for leading than others. Some may have a certain charisma or an inclination to get out in front. But not all effective leaders are charismatic. From American military history, you can compare two principal leaders of the Civil War, Lee and Grant – one noted for charisma and dash while the other quite the opposite. Likewise, from World War II you can compare George Patton and Omar Bradley. Military history is rife with stark contrasts in leadership styles that produced equally impressive results. Flamboyance and dash make for a great movie, but the truth is that for every Douglas MacArthur there was a Dwight Eisenhower, and for every William "Bull" Halsey there was a Ray Spruance.

So if it is not charisma per se, are there other natural attributes that earmark one for leadership greatness or is this something that one can learn? On this burning question, I come down squarely in the middle – in my mind it's both. I believe that some people are born with traits that tend to make them leaders that are more effective. In my own case, I learned at an early age that I was comfortable in a leadership role and that may explain why, at least to some degree, I migrated toward a career in the military. But I wouldn't classify myself as charismatic by any means. If you looked at my Myers-Briggs scores, you'd see a strong introvert. Nonetheless, I always felt a kind of natural comfort when put in a position of leadership. Frankly, at the end of the day, this is about developing whatever abilities we may have to their fullest and that's where training and education come in. Good leaders may be born with certain traits, but it's how you develop those traits that count the most for the majority of us.

Many would say that training is what teaches us how to do our jobs. Okay, I'll buy that. But how does that relate to training to lead? Since the real challenge of leadership is motivating our team to move in a certain direction during difficult times, then leadership training is what prepares and conditions us to react to challenging, stressful situations as the head of the team. It's the stress and the ability to muster the team during those times that distinguish effective leaders. If it were easy, anyone could do it.

Again, I recall my military training experiences. If you're going to take young people right out of high school and prepare them to operate effectively in potential combat situations, you better train them well. And the U.S. military excels in this arena. Training conditions us to know what to do when the going gets tough.

I mentioned my time as a cadet at the Air Force Academy and the training was superb in every respect. Sometimes it was focused on building a thoughtful plan of action and then implementing that plan. Other times, it was about knowing what to do immediately and then reacting. I recall the summer of 1971 when I was enrolled in free-fall parachute training as one of my summer training programs. Airmanship 490 was the course and that number was significant. The course consisted of intense physical and procedural training followed by seven free-fall jumps. It was a graded course and in order to graduate and qualify for parachutist's wings, you had to average a passing score of at least 70% for each jump. Seven jumps times 70% meant you needed 490 points to graduate.

My first six jumps were routine and the training I received enabled me to execute well enough that I had accumulated more than enough points after my sixth jump. So that took the pressure off the seventh jump. As you can imagine, that's when things went haywire. On that final jump, we wore a standard aircrew ensemble that included pilot's helmet and oxygen mask. The mask prevented you from seeing the T-handle when it came time to pull the ripcord so you just had to feel for it. When it came time to pull, I reached for it but couldn't find it with my hand. As I had been trained, I reached up over my left shoulder, grabbed the cable housing and followed it down across my chest. When my hand came to my reserve chute that was strapped to my chest, I realized that the T-handle has slipped down behind the reserve. Fortunately, my training included this very situation as well and I knew what to do – pull my knees up toward my chest causing me to flip over on my back, and pull the reserve. I was trained on what to do in a stressful situation and I acted almost without thinking.

Repeatedly, I have marveled at the quality of training that our military members receive enabling them to perform the routine and the unexpected with equal skill just as I learned to do back at the Air Force Academy. Of course, training to lead an organization isn't normally as cut and dried as preparing for a potential parachute malfunction. But the principle is the same. It takes hard work and practice. There are processes that one needs to learn. That's the book theory that many people often dismiss when they consider what it takes to be a good leader. But if it's not just an inherent trait, then the book theory is important. Forty years later, I still use many of the principles I learned at the Academy studying a number of behavioral theorists. I may not recall who said what, but I've seen many of those theories reinforced time and again in practical situations. I recall the difference between motivational factors and irritants as I learned to distinguish them in the classroom. I appreciate the fact that different situations may require different approaches for the newly assigned leader depending on the organizational climate and clarity of mission. And I learned how to relate one's own personality traits to the specific situation.

Similarly, effective training programs recognize that practice in a controlled environment is just as vital as theory. Again, I think the military is at the forefront in this regard. Standard training programs throughout the military consist of a combination of classroom training coupled with realistic and challenging practical exercises and that includes those who are being trained to lead in those situations. While it's very difficult for private companies to duplicate this approach, it still behooves industry to pay attention to leadership training and build effective internal programs. I feel fortunate to be associated with a company that understands and embraces this approach as key to continued success. It has been my observation that private companies that have endured tough times and seen their business prosper over many years understand the need for this type of approach and adopt it fully.

A Time to Be Bold

With that as background, I turn to one of the more focused ideas that I have had to always keep at the forefront while in a leadership position. Thoughtful people, as I consider myself, know their own weaknesses and work every day to counter these tendencies. That is vital for the leader. It's nigh on to impossible to garner the respect one needs to lead, if you have glaring deficiencies to which you are oblivious or refuse to try and correct. That's not to say that members of the organization expect perfection from their leader. They know the person in charge isn't perfect. They just want to know that that person is cognizant of their own weaknesses and is at least working to get better.

This focus on self-reflection seems to be receiving a lot of emphasis recently. If one compares leadership training and education of a generation ago, we see a lot more tools and techniques aimed at analyzing and identifying a leader's own style and characteristics. There are a number of these tools that have come into vogue in recent years – Myers-Briggs, Strengthsfinder, 360-degree feedback, to name a few – and generally I have found them to be helpful. Their prime usefulness lies in forcing a leader into a self-evaluation mode and provides a framework in which to do so. And this is a good thing, especially if one wants to continue to grow in their ability. Too often, leaders reach a point where they start to believe they have all the answers. When that happens, watch out. Leaders at any level need to periodically consider their performance in a critical way as well as seek the chance to engage in feedback that is more formal whenever the opportunity arises.

It's surprising how far we can miss the mark when we assess our own leadership performance. That's why outside sources, such as those used during a typical 360-degree feedback approach, can be so useful. Having attended a few courses in recent years that employed this type of technique and discussed with my classmates our general impressions, I find that a large number of folks have a very different perception of their abilities than that of their subordinates, peers and superiors. It's surprising but wide misses in this regard seem to be fairly common, at least if one is to believe the far-from-scientific sampling I have taken in recent years.

So feedback and frequent reflection are crucial to leadership effectiveness. That's the best way to identify one's biggest fault. After all, how else are we going to fix a problem if we don't know what the problem is. In my own case, the fault list is substantial, but I will stick to just one for this discussion.

I tend toward a collaborative approach to my job as a leader. There's nothing at all wrong with that and, in fact, I view that as an asset in most situations. But I also know that a collaborative approach doesn't work in every situation and can sometimes lead to timidity or indecision. And that is something I have to work hard to guard against. This pattern of indecision for the sake of collaboration is something I've observed in other cases both in the military and commercial industry.

Every career military officer studies Clausewitz. Many of his concepts, such as center of gravity, are still considered core to basic military strategy nearly two centuries after they were first espoused. Over the years, I've collected a lot of quotes from a wide range of sources, and one of my favorites reflects one of Clausewitz' observations on leaders:

> *"Boldness grows less common in the higher ranks . . . Nearly every general known to us from history as mediocre, even vacillating, was noted for dash and determination as a junior officer."*

Each military service conducts a senior leadership course for its newly selected generals and admirals. I attended the Air Force course back in 1998 soon after I was selected for my first star. And in subsequent years, I had the opportunity to speak to some of the succeeding classes as well. One thing I recall hearing from several of the speakers back in 1998 and something that I always included in my presentation was a reminder to "stick with what got you here." We live in an era when political correctness runs rampant, and it's easy to fall into a trap to do the safe thing even if it's not the very best choice. But when we think about the things that enabled us to reach the upper echelons of our chosen professions, it wasn't always taking the safe road.

Generally, people who achieve more senior leadership positions in an organization do so by knowing when to be bold and then doing so. There's an obvious difference between boldness and recklessness. Likewise, there's nothing wrong with being tactful and diplomatic either. But at the end of the day one has to show boldness when it counts and not fall victim to the trap that grabs many senior leaders – becoming overly fearful of doing something wrong or making a mistake.

In my own case, I came into commercial industry about a year before the major business downturn of 2008. Talk about a baptism of fire. I was just getting my feet on the ground when crude oil hit $140 per barrel sending the aviation industry into a tailspin followed almost immediately by a credit crunch that hit full force. In that environment, I found my confidence shaken almost daily. I had left the known confines of the military and I was in an industry that was being buffeted daily. Our customers were pressing us for reduced rates in an already low margin business, other companies in the industry were declaring bankruptcy at a rate of at least a couple per month, and the overall market was contracting at a rapid rate. It was easy to get into a mode of not wanting to make a mistake rather than being aggressive and seeing opportunity.

Fortunately, I was surrounded by a strong, experienced team who understood that difficulty produces opportunity. We took necessary defensive measures but we also became aggressive, pursuing new customers and ultimately gaining in market share even as the market contracted. It would have been easy to fall back into a completely defensive mode where avoiding mistakes were the only objective.

But this wasn't easy to accomplish. Every day was a challenge. On one particular occasion, I had gathered all of our general managers for a one-day planning session. As I struggled with the agenda and the message I wanted to convey, I was reminded of the boldness issue by one of our vice presidents who was a close personal confidant as well. As I worked on the message I wanted to deliver, he gave me the advice I needed at precisely the right time. "When they come in tomorrow, they need to see the General," he told me. As I thought about it, I realized he was right. I was starting to become too timid in how I conducted business, more interested in avoiding mistakes than anything else.

The situation called for boldness and a leader who conveyed a clear set of objectives aimed at strengthening and expanding our place in the market. When I walked in the next day, they got the General. I was organized, decisive and clear. I laid out our objectives and the actions we were going to take to achieve them. I asked for input as a collaborative leader would do, and I received some good suggestions from the team for some modifications to my plan. But overall, it was clear the team who was in charge and even clearer to me that's what the team needed. The response was overwhelmingly positive.

Tying it All Together

None of this guarantees success in a leadership role. But ignoring these factors will greatly diminish the chances for success. Leaders understand that people are not just another resource and they can't just "manage" them as they would other assets. We may not all be natural born leaders, but training and education are needed even for those who do have considerable inherent ability. And even after the training is long complete, effective leaders continuously seek to understand their weaknesses with a view toward continuous improvement.

I consider myself fortunate to have been afforded the chance to learn leadership in the U.S. military. The training and education were world class, the mentors and people I worked with and observed were truly superb, and the opportunities and experiences I enjoyed were something I could never have received elsewhere. Yes, the world of commercial business is quite different in many ways from the military world I entered at the age of 17 and departed at 55. But the leadership lessons I learned during those years have proven to be something that work in or out of uniform. I'm grateful for the experience and the opportunity.

Wetekam climbing down from an F4

Then Colonel Wetekam, in front of a F117 Nighthawk Stealth Strike Aircraft

Speaking at an AAR event

Chapter 7

Thomas E. Zelibor
Rear Admiral, U.S. Navy (Retired)

"Character in the long run is the decisive factor in life of individuals and nations alike."
— Theodore Roosevelt, Jr., 26th President of the U.S.

Profile

Rear Admiral Tom Zelibor

Rear Admiral Thomas E. Zelibor is a 1976 graduate of the U.S. Naval Academy where he earned a bachelor of science in Oceanography. A Naval Aviator (RIO), during his distinguished military career, he accumulated over 1,000 carrier landings and 3,400 tactical flight hours. Highly decorated his personal awards include the Defense Superior Service Medal, Legion of Merit Medal (three awards), Distinguished Flying Cross (with Combat "V" for valor), the Bronze Star Medal, Meritorious Service Medal (three awards), Strike/Fight Medals (three awards with Combat "V"), Air Medal (with Combat "V"), Navy & Marine Corps Commendation Medal (four awards with Combat "V").

Upon retirement, he was hired as the site manager and Vice President for Strategic Operations - Strategies, Simulations, and Training Business Unit at Science Applications International Corporation (SAIC) in Omaha, NE. Then a unique opportunity was afforded Zelibor when he joined the Naval War College in Newport, RI as Dean of the College of Operational and Strategic Leadership in July 2006. After establishing the new organization in Newport, Zelibor accepted the position as President and CEO of Flatirons Solutions in Boulder, CO in the summer of 2008. He is responsible for the overall strategic guidance and direction of business operations of the company. In less than two and a half years, he has restructured Flatirons, nearly doubled their revenue generation and is recognized as the driving force to changing the culture and leadership development of his employees.

With over 35 years of significant senior leadership positions in government, industry and academia, plus his background in aviation, space operations, information technology and knowledge management, he is widely acknowledged as a leader that maximizes organizational efficiency and effectiveness to achieve mission success.

Onboard USS CARL VINSON (CVN-70)

Leadership Story

Leadership throughout my career has been about learning and seizing the opportunity to shape the lives of those under my sphere of influence. The majority of my leadership capability has come through experience and a natural ability, tempered and coached by several mentors/role models during the course of my life. I learned a lot about myself from each of these individuals, especially during my military career. Utilizing what I learned from them was natural since I had the utmost trust and confidence in their assessments and guidance, but most importantly – I was always willing to listen. I took bits and pieces but did not try to completely emulate one particular leader. It is my belief that your leadership style needs to be personal or it will be perceived as fake. I feel strongly that leadership development is a continuum throughout ones career and not periodic, ad hoc "training" sessions. Leadership skills evolve over the course of a lifetime.

My strength, high energy and the ability to inspire a culture of innovation allow people to flourish and push the limits of their own capability. This combined with a basic philosophy to provide my subordinates with a nurturing style of leadership and guidance allows them to be successful in their work. It is very important to have a clear vision, articulate it, make sure it is well understood and then provide the tools for your subordinates to accomplish the goal or objective. Communicate the vision often. It is imperative to have a balanced approach that addresses the needs of subordinates as well as the need to execute a mission, but the critical component is to deal with facts…not emotion in leading and decision making. You can still make tough calls/decisions while treating people with compassion and respect.

A leader is a leader. Senior leaders can make or break their organizations to a greater extent than the junior ones – this is true in the military as it is in corporate America. The difference between tactical, operational, and strategic leaders lies in their focus and often a leader's focus shifts between different levels; there are no hard lines to define the difference. The driver is that your focus depends heavily on the situation and its requirements—on what is called for. I am a devout believer in situational leadership and that you need to adjust your style to the environment you are faced with.

There is no one single definition for leadership - there are literally thousands of them. Each is correct in some way to each individual. I have found leadership styles to be an individual trait that must be internalized by each person. There are only two definitions of leadership that matter: your personal one and the one for the organization you work within. Every leader must develop a personal definition. Once done, they can complete their own picture of what a leader is and what he/she does for the organization. This requires self-reflection, a process that many senior leaders find difficult to make part of their routine. Leaders need to understand themselves first – before leading others. You have to be able to describe what makes you a leader from your own perspective — not from something you read in a book, a worthless checklist of great leadership characteristics or from what you observed from colleagues. It must be your own style that encompasses your personality. It has to come from the heart.

Genuine leadership manifests itself through thought, word, and action. It can't be faked; if attempted, eventually a person's true character will emerge. If your character is flawed, you become ineffective and will soon lose the trust and confidence of those you are trying to lead. In the military, this is most detrimental and depending on the situation – can even cost lives.

As a leader, you have a critical role as mentor and coach. I believe this is the most important responsibility of any senior leader in the performance of their duties and is an obligation not to take lightly. You should be passionate about the development of those under you who are there to move the enterprise forward and make it better. A culture of improvement means continued growth and stability for an organization. At the same time, you must instill in young leaders the value of character, ethics, and accountability—these are the pillars on which true leaders stand—and on which any organization should be built.

The U.S. Navy is a 235-year-old enterprise that prides itself on developing young leaders who truly understand the legacy they are a part of. The Naval Academy education was the first formal way I was exposed to leadership development and the basic skills of time management, relationship building, change process/management and communication. These are all very important issues and it takes a lot of work and coaching to get them right. However, I think it is even more important to develop higher order leadership traits such as character, ethics and trust. It is an apple and orange discussion. You can teach these, but I believe they are inherent to the capability and makeup of an individual. It is difficult for someone who does not possess these qualities to improve in these areas, no matter how much they are taught and are pushed to change. However, as leader you have a responsibility to try to develop those who report to you and at some point will ultimately replace you.

Leaders should remember it's more important to consider what's best for the organization, not what's best for you or your career. At different times, the two can and most likely will be in conflict. Subordinates given the authority and responsibility will work tirelessly for you. Those who are successful – can achieve levels of authority and responsibility that is unmatched anywhere else in society.

Another critical characteristic of a good leader is solid communication skills. A leader must adapt their communication style to others in order to effectively lead people or the organization. Often the ability to communicate is not taken as seriously as it should be and the simplest task can create problems or challenges for the organization or impede the growth and success of the enterprise because the guidance or mission is not properly communicated by the leader. Simple is better in my book. When Churchill said, "We shall fight them on the beaches," it would not have been as effective or memorable had he said "Hostilities will be engaged with our adversary on the coastal perimeter." You get the point.

When making a difficult leadership decision, my first instinct is to ensure I have the facts about the situation before I decide on a course of action. I make sure I am fair and consistent with previous decisions and actions. I consider the outcome.

Regardless of your job or profession, leadership skills and experiences are completely transferable from one occupation to another. Too often, we see in the papers that many leaders do not apply or adhere to the basic principles of leadership. These are plain old hard work, a strong character and ethical behavior—these are the essence and traits common of those that become a good leader.

The three most important characteristics in development of a good leader are trust, ability to grow quickly into new and expanded roles, and accountability. Leadership is a two-way street and without trust between the junior and senior, you may as well pack your bags and go home. Trusted subordinates/employees should feel empowered to do what it takes to make an organization successful—if you are a good leader, they will. Trusted leaders should have confidence that their decisions and actions will be embraced and carried out. Next, you must be able to transform yourself based on your role. Even though a leader may want positions of increasing scope and responsibility, they cannot seek those positions for personal gain and sometimes this is a difficult challenge. At the end of the day, it is all about contributing to the effort and greater good of the organization. Finally, accountability. The authority and responsibility we enjoy in the military, especially in command, comes from the strict accountability associated with it. That allows us to give a Commanding Officer absolute authority and responsibility commensurate with that authority. Accountability in the business world doesn't enjoy the same status. If it did, the creative energy of people could be unleashed. It's obviously a different type of accountability, but I think most business leaders fail to use it as an effective tool. Being a leader in charge of an organization means being the person who is most accountable. Regrettably, in corporate America this is often not totally embraced, or even worse, is ignored by executive leadership. Blame is largely deflected and catastrophic situations or decisions are allowed to happen with little consequence.

The study of leadership is complex because it is both science and art. There is constant debate over whether leaders are born or made because of this. In my view, anyone can learn the science of leadership. There are basic tenets that simply do not change, and can be learned by anyone. It is the art of leadership that is difficult to master and not everyone can become an artist. Some leaders are born with innate abilities to lead and apply the art. While others have to work hard at becoming effective leaders at each level of their personal development. The fundamentals of good leadership apply broadly in every situation - it's how the leader understands the situation and knows how to apply those fundamentals to the situation that spells success or failure. That's where the art comes in.

When thinking back on my 30-year naval career, there are two experiences that resonate the most with me that are particularly noteworthy and reflect the success I achieved as a leader. Much has been written about the Battle Group I led during the early stages of Operation Enduring Freedom. A great deal of this success is captured in an article I penned for the *Armed Forces Journal 141 (December 2003)* titled *"FORCE net' is Navy's Future: Information-Sharing, from Seabed to Space"*. This leadership experience was a catalyst for a complete case study by University of Arizona on network centric warfare and its effects on leadership. My team totally changed the way we were going to operate (before the 9-11 attacks happened). They had complete freedom to come up with new ways to operate and I gave them the resources to do it. Their creativeness and innovation were unleashed. When responding to the crisis on September 11, 2001, leadership and the creative environment we created was one of the main ingredients to success for this operation.

The other experience, which shaped my life and where leadership was critical, was my appointment as Dean, College of Operational and Strategic Leadership at the Naval War College. The leaders at the Naval War College asked me to establish a new College with two primary objectives. First, create a focal point in the Navy for researching, studying and discussing how to develop operational level leaders. Second, prepare Admirals and their staffs for leading at the operational level of war.

As Dean, I sponsored extensive research with *The Stockdale Group,* a group of senior Naval War College students, to study this topic. (Note: This group was named after Vice Admiral James B. Stockdale who was one of the most highly decorated officers in the history of the U.S. Navy. In September 1965, while serving as Commander of Carrier Air Wing Sixteen aboard USS ORISKANY (CVA-34), he was shot down over North Vietnam. Vice Admiral Stockdale was the highest-ranking naval officer held as a prisoner of war in Vietnam. He was awarded 26 personal combat decorations, including the Medal of Honor and four Silver Stars. His leadership was an inspiration to all held captive until their release in March 1973.)

The outcome of this study was revealing and produced an interesting and detailed discussion of all leadership issues and how we would approach the development of our future leaders. The first objective was to create a working definition for operational leadership. Once this definition was established, the students created descriptive areas where leadership competencies could be binned. These areas were then broken into domains, and defined, as *artistic, scientific* and *personal.* The graphic below depicts a portion of that work and the competencies the students found for each domain through research and survey mechanisms.

From my perspective, the research and study only expands the debate on whether leaders are born or made. There are several competencies required of military leaders, which can also easily be applied to a corporate structure/environment for a business leader. Once the model was developed and the students engaged in debate – the subject of leaders being "born or made" soon disappeared because the answer became obvious that it is both.

2d Trimester Work

Defined Operational Leadership: *the art of direct and indirect influence, both internally and externally, based on a common vision that builds unity of effort while employing tactical activities and capabilities to achieve strategic objectives.*

Draft Traits & Competencies:

Artistic Domain
- Spatial/Visual/Conceptual ability
- Organizational adaptability
- Pattern analysis
- Creative, Innovative, Imaginative
- Intuition, Judgment
- Mental agility, Intellectual depth

Scientific Domain:
- Operational estimates
- Terrain analysis
- Tactical competence
- Joint/Combined Integration competence
- Application of operational art
- Technical development
- Strategic, historical understanding

Personal Domain:
- Courage (moral, physical)
- Character, Integrity, Trust
- Confidence, Boldness, Decisiveness
- Stamina, Drive, Determination
- Communication skills
- Interpersonal skills, advanced
- Patience
- Presence
- Responsibility
- Compassion
- Influential – Persuasive mentor, teacher
- Initiative, Assertiveness
- Strength of will, Determination
- Self Awareness, Assessing

Unclassified

Secondly, it was determined that all three domains intersect. Data gathered by surveying over 100 three-and-four-star Flag and General officers (active and retired) provided feedback on these leadership competencies. The image below – the operational leadership model – was developed from this feedback and depicts how the competencies were ranked in importance by these senior officers. Our analysis of the data showed areas where certain competencies intersected all three domains, leading to the conclusion that one could potentially get more leadership development "bang-for-the-buck" by focusing on those competencies first in developing operational level leaders.

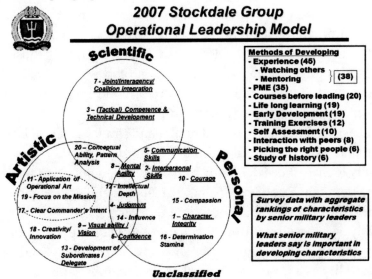

It should be noted, after closer examination, it was their view that the top six characteristics for leadership are: 1-character, integrity; 2 - interpersonal skills; 3- tactical competence & technical development; 4 - judgment; 5 – communication skills and 6 – confidence.

Four of the six fall in the Personal Domain.

I'm often asked, "What is the one leadership style that I admire most?" My response – without hesitation – *my own*. At the end of the day, this is the only one that matters when it comes to accomplishing a mission, developing your people or leading an organization. As mentioned earlier, I did, however, get bits and pieces of my style from a compilation of great leaders who mentored me and whom I observed over the years. I "shopped" every day, was willing to change and adapt, and worked hard to improve over the course of my career. I believe that is how leaders "are made" by their own hand.

Developing leaders must be accomplished through a continuum of education, experience and mentorship - not a one-time shot along one's career. I also don't believe in fostering a zero defect mentality. That means allowing your subordinates to experiment with new ideas, knowing there may be mistakes made along the way. It's important to coach (mentor) young leaders at every opportunity. You are obligated as a leader to effectively develop your subordinates – those "hard charging," young, next generation leaders who will grow to be your replacement. It is imperative that you provide them the guidance, environment and tools to be successful.

Lastly, senior leaders tend to demand similar levels of leadership performance from their subordinates, regardless of their capacity or capability to meet those demands. I always remind myself that it is OK to demand as much as you want from yourself, but expecting everyone else to achieve the same level of commitment to excel and to have the same capability as yourself is unrealistic. Each of us has different capacities to achieve goals and we all have different leadership skills. If your capacity and capability as a leader is higher than someone else and you try to get them to achieve at a higher level than they are capable of the gap will equal nothing more than frustration for both parties. This requires setting realistic objectives for your subordinates and this takes hard work, analysis and coaching to achieve success.

The beauty of the U.S. Navy is that it takes seriously the responsibility to develop young leaders to be the next generation who will ensure we are the preeminent sea service in the world. The U.S. Navy has done this for over 235 years dating back to the days of John Paul Jones, and will continue to build on this proud tradition in the future.

Chapter 8

Dr. Irene Trowell-Harris,
Major General U.S. Air Force (Retired)

"You cannot manage men into battle. You manage things: you lead people."
— *Admiral Grace Murray Hopper*

Profile

Dr. Irene Trowell-Harris

Author of *"Sky High ~ No Goal Is Out of Your Reach"* (Fortis Publishing, 2009), Irene Trowell-Harris, R.N. Ed.D. is the Director of the Department of Veterans Affairs (VA), Center for Women Veterans. In this role, she is the primary advisor to the Secretary of Veterans Affairs on programs and issues related to women veterans. Prior to her appointment, Dr. Trowell-Harris served as Director of VA's Office of Inspector General's Healthcare Inspections Regional Office in Washington, D.C. Concurrent with her position in VA's Office of Inspector General, She served 38 years in the U.S. Air Force/Air National Guard (ANG), retiring as a Major General in September 2001. During her military career, Dr. Trowell-Harris held numerous positions, including chief nurse executive; flight nurse examiner; commander; advisor for nursing and readiness; assistant to the director, ANG; and military representative to the Defense Advisory Committee on Women in the Services for the ANG. She was a 1997 Air Force representative for the Committee on Women in the NATO Forces Conference held in Istanbul, Turkey. She represented the Secretary and spoke at the November 2008 Fédération Mondiale des Anciens Combattants, World Veterans Federation, Standing Committee on Women Meeting in Paris, France. She represents the VA on the White House Council on Women and Girls. Dr. Trowell-Harris is an adjunct graduate faculty member at the Uniformed Services University of the Health Sciences, and serves as an ex-officio member to the Defense Advisory Committee on Women in the Services for VA. She also served as a senior policy specialist for the American Nurses Association.

Born in Aiken, S.C., Dr. Trowell-Harris is a graduate of Columbia Hospital School of Nursing, Jersey City State College, where she earned a bachelor's degree with honors in health education. She earned a master's degree in public health from Yale University and a doctorate in education from Teachers College, Columbia University. In 2010, she received Certification in Public Leadership from the Brookings Institution. A recipient of the Air Force Distinguished Service and Legion of Merit awards, she was the first African-American female in the history of the National Guard to be promoted to general officer. She is also the first to have a mentoring award *and* to have a Tuskegee Airmen, Inc., Chapter named in her honor. In June 2010, she was selected by the Air Force Association, as the National Aerospace Award Recipient as the 2010 VA Employee of the Year.

Major General Irene Trowell-Harris

Leadership Story

My leadership style is clearly participatory with collaboration. This style is based on mentoring, encouraging and guiding others to reach their full potential professionally. I embrace professionalism, political astuteness, continuing education, mentoring others and sustained high performance to be successful as a leader.

A successful approach to sustained performance is called the integrated theory of performance management, which addresses the body, the emotions, the mind, and the spirit. In an article, "The Making of a Corporate Athlete" by Jim Loehr and Tony Schwartz published in The Harvard Business Review, January 2001. The authors called the hierarchy the *performance pyramid*. Each of its levels profoundly influences the others, and a failure to address any one of them compromises performance.

In conjunction with high performance, I stress balancing competing priorities, mastering planning techniques, meeting critical deadlines, time management, collaboration, dealing with frequent change and setting realistic and measurable goals. My experience from serving in numerous senior positions in the military and civilian arenas provides me career broadening in leadership especially in a politically changing environment.

I was born just two generations away from slavery. My journey started in a cotton field in Aiken, South Carolina and has taken me to dozens of countries, a 38-year military career where I rose to become a Major General (2-stars) and became a White House political appointee.

Very far indeed for a young black girl who while picking cotton in the mid-1950s, looked up at a plane in the sky and dreamed of flying. It was an eagerness to learn, and a willingness to step up and seek responsibility that led to where I am today.

There is debate on whether leaders are born or if they are made. I believe there is truth in both beliefs. Some people are born (or raised) to have something within them that makes them stand out or step up, a key trait of those that become leaders—the "making" comes from how experience, their environment and life in general shapes their thinking.

And thinking (whether conscious or subconscious) dictates how you act—and how you act gets you to where you are.

My contribution to this book isn't a dry sermon about "how to be a leader" or even speaks much of "this is what you should do as a leader." There are many books out there like that, which describe leadership. I've found that good leaders learn a lot about themselves in self-reflection on the context of their background and experiences. I believe that this internal dialog cements their sense of who they are—knowing that it is key to lead oneself before you can lead others. So let me tell you a story of what I learned that developed my sense of who I am and in doing so, perhaps it will spark some thoughts of your own.

With most stories, the question is where to start and how to make it a compelling story, appealing, inspirational, eye-catching (and eye-holding) and dynamic. In fiction, they tell the writer to put the reader immediately into the scene, with the protagonist in jeopardy, thereby hooking the reader immediately, making them interested to see what happens next. My life has been an adventure but not necessarily an "adventure story" … but let me tell you about how it was for me … in my beginning (and why it was the impetus to drive my resolve and ambition.

The Cotton Fields

I seemed on fire; the sand burning my feet, a searing heat that never let up—making you want to step faster just for the flash of relief when your foot left the smoldering ground. The heat like a wine press on my head squeezing a flow of stinging sweat into my eyes. Wiping them constantly, a sweep of my hand or sopping kerchief only gave a moment's pause … then stinging again as the unending stream poured into my eyes. Drops of it fall like rain with each stoop and bend. I could feel it pool in my ears, spilling from them like small pitchers as my head turned and moved with the work. My shoulders and neck caught every pounding ray of sun, the only break as a cloud comes over, a small blessing, a shield from the beating of the sun—a breeze, the promise (sometimes false) of relief from the stifling heat that wraps a cotton field with you inside it.

Stoop labor—I knew the definition of it before I ever knew there was such a word. Bend, pick, pull and strip—put the cotton in my bag—do it all again. Over and over, hundreds of times in the heat—thousands of times throughout a full week of work. Fighting the lizards, insects, boll weevils and snakes that infest a cotton field. They wanted to be there—I sure didn't but had no choice.

Eyes stinging, hands and forearms scratched and cut—always roughed up—never healing. The ache in your back, shoulders and how your thigh muscles would feel after only a short while in the field. The chafing under the arms as my shirt, soaked even early in the day, rubbed away skin as my body went through the mechanical motions that had not changed in a hundred years—maybe more. A never-ending cycle—the worst kind of backbreaking work there is. Monday through Friday and a half day on Saturday. It is what I and my ten brothers and sisters had to do, part of what you have to do when you're a family and it depends on each person's efforts. For my family and many like mine it was the past, the present and the future. A bleak and hard life that many never got ahead of or away from.

One day when I was about 15, another day in the crucible—I straightened, stretching to relieve the strain on my back, blinking the sweat out of my eyes. I heard a sound, looked up and sun-sparked metal caught my eye. At first I couldn't spot what caused it, but seeing and following the long white line in the sky, at its end and highest point I saw the plane, a tiny cross of silver … moving higher and farther away from me while I watched it. Sweat no longer gathering in my eyes, running down the sides of my face—I could see clearly now—clear and crisp, sharp like the stars on a winter night. In that moment, the line in the sky, drawn by the small cross of metal that moved with such purpose, I knew what I wanted to do—I knew I would find a way to leave the cotton fields behind me. I'd reach for and take in my hand, something that when I talked about it even amongst family made them smile and laugh—my desire to fly and work on airplanes. To travel in the cool sky on silver wings—leaving a line just like the one above me, marking where I'd been and proof that I was going somewhere.

"Girl, how you going to do it?" they asked. They all knew a girl from a poor black family, farmers with little education and no money did not have a chance. Not in 1950s South Carolina. But I knew I could and someday, in some way … I would … leave that cotton field behind me and never return to it or another.

* * *

Ten years after that day in 1954, where I stood in the cotton field, watching that plane climb high in the sky I proudly walked upon the stage and accepted my silver flight nurse wings at the Aerospace School of Medicine, Flight Nurse Branch, Brooks Air Force Base, and San Antonio, Texas. This is one of my most cherished accomplishments! In a way, it was the end of the beginning for me and the start of the rest of my life.

In spite of numerous roadblocks in my life, my goal was to turn obstacles into steppingstones and move up the career ladder so I could manifest my own form of leadership to directly and positively affect those who worked for me and those I worked with. This was for my family, my community, my state and my country. After serving over 38 years in the military as a leader my vision was to continue to assist my country by helping those who served by becoming a leader able to manifest change in the Department of Veterans Affairs.

Here are some of the core principles I learned from my experience that can help anyone to face challenges, rise above adversity and to become a leader worth emulating:

LESSONS LEARNED

- Stepping up and being proactive teaches you things that are important to success.
- Don't assume that where you are, is where you have to stay. If you want something better—work towards it. Small steps can lead to big accomplishments.
- Learn what you need to learn—do what you need to do—to put the past behind you and move forward to your future.
- There is nothing wrong with hard, honest work. It can build a foundation that can carry you as high as you want to go.

- Sometimes you have to prove yourself before opportunities appear. Waiting for one to come to you does not get it done. Create opportunities for yourself.
- How leaving what is "known" behind you to start something new, in a place you may have never been before—can be a good thing. It promotes self-reliance and simply that is probably one of the most powerful things a young person can learn and have.
- The importance of being responsible and accountable for your own actions cannot be understated.
- Whatever your job is, reach out to learn more. Stretch yourself to learn beyond your job description. When you do that, life rewards you with opportunities that you may not receive otherwise.
- People and systems are not infallible. It's important to take your responsibilities seriously—even though repetition can lead to complacency or even a slack attitude—don't let it be you that makes a mistake.
- Don't just think about your own job. Help those around you by making them more aware of the importance of doing their jobs correctly.

Few people today understand the difficulties faced and personal sacrifices required of minorities and women of past eras who elected to serve their country in the military. For them the journey continues, even though laws and policies are in place on equal opportunity. While we have made monumental advances, there is no time to rest on our laurels.

We still have a lot of work to do. Minorities and women are moving up and are continuing to serve with honor and distinction around this great nation. Many are leaders today and will shape the thinking of those who may become leaders of tomorrow. Like others, they should be recognized for their contributions. Not because they are minority or female but because they are highly skilled and competent officers, enlisted and civilian professionals. Because they chose to serve their country then and now.

I do not forget that I am here today and have accomplished the things I have because the pioneers, that went before me charted the course. They made it possible for me and others to serve in significant military and civilian roles. I simply followed their path—extending it just a little. Young people out there today and tomorrow will extend this path to immeasurable distances because they are destined for even higher roles and greatness!

By working together as a team, we can build bridges for others to pass over and to add value to America—because we have promises to keep for our veterans, our family, our community, our state and our country. To accomplish that takes selfless leadership.

Remember these simple points to help you along the way:

- Embrace a persistent commitment to hard work and always strive for excellence. Just getting by is not acceptable.
- Take advantage of every opportunity to learn and to improve yourself.
- Prepare yourself by seeking advanced education, challenging projects and visualizing the future, and
- seek mentoring from various outstanding leaders, civilian and military.

With this—remember that the future is the bright light ahead of you. Walk toward that light, and enjoy your journey:

- Never evade the challenges—face them squarely. That should be your motto.
- Reach out for opportunities. That should be your goal.
- Accept your responsibilities. That must be your mission.
- With preparation, hard work, education, mentoring and God's help, nothing can stop you.

We have some grave challenges facing us as a nation. Do we have the intelligence, humor, imagination, courage, tolerance, love, respect, and will to meet these challenges?

I say yes, because, it is the human spirit that will propel us to success:

- Money cannot buy it
- Power cannot compel it
- Technology cannot create it

Our success in the future depends on how well we nurture, educate, manage, and instill social consciousness and responsibility in our young people. The success of our nation's military, government and corporate America depends on how well we educate and mentor our youth. Mentoring is perhaps the best tool for ensuring social viability as it is proven to develop people that are better prepared for the challenges that everyone faces in life.

> *"Look for qualities in a mentor that you would admire in a life partner: integrity, good communicator, open-minded, informative, a good listener, dependable, knowledgeable, resourceful, results-oriented, flexible, attentive, and so forth."*
> - *Indigo Triplett Johnson, "Playing by the Unwritten Rules--*
> *Moving from the middle to the top" (2006 page 49).*

As we step deeper into the 21st century, we can rest assured the challenges of competition in a fast-paced, technology-driven, internationally aligned political and economic environment will demand that those aiming for positions of top leadership are the best educated and prepared for those roles.

A key ingredient and trait of great leaders is the ability to shape those who work for and with them—to mold the leaders of tomorrow. It is also one of the most serious of responsibilities. Joseph Conrad said, *"And now the old ships and their men are gone; the new ships and the new men have taken up their watch on the stern-and-impatient sea which offers no opportunities but to those who know how to grasp them with a ready hand and an undaunted heart."* I hope that as a leader you see life as a world of opportunities, that you pursue them with that undaunted heart, and grasp them with ready hands, to make them your own. In doing so you can become the type of leader that shapes and helps others to become the very best, and with that you help not only them, but our nation and the world.

Chapter 9

David R. Scott
Colonel, U.S. Air Force (Retired

"One cannot answer for his courage when he has never been in danger."

— *Francois, Duc de La Rochefoucauld*

Profile

Colonel Dave Scott

Colonel David R. Scott is a retired U.S. Air Force officer and graduate of the U.S. Military Academy where he finished 5th in his class. Because of this high standing, he was able to select which branch of the service he would serve. He chose the Air Force because he wanted to fly jets. After flying school and four years in a fighter squadron in Europe, he earned two graduate degrees at MIT; followed by the Air Force Test Pilot School and the AF Aerospace Research Pilot School.

In October 1963, he was in the third class of astronauts named by NASA. In March 1966 he and command pilot Neil Armstrong flew the Gemini 8 mission. He then served as command module pilot for Apollo 9, which was the first to complete a comprehensive earth-orbital qualification and verification test of a "fully configured Apollo spacecraft." As command module pilot on Apollo 9, he became the last American to fly solo in earth orbit. He made this third space flight as commander of the Apollo 15 mission, the fourth human lunar landing and he was the seventh person, of only 12, to walk on the Moon. Scott was the first person to drive on the surface of the Moon. Using "Rover-1", he and James Irwin performed a geological exploration of portions of Hadley Rille and Apennine Mountains, collecting 180 pounds of lunar surface materials. Nine Apollo missions were launched to the moon and six landed. He is one of 27 members of the lunar family, which stopped taking members in 1972. History has produced more presidents than lunar astronauts. He earned a master's degree from Massachusetts Institute of Technology (MIT) and honorary doctorate from the University of Michigan. After Apollo 15, he moved into NASA management, advancing to appointment as the Director of the Dryden Flight Research Center, Edwards, California. After retiring from the military and leaving NASA in 1977, he founded his own technology company, has co-authored a book with former Soviet cosmonaut Alexei Leonov titled, *"Two Sides of the Moon: Our Story of the Cold War Space Race"*, and consults for films and television. His personal awards include the Air Force Distinguished Service Medal (2 awards); the NASA Distinguished Service Medal (three awards), the Distinguished Flying Cross, the Air Force Association's David C. Schilling Trophy, and the Robert J. Collier Trophy. He is a member of the U.S. Astronaut Hall of Fame and currently resides in Los Angeles.

Leadership Story

Introduction

During the period 1963-1966, my Air Force career took a most fortuitous turn when in late 1963, I was privileged to have been selected by NASA to join the third group of "astronauts" – 2 ½ years later I would fly my first space mission. During that same period, many of my West Point classmates were assigned to join the engagements in Vietnam – one in particular, my close friend Ken Bell, whose Air Force career had paralleled mine, flew *100 missions North* (Macmillan, 1993) in the F-105 Thunderchief "Wild Weasels," and among other honors, was awarded two Silver Stars for gallantry in action. He was fighting my war for me, as were my other classmates so that I could learn and experience leadership in an entirely new field of "combat," the Cold War space race with the Soviet Union. However, although spaceflight has its risks and uncertainties, it does not compare with the risks and uncertainties of enemy fire. To those who engaged the enemy on our behalf and endured the risks and uncertainties of open warfare, I have the greatest admiration, respect, and appreciation.

In order to share with you what I think, (and have learned) are important lessons about leadership and some of the traits of successful leaders; first, it is important to give you some context about the environment and settings that formed my thoughts and the events during, which I observed true leadership traits. Afterwards, I will tell you in detail my own belief about leadership principles and characteristics of leaders.

* * *

In October 1963, I was transferred from Edwards Air Force Base, California, to the NASA Manned Spacecraft Center in Houston, Texas. I subsequently flew three missions, each with increasing leadership opportunities – Gemini 8, Apollo 9, and Apollo 15, for which I was appointed Commander. But my first leadership experience in this new frontier was Gemini 8, launched on March 16, 1966. I was the "pilot" and my commander was Neil Armstrong, a former NASA X-15 research pilot and a veteran of 78 combat missions during the Korean War. As you will note from the following, his leadership qualities were exceptional, and as all leaders know, an aspiring leader must first learn to follow as well as to experience leadership by observation and participation. I am grateful for having had this opportunity, especially under the extreme circumstances in which we found ourselves about seven hours after the launch of Gemini 8.

Briefly, as some background, the "cold war space race" actually began in October 1957 with the launch of the Soviet Sputnik, followed by the first manned orbital mission by Yuri Gagarin in April 1961. The U.S. lagged a year behind in orbital flight, with only the sub-orbital launch of

Alan Shepard in May 1961. However, President Kennedy recognized the situation and essentially declared the race was on in his famous speech to Congress on May 25, 1961. In terms of international visibility and influence (the reason for the race), the Soviet's continued their lead with several notable missions, including the first three-man crew, the first EVA (spacewalk) and the first pair of manned spacecraft in orbit at the same time. By the end of 1965, as the U.S. and USSR programs competed for worldwide attention, the Soviets had launched eight manned missions, while the U.S. had finally caught up, having also launched eight manned missions. 1966, was therefore going to be the key to the race, and the U.S. was determined to take the lead.

The Gemini program was designed to experiment and verify all of the spaceflight operations necessary to land a man on the Moon and return him safely to Earth. But Gemini has experienced some severe "failures" during the past several months; people were beginning to question the progress and rate of the program. The Gemini 6 Titan II launch vehicle shutdown at ignition, but fortunately did not explode. The Agena launch vehicle exploded during launch. Then the Agena rocket engines suffered a hard start and engine failure during ground test. But most tragically, just two weeks before the Gemini 8 launch, the Gemini 9 crew was lost in an airplane accident. Congress is questioning – is Gemini pressing too hard? But Apollo is slipping further behind schedule and overrunning budget estimates, and without verification of such spaceflight operations as rendezvous and docking on Gemini, Apollo will be unable to complete its missions to land a man on the Moon by the end of the decade, and return him safely to Earth.

At the same time the Soviet program was operating in total secrecy and although very little was known about their planning; a series of new spectaculars was expected, very likely further accelerating their lead in the race to the Moon. Congress was getting nervous and many members were becoming even more disenchanted with Kennedy's goal and the "waste of money on the space program," as well as the visible losses of astronauts, rocketships, and airplanes, and the correspondingly high risk of spaceflight as perceived by the public – every failure or loss was front-page news.

These are also troubling times for the United States as a nation. The Vietnam War was escalating, and my West Point classmates are being shot down by SAMs that they cannot attack; political turmoil exists. Communism appears to be gaining worldwide, and Congress is beginning to question the wisdom of spending so much money on going to the Moon when the risks and benefits do not, in the minds of many in Congress and the public, justify the escalating costs, delay in schedules, and most importantly the loss of lives.

In October 1965, during the escalation of both the Vietnam War and the Cold War with the USSR, I am assigned to Gemini 8 as pilot, with Neil Armstrong as commander – we are scheduled to launch five months later, March 16, 1966.

Gemini 8

The Gemini 8 Crew (Dave Scott at left, Neil Armstrong at right)

Background / Preparation

However, the U.S. began to have major problems during the latter part of 1965 and early 1966. Gemini 6 experienced two "failures" in two months:

first, the Atlas Agena target vehicle for rendezvous exploded during launch on October 25, 1965; and then on December 12, 1965, the Gemini 6 Titan II launch vehicle shut down just after ignition, normally requiring a crew ejection (fortunately the crew did not eject). Gemini 6 finally launched on December 15 and joined Gemini 7 in orbit for the first orbital rendezvous. Next up was Gemini 8, scheduled 3 months later, March 1966.

The Gemini 8 mission is designed to demonstrate for the first time the full spectrum of spaceflight operations – rendezvous, docking, combined vehicle operations, extended extravehicular activity (EVA – spacewalk), science, and a precision computer-controlled reentry – four days of intense and carefully planned and coordinated activities. The two-man Gemini spacecraft is stretched beyond its design capabilities – even an auxiliary tape memory had to be added to the overloaded computer, new programs must be loaded and verified in flight.

For Neil Armstrong, and me, it was our first space mission. Our duties in the spacecraft are closely coordinated and communications between us is essential during the dynamic phases of the mission. My main tasks are to monitor the Gemini systems, operate the onboard computer, control the Agena target vehicle when docked, and for this mission in particular conduct the longest and most complicated EVA yet planned for a spaceflight – a 90-minute "walk around the world" with the first "backpack" for life support.

One of the main objectives of Gemini 8 is to dock with an Agena target vehicle and then conduct combined vehicle operations whereby the Agena is used to control the location and orientation of the docked vehicles, including orbital change maneuvers. The Agena is a modified Air Force upper stage that has been plagued with problems.

My job as pilot is to "fly" the Agena when we are docked – I have a small control box that sends 3-digit digital signals through the docking interface to the Agena control system. The function of these signals is to activate-deactivate the Agena as well as to control the orientation and the maneuvers of the docked Gemini-Agena combination. But of course, when docked, only one spacecraft controls the combination, either the Gemini or the Agena – when one is "on" the other must be "off," obviously requiring close coordination between the commander, who flies the Gemini spacecraft, and the pilot.

However, in the interim, more problems with the U.S. space program ensued. A month before launch, troubles with the Agena target vehicle continued with another failure -- a hard start and engine loss during a ground test (12 February). Two weeks later and just two weeks before the scheduled G-8 launch, the Gemini 9 crew died in an aircraft accident, another highly visible failure. With these several and apparent compounding failures, the pressure was on Gemini 8 – it had to demonstrate a highly successful multi-objective mission – because another failure, especially in the eyes of Congress, might very well doom the U.S. side of the race to the Moon for political, budgetary, and technical reasons – success of Gemini 8 was paramount.

(Left) Neil Armstrong – (Right) Dave Scott

Preparations for Gemini 8 are thorough and complete. We know that we have only one chance – regardless of the outcome, as soon as we are launched, everything must work, there will be no second chance, and there will be no more Gemini 8s. Should any part of our mission be unsuccessful, it will be repeated by Gemini 9, now in final preparation only 10 weeks from launch. During these days of Cold War competition, one of the driving forces behind the U.S. approach is the realization, and promotion, that "space is the only arena of worldwide interest in which the U.S. can demonstrate at the same time its scientific expertise, its technological strength, its peaceful intentions, and the openness of a free society." Our mission will be open to the world, every step of the way. (We will later learn that for the first and only time, NASA will withhold from the public the normally open communications between the spacecraft and Mission Control.)

The Mission

Seven hours into the mission, after a perfect pair of launches (Agena and then Gemini 90 minutes later), a precise rendezvous, and smooth docking (the first in space), we enter darkness. As a final maneuver before our first rest period, I command the Agena to yaw the combined vehicles 90 degrees to test the Agena control system and response as well as the structural interface between the two spacecraft. Again a very smooth maneuver. Satisfied that all of our objectives to this point have been right on, we depart the "range" of near-continuous communications and contact with Mission Control Center (MCC). We are now in an orbit that only passes over two ships at sea with keyhole coverage of only about 10% of our flight and no direct links to MCC. We settle down for a meal and begin our night activities, relaxed and comfortable in our secure little spacecraft with our Agena target satellite in smooth tight control of the combined vehicles.

However, just before we depart the final remote comm link with MCC, we receive a somewhat troubling call from the CapCom: "*If you run into trouble and the Agena goes wild, just send in command 400 to turn it off and take control of the spacecraft…*" Our first thought is uh oh, trouble again. Even so, the Agena has performed flawlessly to this point, and we see no signs of any abnormalities, it's a smooth tight bird. Nevertheless, we are on notice, and remain keyed to any potential malfunction. I review my Agena procedures to make sure I am ready should any malfunction occur.

Darkness, no horizon out the small Gemini windows, cabin lights up, all is well as the Agena holds the combination horizontal – soon we should pass over Australia and see the ever-sparkling lights of Perth. I happen to glance toward Neil's side and notice that his "8-ball" (attitude indicator) shows a 20-degree bank – we should be level. "Look, Neil, we're in a bank." He checks his and then mine and says, "OK, we better shut the Agena down and I'll take it." In goes command 400. Neil calmly grabs the hand controller in the console between us; and rolls the spacecraft back to horizontal – all is well. We look at each other quizzically – wonder what caused that? Suddenly the combination begins to roll again, 8-balls showing increasing bank. Neil grabs the hand controller and says firmly, "Agena Off." I send 400 again and respond with the "the Agena IS off." "OK, then turn it back on." I insert command 401 to reactivate the Agena; Neil shuts down the Gemini thrusters – but we continue to roll, slowly at first, but then increasing in roll rate and now pitch rate – we are in an uncontrolled "tumble," now combined roll, pitch and yaw.

We repeat this process several times – Gemini on/off, Agena off/on – but the rates continue to build and response from the hand controller is sporadic; sometimes it helps sometimes it does nothing. We begin to emerge into daylight and can faintly see the horizon sweeping through the windows. Finally, I notice that we are down to only 13% propellant remaining (at this point in the mission we should still have about 75%). And I begin to think about this new untested structural interface between the Gemini and the Agena – time to make a decision. "Maybe we better get off," I say to Neil. "Yes," he says – "let me get it slowed so we don't re-contact and standby to undock." But while Neil is working the handcontroller, I quickly assess the situation with "my" Agena – set so that it can be recovered by MCC ground command and activate our window camera so that the separation can be recorded. He finally reduces the tumble rate as best he can; then with calm determination, says "Ready?" I reach for the Undock switch "Ready." "Rog, undock NOW" he commands. I throw the switch and we immediately disengage. We watch the Agena slide away against the sunlit background of the Earth. Based on the warning from MCC, that should have enabled us to stabilize the Gemini, figure out what had gone wrong. But seconds later we began to roll even more violently – ah ha, another surprise. The moment we undock, the Gemini begins to really spin up, rates increasing and increasing. Just then, we pass over one of the two NASA tracking ships that remote the comm to MCC in Houston. We report our situation, which is not good – "We have a serious problem," I say, as coolly as I can, "We're tumbling end over end up here. We're disengaged from the Agena." Then enters more confusion on the ground, the comm link with MCC is distorted and the quick exchange between the CapCom on the ship and the Flight Director in Houston both complicates the situation for the CapCom as well as alerts MCC that there are major problems with Gemini 8. PAO shuts down the relay of our communications to the public – silence from the NASA Mission Control Center (for the first and only time). MCC Flight Controllers gather the little information they can, all are mystified – the mission has gone so smoothly up to now.

In the meantime, onboard Gemini 8 the tumble rate is increasing, and slowing the rates with the handcontroller seems less and less effective. We are now in full daylight, and as we approach one revolution per second (the camera is still recording), the bright horizon is flashing through the windows almost once a second. Neil looks at me and says, "All we have left is the Reentry Control System" (a separate set of thrusters to be used only during reentry), what do you think?" "Do it," I agree. And then he somehow reaches above his head to an overhead panel and finds the switches to turn off the main thrusters and activate the RCS (I'm still amazed that he could do that while we were spinning so fast). Gemini main thrusters off, RCS on, and finally the handcontroller begins to respond – slowly but surely, Neil recovers the spacecraft and we return to stable horizontal attitude. We look at each other with relief and curiosity -- it wasn't the Agena after all, the problem must have been with the Gemini itself, the reliable, and after seven previous missions, the fully proven Gemini spacecraft.

It has been over 25 minutes since the 20-degree bank was first noticed, we are now in full daylight, but we have just departed the keyhole comm link with the tracking ship and will again be on our own for another 30 minutes until we pass over the next ship. Mission Rules say that once the Reentry Control System is activated, the spacecraft must reenter at the next available opportunity – for if the RCS leaks or fails, there would be no way to get down. The bad news is that our "full-spectrum" spaceflight mission is over with only one ray of light (the first docking), but the good news is that we have recovered from a major failure and can still perform our precision reentry – but for the first time to a secondary recovery area in the South China Sea; over 9,000 miles from the prime recovery forces in the Atlantic. But that's another story; and although there will be no repeat of Gemini 8, Neil and I will each have another day.

Apollo 15

Air Force Colonel David Scott salutes the flag during the Apollo 15 mission

Background / Preparation

On November 30, 1969, I was appointed Commander of Apollo 15, scheduled for launch in July 1971. I spent the next 20 months with my all-Air-Force crew (Lt. Col. Alfred M. Worden and Lt. Col. James B. Irwin) totally focused on those leadership principles that had worked so well on Gemini 8 (and Apollo 9) and that would maximize our chances of success (and survival) on Apollo 15.

First, came an estimate of the situation. Our mission was to land and explore one of several landing sites on the Moon then being considered. Our basic objective was to extend the scientific exploration of the Moon with new more flexible space suits and longer duration "backpacks" (life support systems). Apollo 12 had just demonstrated a "pinpoint" landing and I had been backup Commander so I was comfortable with the flight operations expected of us. However, our mission was primarily "field geology." During the Apollo program, the Commander of the mission, once appointed had considerable flexibility in the manner in which he prepares his team and conducts the mission. Therefore, my first action was to ensure our training encompassed as much realistic field geology training as practical – learn as much as we can, practice in as high a fidelity environment as we can, and maximize the returns for the scientific community. A somewhat new challenge for three fighter pilots none of whom had even been "rock hounds' before we joined NASA. But we were determined to demonstrate new skills in a new discipline, and at the same time ensure the corresponding success of our spaceflight operations – including another pinpoint landing.

Five months later, in April 1970, as we were really getting geared up, Apollo 13 suffered a near-fatal explosion on the way to the Moon. Leadership and teamwork by both the crew and MCC got them back safely. But the NASA lunar exploration program suffered a major setback, and perhaps a terminal failure in the eyes of the public and Congress. However, less than three months later, NASA leadership made one of its boldest decisions. In the face of the near disaster of Apollo 13, dwindling public support, and a rapidly declining budget, NASA leadership decided to skip the final "H" type mission (Apollo 15 after

Apollo 14); press on with upgrading the complete Apollo "system" (hardware, software, science, and operations) to the "J" configuration, and launch three full-up "J" missions to the most significant scientific sites on the Moon. This upgrade from "H" to "J" included the Lunar Roving Vehicle, double the lunar stay time, double the EVA surface excursion time, significantly more scientific equipment and experiments, and many other enhancements.

To go beyond the first lunar landing, the Apollo 11 "G" mission in July 1969, demonstrated considerable courage and confidence, especially after achieving the political objective of "landing a man on the Moon and returning him safely to Earth." But to advance beyond "H" into even one "J" mission (much less three J missions) required a very bold and aggressive decision. But this commitment to the enhanced "J" missions was surely one of the most rewarding decisions of the Apollo Program. It would have been a lot easier, safer, and cheaper to finish the program with the final two "H" missions as scheduled (for if one of the final missions were to be a failure, the Program would surely end and "Apollo" would forever have been considered a "failure"). Fortunately for the overall results and success of Apollo, as well as for providing a great opportunity for the Apollo 15 team – Apollo 14, seven months from launch, continues as the final "H" mission, but Apollo 15 was immediately upgraded from the final "H" mission to the first "J" mission – the first "extended scientific exploration of the Moon."

Apollo 15 Mission

July 26, 1971, at precisely 0936 EST, Apollo 15 lifts off from Cape Kennedy – cargo: our Air Force crew of three, the Command and Service Module (CSM), *Endeavor*, the Lunar Module (LM), *Falcon*, and *LRV-1*, the first Lunar Roving Vehicle -- destination: the Hadley Rille at the base of the Apennine Mountains, the northern-most landing point in the Apollo program. We are ready and eager to go -- on what *Time* magazine calls "*Apollo 15: The Most Perilous Journey*" – a journey that includes a descent twice as steep as prior missions which passes directly through a gap in the Apennine Mountains to a small area just short of the vast "Hadley Rille," a canyon 1,000 feet deep and a mile across.

During launch, lying in the left, Commander's couch, every second I monitor every instrument in front of me; I listen to every word from Al in the center couch and Jim in the right couch; and of course the ever-present MCC CapCom. The Abort handle is in my left hand – a 45 degree <u>left</u> twist and we abort the launch – and the mission; a 45 degree <u>right</u> twist and I take control of the entire stack with the hand controller in my right hand – the entire Saturn V launch vehicle can be flown manually from lift-off to all the way to orbit in case the Saturn guidance system fails.

Arrival in Earth orbit is right on. One orbit later, Trans Lunar Insertion sends us on our way to the Moon. During the three-day transit, we encounter only minor problems: a water leak in the Command Module cabin and broken glass from an instrument in the Lunar Module. Finally, after 240,000 miles, we enter a lunar orbit 60 miles above the surface and spend a day preparing both spacecraft for the landing. As we close the hatches between the CSM and the LM, Jim and I shake hands with Al (who will fly solo in lunar orbit for three days), disconnect from the CSM and begin our descent. On the far side of the Moon during initial descent, Jim solves a problem with the Environmental Control System, and as we begin our final approach, we pass below and between the tops of the Apennine Mountains – a striking visual surprise out the sides of our windows that simulators never show.

Final approach and touchdown with fuel to spare, well above minimums, the training has been superb – the Abort button is right in front of me, but I never even give it a second thought – once we are on final approach, our minds go to the "land" mode, not the "abort mode" as we have practiced so many times in our simulators. There follows three days of "planetary field geology" in the most spectacular setting I have ever seen; only being there can bring the experience to reality. We press through this high-intensity but fulfilling exploration on this pristine area of our vast and lonely Moon, making time-critical and risk-critical decisions moment by moment. But of course, while living on the Moon with such complex equipment, we have our share of problems: an oxygen leak in the LM the first morning; and a water leak inside the LM the third morning, both of which are solved, but they cut into our brief sleep periods.

After three days of living and working on the Moon, liftoff to join Al in the CSM, precise rendezvous and docking, transfer of our lunar treasures, followed by two more days of science around the Moon, including the launch of a small scientific satellite into lunar orbit. Then the final maneuver by the CSM -- Trans Earth Insertion for the three-day trip home. But even more science on the way: we take the first photos from space of "black holes." A precision reentry takes us to our landing point next to the USS OKINAWA (LPH-3), our recovery carrier in the Pacific, but not before the final surprise – one of our three parachutes collapses during final descent. But the "system" is designed to land safely with two chutes; imagination, anticipation, and brilliant engineering prevail again. The Navy picks us up and takes us home; we debrief science and engineering, and write our reports; and then our new careers as ambassadors begins – seven interesting months of travel and telling our story: many U.S. cities and many European cities, West and East, including Yugoslavia and Poland (the second official U.S. delegation since WW II).

Back in Houston, the scientists and engineers are hard at work, compiling and analyzing the data; with the results of the mission probably best summarized four months later in the Foreword to the Apollo 15 *Preliminary Science Report*:

Foreword

In richness of scientific return, the Apollo 15 voyage to the plains at Hadley compares with voyages of Darwin's H.M.S *Beagle*, and those of the *Endeavour* and *Resolution*. Just as those epic ocean voyages set the stage for a revolution in the biological sciences and exploration generally, so also the flight of *Falcon* and *Endeavor* did the same in planetary and Earth sciences and will guide the course of future explorations.

The boundary achievements of Apollo 15 cannot now be established. As the author of the following paper points out, the mission was not finished at splashdown in the Pacific, nor later with painstaking analysis in scores of laboratories of the samples and cores brought back, nor with careful study of the photographic imagery and instrument traces returned home. For the distinctive fact is that the mission is not yet over. Data still flow in daily from the isotope-powered station emplaced on the plain at Hadley, and from the Moon-encircling scientific satellite left in orbit. This data flow is of exceptional value because it now affords, for the first time, a triangulation of lunar events perceived by the three physically separated scientific stations that man has left on the Moon.

This volume is the first, though assuredly not the final, effort to assemble a comprehensive accounting of the scientific knowledge so far acquired through this remarkable mission.

Dr. James C. Fletcher, Administrator
National Aeronautics and Space Administration
December 8, 1971

And because of the mission, I was gratified to receive the Air Force Distinguished Service Medal as well as NASA's highest award with the citation:

"For leading the most complex and carefully planned scientific expedition in the history of exploration..."

Leadership Characteristics & Principles

The characteristics of a leader can be described in many forms. From my experience and observations, I believe that they can best be described in terms of certain individual characteristics and basic principles of behavior. Three requirements are paramount for a leader: (1) prepare for the "mission" in all manner of known and expected "opportunities" and "challenges;" (2) make sound and timely decisions, but make decisions; and (3) remain calm, cool, and collected under "fire."

Other very important qualities of a leader include: (a) maintain the highest standards of appearance as well as mental and physical capabilities; (b) encourage open communications and be receptive to inputs from your charges; (c) communicate instructions and orders with clear, concise, and understandable terms; (d) take responsibility for all actions of the team; (d) keep pressure on the team for maximum performance every day, whether in preparation or during the mission; let no minute pass without max performance from everybody; (e) encourage others to take action, then judge their action; (f) make your position known to your supervisors, but with respect; (f) work as a team, rely on your colleagues just as they must rely on you.

"Leadership" can be characterized by personal qualities and traits as well as principles of action and (analysis, leading, commanding). Leaders are born with certain personal qualities, and leaders are made by experience and training. Successful leadership must include major elements of each. Further, the applications of military leadership must also be qualified by whether or not the leader is acting under arms – lessons for corporate America will in general exclude those military leadership qualities that are expressed under arms. Leadership activities during a space mission are probably a good example of a mixture or hybrid of both (at least during the Apollo program days).

Because of the unique nature of space missions, leadership requires special emphasis on certain qualities, especially anticipation, imagination, and most-importantly preparation. But unlike the military, space missions were not "under arms" (nobody was shooting at us), although conducted in a hazardous environment (where even small mistakes had life or death consequences). A space mission is a one-time event, usually of national or international significance, and, especially for the US, with high public visibility; there are no second chances – if the mission fails, there is no fallback or regrouping for a second try. Therefore, the leader must anticipate the requirements for performance, imagine the "what-ifs," and prepare his team for both nominal and off-nominal situations.

We learned many things from the Gemini 8 experience. One thing of course was the cause and fix of the thruster malfunction – the electrical command to open the thruster propellant valves was changed from the application of a ground to the application of electrical power, thus an incidental "grounding" of a loose wire could not cause a thruster to fire, as it did intermittently during our tumble. But many leadership qualities and principles were also demonstrated.

Planning and preparation prior to the mission were thorough and complete, including a wide range of "what ifs" – however, at the time, a simulator representing the combined vehicles (Gemini and Agena) was not available, and nobody thought much about combined vehicle operations under emergency situations. Gemini 8 was to demonstrate the operations of all of the space "technology" and concepts available at the time. Through our training and preparation, (albeit absent the combination) Neil and I built confidence in the system, the procedures, and especially ourselves – we were ready to go, and we felt that as a team, we could handle any unusual situation. And an unusual situation we had. The successful recovery of Gemini 8 can be attributed to many leadership principles, most of which can be applied to corporate leadership.

Although the problem occurred as a surprise and increased in intensity, we remained cool and calm throughout. Decisions were made quickly but thoughtfully analyzing and interpreting the options. Teamwork was essential because of the nature of two active vehicles joined together but necessarily being controlled by only one; however, Neil was commander and his lead was key to success; i.e., unity of command. Orderly discipline but coordinated teamwork was continuous. The problem was a surprise that nobody had anticipated, and we had even been directed along the wrong path (*"send Agena command 400"*) – therefore it was necessary to improvise both the procedures to be used and their sequence of application. Throughout the tumble, even when it reached its most violent, we were determined to solve the problem and we had confidence in ourselves, individually and as a team. And when the problem was solved, even though the mission had to be terminated early and most objectives had to be abandoned, the mission was still a "winner."

At the time, NASA and the space program were having major problems – had Gemini 8 been "lost in space," and not recovered, it can be argued that the entire program might have been terminated – with the high rate of roll, MCC would have been unable to obtain data from the spacecraft and had no control over the spacecraft anyway; Gemini 8 with its crew would have remained in orbit for many years. But regardless of conclusions, a very long period of analysis and uncertainty would have ensued, perhaps allowing the Soviet Union to regain the lead and eventually win the race to the Moon.

NASA vs. Military Culture

To understand better the leadership principles discussed above, it is important to understand the organizational culture and command structure of the National Aeronautics and Space Administration (NASA) during the Apollo era as well as the roles and responsibilities of the mission Commander. In essence, NASA was somewhat a hybrid organization between the military and corporate cultures.

However, within this context, the NASA mission must also be understood – NASA of Apollo was an R&D organization formed for the specific objective of human exploration of the Moon. The leadership principles described in this relate to both the conduct of the mission as well as the effects of planning, preparation, and training. This NASA management (or command) culture could be seen as a mid-point between the military command culture and the corporate management (or governance) culture – not as rigid as the military, but at the same time not as flexible as the corporate culture.

During the mission, the commander had absolute authority over real-time decision-making, especially any decision he deemed appropriate to ensure (1) the safety of the crew and (2) the success of the mission. However, major factors in this decision-making were the support and recommendations of the Mission Control Center (MCC). During the mission, just as in the field during a military operation, seldom is there any override by senior management (command), almost as if the unit were isolated without communications with headquarters. In fact, should communications with Earth be lost, the crew must be prepared to complete the segment of the mission in which they were engaged and return to Earth successfully on their own. However, correspondingly, the commander is directly and personally accountable for his actions to the entire chain of command of NASA as well as to Congress (and ostensibly to the President, but unlikely in practice). That is, should a fault occur, the commander could be required to testify directly to Congress as the responsible individual in NASA, essentially absolving the entire chain of command from the action in question. The burden of responsibility remains with the commander. Prior to and directly after the mission, the commander reports to the NASA chain of command in a manner similar to the military; but with the unique flexibility (albeit seldom used) to be able to bypass the chain of command and present his case directly to the NASA Administrator without fear of retribution or condemnation (although would not be tolerated on my watch). Thus the responsibility and authority flows both ways from top to bottom and vice versa, with no barriers in between, other than perception of colleagues.

To illustrate the responsibility and authority of the Commander of an Apollo mission, during a mission to the Moon, the operations and even existence of the spaceship traveling through the vast and lonely universe was very similar to that of a sea ship traveling the oceans of Earth about 400 years ago. The captain of the ship had absolute authority; he was truly master and commander. During an Apollo mission, the Commander (CDR) has direct control over only two individuals – the Command Module Pilot (CMP) and the Lunar Module Pilot (LMP). The CMP is second-in-command of the mission and flies the orbiting Command Module solo while the CDR and the LMP explore the surface of the Moon. However, the CDR is ultimately responsible for the results of the entire mission -- if the CDR fails, the mission fails.

But a major difference from ships at sea was that the very complex spaceship required a support team of 400,000 dedicated individuals to maximize the success of the mission and the safety of the astronaut crew; and once launched into the sea of space, this team supported the spaceship via almost continuous communications links. However, similar to the ships at sea 400 years ago, the captain of the ship could not be replaced, effectively, that is (even under direct orders) – he was the only member of the crew who had the experience and had been trained to perform and direct his crew in certain high-risk tasks (such as launch aborts, landing aborts, and the lunar landing itself).

Further, an Apollo mission represented the capability and culture of the United States which was openly exposed to the entire world – it has been said that human space exploration is the only arena of worldwide interest in which the United States can demonstrate at the same time its scientific expertise, technological strength, peaceful intentions, and the openness of a free society. During our information age, the eyes and ears of the world are on the mission at hand and especially the performance of the astronaut crew.

In Gemini 8, I was very fortunate to have been able to support a true leader who in all likelihood saved the U.S. space program and the race to the Moon. Had Gemini 8 been lost, a long delay, or even termination, of the program would have occurred. In fact, the race was even closer than we imagined at the time. 2 ½ years later we learned that as Apollo 8 was preparing to launch to the Moon during the third week in December 1968, the Soviets had a launch window and a two-man Soyuz lunar spacecraft on the pad during the first week of December 1968, an opportunity two weeks ahead of Apollo 8 (but they decided to delay until January) – for whatever interpretation may be made of the space race, it was very, very close – because, given slightly different circumstances, Soyuz __ might have returned the first photos of Earthrise from the Moon, and Apollo 8, with its now-famous Earthrise photo, would have been a footnote.

I am most thankful to my colleagues, my mentors, and my own special leaders for those lessons of leadership that I learned at West Point, in the Air Force, and on Gemini 8 and Apollo 9 that enabled me to contribute to the success of most challenging and rewarding mission of my career. We had taken the challenge, we were proud of our achievements, and we all hope that Apollo 15 contributed to both science and "winning" the Cold War, for those were the real reasons for this exciting voyage to the mountains of the Moon.

Dave Scott on the Moon (the lunar rover in the background)

Chapter 10

Elmo R. Zumwalt, Jr. (Deceased)
Admiral, U.S. Navy
By James G. Zumwalt

"All that is necessary for the triumph of evil is for good men to do nothing."

— *Edmund Burke*

Profile

Admiral Elmo R. Zumwalt, Jr.

Admiral Elmo Russell Zumwalt, Jr., was born in San Francisco, California, on 29 November 1920, son of Dr. E. R. Zumwalt, Sr. and Dr. Frances Zumwalt. In 1939, he received an appointment to the U. S. Naval Academy, Annapolis, Maryland, from his native state. Zumwalt graduated in the top three percent of his 1943 class, which, due to the war, had an accelerated graduation in 1942. Commissioned Ensign on 19 June 1942, he was promoted just 28 years later to the rank of 4-star Admiral (1 July 1970).

Following graduation from the Naval Academy in June 1942, he joined the destroyer USS PHELPS (DD-360). In August 1943, he was detached for instruction in the Operational Training Command, Pacific, at San Francisco,

California. In January 1944, he reported onboard USS ROBINSON (DD-562) where his actions later earned him a Bronze Star with Combat "V" for "heroic service, in action against enemy Japanese battleships during the Battle for Leyte Gulf, 25 October 1944.

Just before hostilities ended in August 1945, until December 8th, Zumwalt commanded (initially as prize crew officer with ten sailors) HIJMS ATAKA, a captured 1200-ton Japanese river gunboat with two hundred enemy officers and men onboard. In that capacity, he sailed the first ship to fly the flag of the United States, since the outbreak of World War II, up the Whangpoo River to Shanghai. There he helped restore order and assisted in disarming the Japanese. It was there that he met his future wife.

He next served as Executive Officer of the destroyer USS SAUFLEY (DD-465) before being transferred in March 1946 to the destroyer USS ZELLARS (DD-777), as Executive Officer and Navigator. In January 1948, he was assigned to the Naval Reserve Officers Training Corps Unit of the University of North Carolina at Chapel Hill, remaining until June 1950. That month, he assumed command of the destroyer escort USS TILLS (DE-748), in commission in reserve status. When USS TILLS was placed in full active commission at Charleston Naval Shipyard on 21 November 1950, he remained in command until March 1951, when he reported onboard the battleship USS WISCONSIN (BB-64) as Navigator.

The Commander, Seventh Fleet, recognized Zumwalt "For meritorious service as Navigator of USS WISCONSIN during combat operations against enemy North Korean and Chinese Communist forces in the Korean Theater from 23 November 1951 to 30 March 1952...," awarding him a Letter of Commendation, with Ribbon and Combat "V."

Detached from USS WISCONSIN in June 1952, Zumwalt attended the Naval War College, Newport, Rhode Island, and in June 1953 reported as Head of the Shore and Overseas Bases Section, Bureau of Naval Personnel, Navy Department, Washington, D. C. In July 1955, he assumed command of the destroyer USS ARNOLD J. ISBELL (DD-869), participating in two deployments to the Seventh Fleet. In this assignment, he was commended by the Commander, Cruiser-Destroyer Forces, U.S. Pacific Fleet for winning the Battle Efficiency Competition for his ship and for winning Excellence Awards in Engineering, Gunnery, Antisubmarine Warfare, and Operations. In July 1957, he returned to the

Bureau of Naval Personnel for further duty. In December 1957, he was transferred to the Office of the Assistant Secretary of the Navy (Personnel and Reserve Forces) and served as Special Assistant for Naval Personnel until November 1958, followed by a tour as Special Assistant and Naval Aide until August 1959.

In December 1959, he took command of the first vessel built from the keel up as a guided missile ship, USS DEWEY (DLG-14), remaining in that position until June 1961. During his tenure of command, USS DEWEY earned the Excellence Award in Engineering, Supply, Weapons, and was runner-up in the Battle Efficiency Competition.

During the 1961-1962 academic year, he was a student at the National War College, Washington, D. C. In June 1962, he was assigned to the Office of the Assistant Secretary of Defense (International Security Affairs), Washington, D. C. From December 1963 until 21 June 1965, he was Executive Assistant and Senior Aide to the Honorable Paul H. Nitze, Secretary of the Navy. For his service in the offices of the Secretary of Defense and the Secretary of the Navy, Zumwalt was awarded the Legion of Merit.

In July 1965, after his selection for Rear Admiral at age 44, Zumwalt assumed command of Cruiser-Destroyer Flotilla Seven. in that capacity, he was awarded a Gold Star in lieu of a Second Legion of Merit. In August 1966, he became Director of the Chief of Naval Operations Systems Analysis Group, Washington, D. C. As Director, Systems Analysis Division, Office of the Chief of Naval Operations, Deputy Scientific Officer to the Center for Naval Analyses, during the period from August 1966 to August 1968, he was awarded the Distinguished Service Medal.

In September 1968, he was promoted to Vice Admiral at age 47 to become Commander U.S. Naval Forces, Vietnam and Chief of the Naval Advisory Group, U. S. Military Assistance Command, Vietnam. On 14 April 1970, President Richard M. Nixon nominated him, at age 49, for a fourth star to serve as Chief of Naval Operations. Upon being relieved as Commander Naval Forces, Vietnam, on 15 May 1970, Zumwalt was awarded a Gold Star in lieu of a second Distinguished Service Medal for exceptionally meritorious service. He assumed command as Chief of Naval Operations on 1 July 1970 and retired from that position on 1 July 1974. For nearly the next quarter century, Zumwalt enjoyed a very successful career as a businessman, author, speaker and contributor in time and resources to numerous charitable initiatives.

Admiral Zumwalt died on 2 January 2000 at the Duke University Medical Center in Durham, NC. His home was in Arlington, Virginia. He was married to the former Mouza Coutelais-du-Roche of Harbin, Manchuria. They had two sons, Elmo R. Zumwalt III, who died of cancer in 1988, and James Gregory Zumwalt, and two daughters, Ann F. Zumwalt Coppola and Mouza C. Zumwalt-Weathers. He is also survived by six grandchildren.

Leadership Story

MAKING WAVES

It is difficult to define leadership. In some ways, it lends itself to the same description of "obscenity" given by Supreme Court Justice Potter Stewart in a 1964 ruling in which he said, although he was unable to describe it, he knew it when he saw it.

This effort is magnified with great leaders as they rarely share all the same strengths. One's strength may well be another's weakness. But leaders achieve greatness because they have come to recognize what their weaknesses are, balancing them against their strengths. They mold these into a leadership blend unique unto themselves.

Because of this distinctiveness, any new leader taking charge of an organization automatically introduces into it an element of change. But when that organization is not performing as it should or as needed to meet future challenges, sweeping changes are required to set it on the right course. Great leaders implementing such changes inevitably make waves. And those waves generate either supporters or critics.

My father, Admiral Elmo R. Zumwalt, Jr., headed the U.S. Navy as Chief of Naval Operations (CNO) from 1970-1974. Given this responsibility at the age of 49, he was the youngest admiral ever to do so. He inherited a Navy suffering on many fronts that was quickly finding itself unable to meet future threats posed by an expanding Soviet Navy during the Cold War. With only a four-year tour in which to turn the Navy around, he embarked upon some very radical programs to shake the service up in order to effect the necessary course changes. He was a wave-maker. In doing so, he generated both controversy and critics.

Let me acknowledge at the outset, as a son who is writing about the leadership of a father who was his life's hero, I open myself up to criticism for lack of objectivity. But to such critics, I proffer the following: As one who observed firsthand the challenges facing my father and the battles he had to fight, I feel I bring to the reader certain personal insights and considerations to which a more detached observer would not be privy.

I will begin with just such an insight—a lesson of leadership about loyalty conveyed to me in the hours soon after my father's death.

* * *

As New Year celebrants were recovering from the dawn of a new millennium, I was mourning my father's loss. He died, at age 79—a victim of mesothelioma— during the early morning hours of January 2, 2000.

During his last days, I had been keeping friends apprised of his deteriorating health via periodic email communications. As I struggled to put together the words of his death in the final email, there was one person I felt a personal responsibility to call to tell of his demise.

In the late 1960s, Admiral Chon was my father's counterpart during the Vietnam war. While Chon commanded the South Vietnamese Navy, my father commanded all U.S. Naval Forces there from 1968-1970. A criticism sometimes made by our South Vietnamese allies was the failure of their American counterparts to treat them as equals. Such criticism was never leveled against my father. Working with my father, Chon quickly found him to be a man of compassion and intellect. And, understanding the cultural barriers that sometimes existed between allies, my father made sure Chon was always included in strategy sessions—his counsel sought on any issue affecting US/South Vietnamese naval performance. It created a bond between the two by which they became brothers—a bond evident during the twelve years Chon later spent in a re-education camp after the fall of Saigon in 1975 as my father worked diligently to win Chon's release. Soon after Chon was finally allowed to leave Vietnam in 1991, among those to greet him was my father.

When I reached Chon by phone that January morning to share the news about my father's death, I got no further than a greeting. Chon interrupted to say, "Your father died, didn't he?" I responded in the affirmative. But what Chon said next was telling to me, not only about the strength of their friendship but also about the leadership trait that gave rise to it.

"I had a dream last night," Chon explained. "Your father and I were on a ship that was sinking. Your father pushed me through a hatch to safety. I then turned around and extended my hand to help him up through the hatch. But he shook his head 'no,' closing the hatch behind me. I knew this morning as I awoke that he had passed — and I had been separated from my brother."

Chon came to respect Zumwalt as an innovative leader who developed a winning naval strategy during the Vietnam war. In fact, it was the remarkable success of that strategy that gave Zumwalt a high profile with his superiors — the Commander of the Military Advisory Command Vietnam, General Creighton Abrams, and Secretary of Defense Melvin Laird — eventually propelling him to the Navy's top position.

But Chon also came to respect Zumwalt for leadership traits demonstrating a tremendous capacity to seek the counsel of others, nurturing a team mindset, sorting through issues, analyzing them critically, and then making decisions on how best to proceed. Everyone's opinion was valued so that every potential impact of a strategic decision was considered in advance. Only after all the "knowns" were considered did Zumwalt then make his final decision.

Interestingly, while valuing the counsel provided by others, Zumwalt did what great leaders sometimes have to do — opting to exercise a decision running contrary to the team's popular opinion based on his own determination the gains far exceeded the risks.

Nowhere was this more evident than Zumwalt's decision to defy conventional wisdom by creating an isolated base deep in enemy territory.

* * *

The Cau Mau Peninsula makes up the extreme southern tip of Vietnam. It is a place of streams and mangrove swamps with very difficult access. For years, the Viet Cong used the area as a sanctuary. It was deemed so irremediably enemy territory that locals were evacuated to enable B-52s to bomb it. The region, normally fertile with people, was uninhabited and thus devoid of the daily commercial activities usually pursued.

Zumwalt analyzed the feasibility of establishing a resettlement effort for locals on the peninsula if the Navy could succeed in gaining control of a section of a principal river in the area. He envisioned such a resettlement effort beginning on the riverbanks, gradually spreading up and down river and, eventually, inland.

Zumwalt initiated his normal team decision-making process in which the U.S. Army also participated. The majority of the team deemed it foolish risk to establish a base on the riverbank in that part of the country. So Zumwalt hit upon the idea establishing a floating base—built upon pontoons—in the middle of the river. The majority's input deemed this even more foolish as such a base could easily be targeted for mortar or sapper attacks.

But Zumwalt believed the concept, dubbed "Sea Float," would work. Riverine patrol boats would operate up and down river from the base to provide security and show the flag. A helicopter pad would be available to shuttle men and supplies to the base. Nets and various warning devices would be installed to prevent mines from floating downstream to it and to detect swimmers. Zumwalt convinced General Abrams that Sea Float could succeed. Against the advice of his own Army and Air Force subordinate commanders, Abrams approved it.

Sea Float went on to become one of the most successful military operations undertaken by the Navy during the war as local Vietnamese, feeling safe under a U.S. security umbrella, began occupying the riverbanks. As Zumwalt envisioned, the resettlement spread up and down the river and eventually inland. As the locals returned, so too did commercial activities: they began re-planting pineapples, re-building pottery kilns and re-started fishing and shrimping operations. Safety gave rise to prosperity. The loyalty of the local citizenry was directed at Saigon rather than the Viet Cong. That loyalty became so entrenched that the Cau Mau Peninsula proved to be one of the most difficult areas for North Vietnam to secure after Saigon fell in 1975.

* * *

As Commander, U.S. Naval Forces Vietnam, Zumwalt—a veteran of World War II and Korea—found his Vietnam war experience quite different from his experiences in other wars. In both World War II and Korea, the decisions he made in combat placed his own safety in peril equally with that of his men. If the right decision was made, all benefitted; if not, all suffered its consequences.

In Vietnam, however, the decisions Zumwalt made placed only his subordinates at risk as he remained safely at command headquarters. This concerned him, causing him to embark upon a policy in which he started accompanying patrol boats on their combat missions. While the policy boosted the morale of his sailors, General Abrams soon stopped it. Abrams' concern was should Zumwalt be killed, wounded or captured, the loss of such a senior level commander would provide the enemy with a great propaganda victory.

No longer able to join his men on patrol, Zumwalt did whatever he could, within the letter of Abrams' order, to continue to show them he was willing to share their risks as well. He dutifully visited units at isolated locations, showing the command flag. To further boost morale, he expedited the awarding of medals after a combat action occurred, resulting in his personal appearance at such unit locations, regardless of where they were, to pin the medal upon a deserving sailor's chest days after earning it.

* * *

When Zumwalt was promoted to the Navy's highest position—catapulted over 33 senior admirals—some people were surprised; some not. A person who experienced both emotions was Jason Hammer. In a very moving tribute to Zumwalt he wrote after the admiral's death in 2000, Hammer recalled with fondness and admiration a man for whom he held immense respect—despite the fact 55 years had passed since his last contact with him.

"My immediate reaction was surprise," Hammer wrote when he first read about Zumwalt's selection as CNO, "the happy surprise of someone falling heir to a small degree of vicarious fame that somehow lends credence to his own, shared experiences. And yet, no surprise. I was not surprised he had become the youngest Chief of Naval Operations in U.S. naval history. I figured he simply set his mind to it. It was merely a logical extension of my idea of what kind of a man he was."

Combat tests the mettle of a man—and no higher compliment can be paid a leader by a subordinate than to praise that leader for having maintained a calming command presence in battle that served to instill peaceful confidence into his men. It was just such a moment in his tribute that Hammer recounted more than half a century after the incident happened.

Zumwalt, explained Hammer was, "the epitome of what an intelligent, good-humored and efficient naval officer should be and at the same time one of the kindest and most considerate men it was my good fortune to have served with...a wonderful human being deeply dedicated to equality and justice in word and deed for all people...In most instances, naval protocol effectively stifled any meaningful socializing between officers and enlisted men. That's the way it was, and each accepted it as a fact of life. We were shipmates in the sense that if something went radically wrong, we were all, regardless of rank, literally in the same boat. In any event, socializing with him certainly was not a prerequisite for recognizing that seemingly unflappable aura which seemed to surround him even under the most nerve-jangling circumstances. That calm command would have been memorable even to someone knowing nothing else about him beyond what they could observe. It left an indelible impression. Anyone dependent on another human being for leadership, and in desperate need of some degree of assurance under hazardous conditions, immediately will recognize the feeling. Here was a man from whom I repeatedly gained some measure of peace of mind. His quiet strength and obvious calm, whether during torpedo run, kamikaze attack or retaliatory fire from hostile shore batteries, never failed to reassure me with his always observable control of any situation. There was, however, one occasion when the lieutenant's decorum proved his human vulnerability and belied his usual stoic approach to danger."

In his tribute, Hammer goes on to detail a nighttime combat action involving USS ROBINSON (DD-562) in October 1944 during the Battle of Surigao Strait. The action was the second of four that took place against the Japanese during the Battle of Leyte Gulf—considered the biggest battle in naval history.

As a Radioman 3rd Class, Hammer worked directly under Lieutenant Zumwalt in the Combat Information Center (CIC) of the destroyer USS ROBINSON.

CIC was the ship's nerve center, where all information about threats to the ship and the ship's status was constantly monitored and relayed to the bridge. The CIC officer was charged with responsibility for assessing all such information and keeping the Officer of the Deck (OOD) and captain apprised of all dangers. While these dangers were also to be monitored by the OOD on the bridge, the CIC officer served as back-up to ensure action was taken in a timely manner.

ROBINSON was operating with other ships of the U.S. Navy's 7th Fleet, including some of the battleships damaged at Pearl Harbor. These ships, Hammer said, "savored the pungent smell of revenge by firing devastating salvos at… (the enemy's) cornered fleet… (which) without success… (was) trying desperately to clear the Surigao Strait and take evasive action."

One can only imagine the intense activity taking place in the CIC as ROBINSON—making a nighttime torpedo attack against enemy battleships—dealt with evading enemy shells from the Japanese battleships as ROBINSON closed in on its target, releasing those torpedoes and then veering away from a disturbed hornet's nest of

Japanese battlewagons, while simultaneously listening for the sonar ping of an enemy submarine and trying to determine the threat posed by an unidentified blip on the radar screen. Yet, in the midst of all this activity, in the midst of the ever-changing flow of information and in the midst of having to assess all viable threats and prioritize them, a voice of calm maintained constant control over a dangerous situation that only seemed to be getting worse.

Hammer's tribute sets the tone for the events of that evening:

"It was a black velvet night in October—total darkness, except for the eerie phosphorescent glow of the ship's wake. The only stars in the sky were man-made bursts of heavy-caliber gunfire. If there was a moon, it was obscured by a heavy pall of thick, black smoke...

"Aboard ROBINSON, I was at my battle station, operating a radio in the Combat Information Center...Exact courses were plotted, and radar information was interpreted. At that moment, sonar antisubmarine information punctuated the tense air with its rhythmic and penetrating ping, mixing with staccato instructions and questions from the bridge.

"All this diverse and critically important information was being directed at Lt. Zumwalt, standing at my left studying a large, circular, table-like radar screen brightly lighted from the underside of its clear plastic top. The ever-changing crayon marks offered a kaleidoscopic overview of our position in relation to other ships in the formation.

"To the practiced eye, the hieroglyphics told an accurate picture of a potentially chaotic and deadly game of 'Listen to all instructions, see all potential hazards in advance and ABOVE ALL EXECUTE ALL ORDERS IMMEDIATELY!

"Any miscalculations could spell disaster. We were the electronic eyes and ears on which so many matters of life and death depended.

"Strangely, I was not worried—excited, yes, but not worried.

"In addition to a heavy sense of adventure which seemed to shield me from the reality of the danger, I totally was reassured by the expected calm efficiency being displayed by the lieutenant.

"Lt. Zumwalt was showing his proven ability to transmit a quiet serenity to everyone around him—his voice always even, his actions always carefully considered and calm, regardless of the urgency of the situation—and the circumstances at hand certainly called for all the calm we could muster.

"We were, at the moment, on a torpedo run and closing rapidly with a Japanese battleship while running directly under large and small-caliber shells being exchanged by the opposing fleets.

"We fired five torpedoes at our flaming target, now totally obscured by a thick pall of smoke. No waiting around to see the results, if any. We turned sharply and, at flank speed, rushed for the relative safety only distance could provide. Our capital ships (battleships) still fired relentlessly over our head at their designated targets.

"Enemy star shells hung in the sky directly overhead pointing a bright accusing finger of light at our naked vulnerability as the crew heard the ominous sounds of shells chasing our wake and often landing dangerously close to our thin-skinned hull.

"As the seconds ticked by, our lease on life seemed to lengthen in proportion to the distance we rapidly put between us and our desperate foe in the throes of its own funeral pyre.

"Suddenly, our mounting euphoria was tempered by a suspicious-looking blip on the radar screen. Was it one of our own or an enemy ship?

"The lieutenant reported to the bridge: 'Radar contact. Unidentified object in the water dead ahead.'

"No answer from the bridge.

"The tension mounted to an almost audible level as the lieutenant at this point observed that the ship had changed course and, in fact, was heading toward Little Hibuson Island.

"'On collision course,' (advised Zumwalt).

"'Bridge! Little Hibuson Island dead ahead. Closing rapidly,' (Zumwalt again warned).

"Still nothing but ominous silence from the bridge. No doubt, something happening above deck was taking priority in the order of command. One more time, this time with a rising note of urgency: 'Bridge! On collision course with Little Hibuson Island dead ahead! Acknowledge! Acknowledge!'

"Obviously we were heading for disaster if evasive action was not taken immediately. At a speed of 30 knots plus, we were approaching the island at the approximate rate of one-half mile every minute and impact undoubtedly would accomplish what enemy fire had so far failed to do.

"The lieutenant increased the volume in his voice and, finally, with a great degree of unfamiliar urgency bordering on total disbelief and frustration, shouted: 'Bridge! Back all engines emergency full immediately! You are going aground!'

"The lieutenant questioned the radar operator repeatedly.

"'What's the range? Keep the ranges coming.'

"It obviously was too late for a course correction and, without an immediate change, we definitely were going aground! The only questions now were, 'How fast?' and, 'Could we survive the impact?'

"A collision at this speed, with an accompanying boiler explosion, would demonstrate very spectacularly why these ships were called tin cans.

"Finally, a response:

"'Bridge aye.'

"The significance of the answer coming from 'above' was not totally lost on me. 'Providence' finally had responded.

"The order reached the engine room. There was the expected loud whine from the engines as the ship began to shudder violently.

"Was the maneuver in time? Our speed was not noticeably reduced.

"I looked at the lieutenant for reassurance, and he had chosen that moment to make an assessment of our situation.

"His words were electrifying and anything but comforting: 'Hang on. This is it!'

"This grim declaration from the person I correctly deemed to be the ultimate authority of our rather precarious situation prompted me immediately to embrace the steel post directly in front of me with the passion born of numbing fear mixed with the certainty that this was, indeed, 'it.'

"Based on numerous past experiences, if the lieutenant was certain then I have no doubt whatsoever about the outcome. Sentence just had been passed and we awaited the final moment.

"I prepared myself as best I could for the inevitable impact and turned once again to the lieutenant, fully expecting to see him carrying out his assigned duties right up to the explosive end.

He indeed was doing just that. But, frankly, I was not prepared for what I saw.

"I was looking at a tall, dignified, impeccably dressed naval officer in spotless tans looking quite militarily proper in every way except, could this be? He had prepared for this inevitable collision by PULLING HIS HAT DOWN TO THE TOP OF HIS EARS, with the bill resting slightly above the bridge of his nose! At least his vision was unimpaired if not his dignified appearance.

"Under less ominous circumstances, I would be desperately trying to suppress an uncontrollable urge to laugh but, understandably, the humor escaped me for the moment. Instead, it occurred to me as a fleeting thought that perhaps the human desire to die with dignity (with his hat on) was at least as powerful as the attempt to live with it.

"Very obviously, the lieutenant had made a silent but forceful statement: He was prepared to die, but he would die on his own terms, with the symbol of his dignity and pride as a career naval officer firmly on his head.

"But my mind immediately was drawn back to the compelling priority of our present situation, and the moment called for undivided attention—no matter how profound the philosophy.

"The reversed engines screamed their displeasure while the ship seemed incapable of surviving the by-now-horrendous shuddering and creaking sounds of metal plates straining to put rivets and welds to their ultimate test. The sounds and palpable tension there created a continuing aura of unreality.

"The silent countdown continued and, almost as an anticlimax, I felt the expected thud. Some ominous scraping beneath our feet, and then silence! Miraculously, we had made it. We eased to a total stop, still very much in one piece.

"Then a momentary pause, as though the ship was gathering strength for the supreme effort.

"Suddenly the engines once again come to vigorous life with a thunderous roar as the ship slowly started to back off, straining to free the bow from the clutching coral, mud and assorted debris scattered across the deck.

"Above, star shells still were turning night into day, but now with a significant difference. We were no longer a moving target.

"Another terrifying scraping sound. Another roar of the engines and I felt a gradual but steady movement of the ship in reverse. Another few, elongated seconds and we were once again afloat, drifting for a few more heartbeats while the ship was backed into the channel and turned; with full throttle, we were heading for home back to the relative safety of our capital ship line.

"Once more, it was obvious, 'Robbie,' the ship's imaginary guardian angel at the top of the mast, had been working overtime. Miraculously, we had made it through unscathed.

"I wiped my forehead with a rumpled sleeve and once again glanced at the lieutenant. As I expected, he was unruffled and totally in control of the situation. He was at ease, and so, incidentally, was his hat. It was on his head at the proper elevation and, like everything else around us, no worse for wear.

"I was certain he was unaware of the touch of unintended humor he had provided.

"Nor was he aware, I'm sure, despite that dramatic pronouncement of impending disaster, of my gratitude for once again supplying the quiet reassurance I so often needed—especially on that unscheduled rendezvous with Little Hibuson Island.

"Thanks, admiral. Well done."

No single story about Zumwalt's career provides a more telling example of good leadership saving a career than how his involvement in an incident, normally deemed career-ending, left not a blemish on his.

In the natural order of things, ships stay afloat because the men to whom their captains have entrusted a vessel's safe passage have performed their responsibilities in a professional manner. In particular, the captain looks to his navigator to make sure a course is followed to keep the ship and its crew safe at all times.

But there have been successful naval officers who, in the blink of an eye, have had a promising career come to an abrupt end when their ship went aground. When groundings occur, it is normally because the navigator has failed in the performance of his duties with the result at least two careers — the navigator's and his captain's — are terminated. Few times in U.S. Navy history, have persons in positions of responsibility onboard a ship involved in a grounding walked away without suffering adverse impact.

In March 1951, the battleship USS WISCONSIN (BB-64) was recommissioned. Her new skipper was Captain Thomas Burrowes — an officer whose promising career had him headed for flag rank. Zumwalt, then a Lieutenant Commander, reported for duty as navigator onboard WISCONSIN about the same time. As the ship went to sea for shakedown training, Burrowes quickly developed confidence in Zumwalt as a highly professional officer and an outstanding navigator.

In August 1951, WISCONSIN entered New York Harbor. The ship was ordered to navigate between and secure to buoys anchored in deep waters in the harbor. The water was rough and Zumwalt had an immediate concern the buoys to which WISCONSIN was assigned would be unable to hold her. He reported this to Captain Burrowes who immediately contacted senior authority to register this concern. Burrowes was assured by that authority the buoys would hold as only a few weeks earlier they had securely held an aircraft carrier without incident.

Ordered to continue, Zumwalt navigated WISCONSIN into position and the ship was secured in place. However, before shutting down power, Zumwalt again raised his concern with Burrowes, who again contacted senior authority. This time there was little discussion as it was made clear to Burrowes he would execute as ordered.

As power onboard WISCONSIN was shut down, a worried Zumwalt continued to walk the bridge, repeatedly taking readings to various shore positions to ensure the ship was not moving. It soon became evident the buoys were dragging—and the current was carrying WISCONSIN into shallow waters. However, before power could be regained to get underway, WISCONSIN grounded on the mud flats.

Navy tugs arrived on the scene and, after a few hours, were able to pull the ship back into deeper water. No damage was suffered by WISCONSIN. Within a few days, a board of inquiry was launched to ascertain the cause of WISCONSIN's grounding. When completed, the investigation's findings completely absolved Burrowes and Zumwalt of any responsibility. Burrowes went on to be promoted to rear admiral while Zumwalt's rise to the Navy's top position was unimpeded by the incident as well. The grounding did prove, however, to be a career-ender for the senior authority that chose to ignore completely the concerns of subordinates much more familiar with how adverse weather conditions would impact on WISCONSIN.

A post-script to this incident occurred years later when Zumwalt, after becoming CNO, had a discussion with a prominent U.S. Government official. The official shared with Zumwalt a story he would periodically share with audiences to underscore the importance of teamwork. Unaware Zumwalt had served onboard the ship at the time, the official explained he was a midshipman onboard the WISCONSIN when it went aground in 1951. But what had impressed him most was what he observed afterward. He watched as several Navy tugs arrived on the scene and, through a well-coordinated effort of teamwork, began working together, pushing and pulling, to eventually get the behemoth off the mud flats.

Only after the official finished his story did Zumwalt share his role in the incident. However, Zumwalt went on to explain one other factor came into play that day to bring the Navy's team effort in pulling WISCONSIN off the mud flats to a successful conclusion—high tide. The official said the next time he told the story about WISCONSIN's teamwork, he would be sure to add the caveat that sometimes it helps too to get a hand from Divine Providence!

The former midshipman and government official was Donald Rumsfeld.

* * *

Zumwalt took a unique approach to each of his naval assignments. He believed a leader should approach each job as if it were his last assignment. Such an approach focused one on doing whatever was necessary to get the immediate job done, without concern about waves being generated. If doing so resulted in political fallout that closed a door to a future opportunity, then so be it.

When Zumwalt became CNO in July 1970—a job representing both the pinnacle and twilight assignments of his career—he followed the same approach. He knew there were major changes that had to be made in the Navy. He knew he would be working against an institutionalized mindset that made such change difficult. He knew, with four years in office, he only had a limited amount of time to implement the changes needed to alter the Navy's course.

The changes Zumwalt sought to implement were of both short and long-term impact. While this impact would span from immediate as well as into the next decade, change had to be implemented quickly in order to start effecting the course change he desired. A December 21, 1970 Time magazine cover story about the Navy's dynamic—and controversial—new CNO described him as taking the Navy "kicking and screaming into the 20th century."

* * *

The Navy of which Zumwalt took command in 1970 was afflicted with problems. It suffered from the worst retention rates in history and its aging fleet had lost its ability to fight and defeat a much larger, more modern Soviet navy.

The low re-enlistment rates resulted from an unpopular war and the anti-military sentiment it generated. Ninety percent of the enlisted sailors opted to get out of the Navy after serving their obligated time. These numbers drained the Navy of experienced sailors, requiring more money to be spent on training new recruits and thus leaving less money available for research and development and building new ships. Something had to be done to make the naval service more appealing for sailors reaching the end of their obligated service.

Nearly three decades of war and peacetime service in the Navy had sensitized Zumwalt to the demands put on those wearing its uniform. Coming off his Vietnam command, he had the utmost respect and admiration for the young sailors and officers fighting that war. As CNO, he saw no reason why many of the more stringent Navy regulations should not be liberalized to humanize military service for them. To achieve this, he implemented a broad range of Navy-wide changes, promulgated to All Hands as "Z-grams."

Zumwalt targeted four areas to make the Navy more attractive and satisfying to its sailors:

1. Re-examining regulations and practices dealing with personal behavior, i.e., dress, grooming, etc., to bring them in line with the customs and tastes of the 1970s and embarking upon people programs to improve Navy life. This involved the elimination of "Mickey Mouse" regulations that were demeaning or onerous. (It included regulations such as one requiring sailors and officers shift into the uniform of the day from their working uniform for evening meals—then shift back into the working uniform after the meal if returning to work.)

2. Developing operational schedules, job rotation systems, and home-porting facilities to lighten the Navy's heaviest burden— long separations from family.

3. Increasing job satisfaction by finding ways to give bright and talented young men and women more responsibility earlier and greater opportunity for advancement than they were getting. (One very innovative and successful program to evolve from this, named after a popular 1970s TV show—"the Mod Squad,"—gave command and subordinate billets within a squadron of ships to lower ranking, by one rank, personnel in order to provide them with responsibility earlier in their careers.)

4. Ridding the Navy of those "silent" regulations that inhibited recruiting, training, job assignments and promotions for minorities, fostering institutional racism. (For example, Filipinos were restricted from serving in ratings other than stewards, drastically curtailing their promotion opportunities.)

Zumwalt knew the changes he sought to implement would be contentious. They would be welcomed by the younger sailors and officers but opposed by the "Old Guard." But very poor re-enlistment rates made it clear the Navy was in trouble. It had to become a "kinder, gentler" service, while still maintaining discipline, if low re-enlistment rates were to be turned around.

The effort to make a kinder, gentler Navy was not appreciated by all. Some senior officer and enlisted leaders felt the Z-grams impinged on their authority. As a result, Zumwalt's efforts met with resistance and challenges from those who balked at implementing their intent, choosing instead to cling to the more strict and abusive standards of the old Navy. Anything less, they believed, would undermine discipline.

* * *

Zumwalt's efforts to implement his course change for the Navy with his Z-grams encountered problems. Between October and November 1972, three major racial disturbances occurred. The first was October 12 onboard the aircraft carrier USS KITTY HAWK (CV-63), followed four days later by a second onboard the fleet oiler USS HASSAYAMPA (AO-145). The final disturbance, onboard the carrier USS CONSTELLATION (CV-64), occurred November 3.

Investigations into the first two incidents proved intriguing in that the conditions onboard the two ships giving rise to these disturbances were so very different—one was a very positive environment; one very negative. Investigation findings reached but one conclusion: racial animosity, unavoidably, was afflicting the entire Navy. Similar incidents had occurred in the other military services facing the integration issue earlier on. It became clear, therefore, this affliction was societal—with each of the services merely representing a microcosm of American society.

Accordingly, Zumwalt felt it was incumbent upon him not to allow an argument for "maintenance of discipline" in the Navy to become a euphemism for slowing down his racial integration plan. In the war against racism, the Navy was in the rear among all the military services. Zumwalt sought to put the Navy in the vanguard, but before he was able to continue his racial equality initiatives, trouble broke out onboard CONSTELLATION.

The first two disturbances had received little attention by Washington and the press. That changed with CONSTELLATION. The racial problem onboard CONSTELLATION began just before the 1972 presidential election, remaining in the spotlight several days afterward. While the issues triggering the riot need not be detailed here, the incident is referenced for the leadership challenge it presented to Zumwalt by generating an angry President's wrath—and illegal order.

Problems began for CONSTELLATION while on a training exercise at sea off the California coast. A large group of mostly black protestors took over part of the mess hall, causing the ship's captain to order the ship to San Diego. While good leadership prevented this racial tension powder keg from exploding, the protest ended pierside at

CONSTELLATION's berth a week after troubles first began. Violence had been avoided when the final dockside protest was broken up. But the evening news aired footage of protestors raising clenched fists and uttering militant statements as they were placed on buses for processing.

The day after the CONSTELLATION incident ended, Zumwalt delivered a speech to assembled flag officers in the Washington D.C. area focusing on the issue of dealing with discrimination openly and fully. The bottom line of the speech was that new programs designed to defuse racial and sex discrimination tensions in the Navy were proving successful where they were implemented in the same spirit with which they were designed. He concluded by pointing out, in the end, it is not the administration of programs that is important but, rather, the even-handed leadership of the Navy's men and women that is. The speech generated a media frenzy — the New York Times making it a lead story and citing the statement in Zumwalt's speech "Equal means exactly that, Equal" as its "Quotation of the Day."

Three days before Zumwalt's speech, President Richard Nixon had been re-elected in the biggest landslide victory in history. But the news footage of Navy sailors protesting, raising clenched fists and making militant statements did not sit well with him. Apparently, neither did the media attention Zumwalt's speech garnered.

Henry Kissinger, serving as the Presidential Assistant for National Security Affairs, called Zumwalt the day after the speech was given. Yelling at Zumwalt for most of the five-minute call, Kissinger had but one message to deliver. Nixon was furious over the media attention and, as Commander-in-Chief, wanted CONSTELLATION's protesters immediately to be given dishonorable discharges.

Zumwalt attempted to explain to Kissinger that this was an impermissible penalty to impose without the accused first undergoing a (lengthy) general court-martial trial to determine whether he was guilty. Nonetheless, Kissinger abruptly ended the conversation by saying he would call back the next working day to see what action had been taken towards the President's directive.

There was never any doubt in Zumwalt's mind what his response would be when Kissinger called back. He later wrote, "As you might suppose, that conversation shocked me. Even though a professional military man has been prepared by training, by habit, and by conviction to obey unhesitatingly the orders of his superiors, including specifically orders he disagrees with, he cannot but be taken aback when his Commander-in-Chief, of all people, relays to him a peremptory, angry, illegal order such as that which had just been given me. The fact that it was clearly illegal spared me the pain of an internal conflict between conscience and duty: conscious and duty both dictated that I not obey it." Perhaps, after further reflection, Kissinger arrived at the same conclusion as he failed to make the promised follow-up call.

* * *

Another challenge facing Zumwalt when he became CNO was the accelerating obsolescence of the U.S. naval fleet and how best to offset a growing Soviet naval fleet undergoing modernization.

One of the greatest challenges for a leader—whether military, political or business executive—is making the tough decisions that will have a negative impact on an organization's current capabilities, recognizing that the beneficial impact will become evident only after the decision-maker is gone. Zumwalt faced three delicate decisions in addressing the faltering capabilities of the U.S. Navy to meet the Soviet threat—decisions that would then demand innovative solutions be taken:

1. With the Soviets building two ships for every one built by the U.S. Navy, with President Nixon determined to reduce defense spending and with no new "money pot" available for new construction of ships, Zumwalt had to find funding. This involved making a decision no CNO likes to make—drastically reducing existing naval force levels. Only by immediately retiring aging ships and aircraft that were draining off significant operational funds could monies be freed up to build ships and planes of the future capable of meeting the increasing Soviet threat. The first delicate decision involved determining the price the Nation was willing to pay, by seriously reducing its 1970s

naval capability, in order to have a sufficient and appropriate 1980s naval capability—i.e., it involved determining the number of ships that could immediately be retired. It was truly a balancing act—for retiring too many ships could well embolden the Soviets who might perceive an American naval weakness. When Zumwalt completed this exercise, removing the obsolescent ships from the active roles, one-third of the Navy's ships had been retired. It prompted critics to accuse him of putting more ships out of action than the entire Japanese Navy did during World War II. No doubt this decision was an unpopular one—but one for which Zumwalt knew he had to take the heat now so that the Navy would be better prepared to meet an increasing Soviet threat of the 1980s. Crediting Zumwalt for making this difficult decision, one historian later wrote: "Zumwalt was not one to leave troubles for future CNO's to handle, but began a meticulous and sweeping program to restore numbers back to the fleet and create one ready for war." (Mike Burleson, "Zumwalt Replacing Mahan", July 15, 2009.) It is clear great leaders often have to make unpopular decisions.

2. The second delicate decision was how to design a ship-building program—fitting within the constraints of the money pot Zumwalt created by retiring ships—while providing the Navy with the biggest bang for its buck. This was another balancing act—i.e., determining how best to supplement high-performance ships—being built in small numbers due to their high cost—with new ship types having adequate capability for multiple missions—but inexpensive enough to be built in the larger numbers needed to maintain a global naval presence. The cost of building one expensive "supership" had to be weighed against the costs of building several less expensive ships with moderate capabilities able to accomplish the same mission. Yet this balance had to be struck while maintaining the Navy's dual-mission capability of keeping the seas open for the world's commercial and military traffic (known as "sea control") and making it

possible to apply military power overseas (known as "projection").

3. The third delicate decision Zumwalt faced was allocating Navy resources between general purpose (conventional) and strategic (nuclear) forces. This too was a balancing act—i.e., ensuring the enormously important and enormously expensive strategic forces would not drain funding needed to maintain an adequate conventional force deterrent. Pumping too much money into the strategic force and too little into the conventional force was dangerous. An insufficient U.S. Navy conventional force in time of a crisis in which it was threatened by a superior Soviet conventional force would leave as our only option escalating that crisis to a strategic force level (nuclear) response.

Having identified the key issues necessary to move the decision-making process along to design a program to improve future U.S. Navy capabilities vis-à-vis the Soviet Union, Zumwalt determined his first imperative was for such a program to be conceptually ready within the shortest period. He was well aware of the road such a program would have to travel—surviving critical salvos as it was sent through Department of Defense (DOD) channels, the White House budget apparatus, four Congressional committees and two Houses of Congress. Although this road was one well-traveled, the length of time it would take to complete the program's journey was worrisome. As additional motivation to his staff, Zumwalt named this initiative "Project 60" to signify his own determination to have a plan for review by the Secretary of the Navy and Secretary of Defense no more than sixty days after becoming CNO. Project 60 became nothing less than a comprehensive plan for Zumwalt's four year term, including a variety of programs for meeting two other major issues confronting the Navy in 1970: how to maintain a high quality all-volunteer force once the draft ended and how to maintain sufficient capability during the modernization process for the Navy to continue to perform its assigned missions.

As completing the Project 60 plan within the first 60 days had top priority for Zumwalt, he was able to call together a team of subordinates he had identified from previous assignments who were capable of helping him meet this deadline. Throughout his naval career, Zumwalt had a reputation for molding personnel under his command into effective team players in whom he had tremendous faith and confidence. As CNO, such confidence enabled him to spend less time on details—leaving them to the team to work out—and fit well within the way he structured his working day.

Zumwalt's typical day ran from five in the morning to nine or ten at night. He broke up his working day at the office into 15-minute blocks, with a separate task assigned to each. More important matters might occupy several such blocks of time, but he trusted his assembled team to run with assigned projects, briefing him when time was blocked into his schedule for an update. Zumwalt saw his role more as a coach who, having outlined the game plan, left it up to the team to determine how best to drive across the goal line.

* * *

Zumwalt noted that during his career there were times a leader only needed to undertake little changes to have a positive impact on subordinates' morale and motivation. Challenging his subordinates to have a plan available for timely review simply by calling it Project 60 to inspire them to meet the 60-day deadline was but one example. Another occurred onboard a destroyer he commanded much earlier in his career.

In 1955, Zumwalt took command of the USS ARNOLD J. ISBELL (DD 869). Isbell comprised one of eight ships in a squadron in which it repeatedly finished last in competitions testing various crew skills. After taking command, Zumwalt immediately interviewed crewmembers to identify the reasons for Isbell's consistently poor performance.

It quickly became clear a number of factors were responsible for a lack of morale and motivation onboard the ship—some of which would require more time to effect than others. One that seemed relatively simple involved the ship's lackluster call sign—"Sapworth." Isbell's sailors complained hearing this name called out during operations in the presence of ships with more impressive call signs such as "Viper" and "Fireball" was not particularly motivating for them. As Zumwalt discovered, changing a ship's existing call sign nearly required an act of Congress. In a major campaign that took six months, he finally convinced the Navy of the need to change Isbell's call sign — resulting in Sapworth being replaced with "Hellcat." Ship patches for Isbell's crew were immediately created showing a cat with a pitchfork as a tail, emerging from the flames of Hell, breaking a submarine in half with its paws. This change, plus many others implemented by Zumwalt, propelled Isbell from last to first place in later squadron competitions where it won every efficiency award.

* * *

Occasionally, Zumwalt's team building efforts involved counseling a poorly performing subordinate. Zumwalt was a firm believer in praising subordinates in public when they did well and admonishing them in private when they did not. Such an approach was critical to ensure subordinates retained confidence in their ability to get the job done after such a counseling session. One incident in particular during Zumwalt's career demonstrated the importance he placed on re-establishing a subordinate's confidence after it had, necessarily, been shaken.

When Zumwalt first took command of the Isbell in 1955, the crew did not yet know the cut of their skipper's jib. They would quickly find out. Isbell was ordered underway to participate in a nighttime operation with the rest of the squadron. A member of the crew manning his station on Isbell's bridge gave the following account of what happened that first evening.

Apparently a very junior naval officer who had only qualified weeks earlier as "Officer of the Deck Underway" (OOD) — a position that effectively put him in command of the ship's movement and safety while operating underway — had the "conn," i.e., he was personally responsible for the ship's safe operation.

Zumwalt came up to the bridge to observe the night's activities. Fate often proves a factor in one's career and, fortunately for Zumwalt, it did this evening by putting him on the bridge when it did. The junior officer's inexperience soon became apparent as a situation of extremis developed in which the ship was increasingly in danger of colliding with another vessel. Waiting as long as he could to allow the OOD to take appropriate action, Zumwalt finally had to act. "This is the captain," he announced to those on the bridge, "I have the conn." This effectively meant Zumwalt was relieving the OOD of his operational responsibilities, taking them upon himself. Immediately ordering a course change, Zumwalt avoided a certain collision. Danger averted, the bridge became deadly silent as the OOD and other watch-standers fully expected their new captain to deliver a scathing reprimand. What happened next surprised all—but was typical of Zumwalt's compassionate leadership.

Zumwalt immediately informed the bridge he was returning the conn to the young OOD. Without saying another word, he left the bridge and disappeared below decks. By this action, Zumwalt made it clear, while a dangerous shiphandling error had been made, he retained confidence in his OOD. Zumwalt knew the OOD had been embarrassed by being relieved of the conn in the presence of others—shaking his confidence. While it had been necessary to do for the safety of the ship and crew, Zumwalt also understood returning the conn to the OOD and departing the bridge would work towards restoring that confidence. (It apparently did as this junior officer eventually went on to command a ship of his own.)

* * *

The vision Zumwalt had for Project 60 was one he had actually proposed in an article that he had written for a military professional magazine eight years earlier. It was a concept that came to be known as "High-Low." "High" represented the use of high-performance ships and weapons systems that were so high cost that only a few could be built at a time. Though expensive, such ships provided great flexibility and versatility that some Navy missions required. "Low" represented the use of more moderate-cost, moderate-performance ships and weapons systems that could be produced in rather large numbers to ensure the Navy could have sufficient assets to strategically deploy when needed in different parts of the world. When Zumwalt became CNO, there was plenty of High but not enough Low. The Low became the innovative part of Project 60.

Project 60 visualized starting construction of four new ship classes — all designed to meet the Navy's sea control mission. While three were relatively inexpensive, incorporating existing technology, one involved long-term research and development.

The simplest and cheapest of the three was a high-speed 170-ton hydrofoil patrol boat (PHM), armed with the Navy's new Harpoon cruise missile. The second was the patrol frigate (PF) — a much smaller platform than the higher cost destroyers it would replace, but almost as fully armed. The third was an extremely austere carrier called the "Sea Control Ship (SCS)," capable of carrying 14 helicopters and three VSTOL aircraft.

The fourth of the Low components was the "Surface-Effect Ship (SES)" — a high speed vessel that would skim just above the ocean's surface at speeds of 80-100 knots. Capable of crossing the Atlantic Ocean in a single day, the SES would virtually be immune from underwater or surface attack due to its speed. Development of SES involved a ten-to-fifteen year period, even though its propulsion system was already in existence.

When Project 60 was finished, it involved 52 separate points delineating programs to be implemented affecting the Navy's ships, aircraft and weapons systems — in addition to a number of electronic systems factored in to be strengthened. Briefly, Project 60 sought to "re-optimize" the Navy's capabilities to meet the specific threats posed by the Soviet navy. Within 60 days of Zumwalt having been sworn in as CNO, the Secretary of the Navy had approved Project 60. Twelve days later Secretary of Defense Laird was briefed on it. Major battles remained to be fought by Zumwalt against two of the Navy's cabals — the aviation and the nuclear power communities — to implement Project 60. Some would be won and some would be lost.

* * *

By the time Zumwalt retired in July 1974, he had issued 121 Z-grams. Their impact on morale and the Navy's image was phenomenal as retention rates soared threefold during his watch. Having devoted so much of his energy to improving Navy life, those benefitting from the improvements he implemented understood why Zumwalt and the Patron Saint of Sailors—Saint Elmo—shared a common name.

The course Zumwalt had set for the Navy and underscored in his 1972 speech to his admirals had been reached. Even-handed leadership of the Navy's men and women had been attained. Two days before retiring—content the course change he had set was now fully incorporated into the Navy's collective mindset—Zumwalt cancelled all 121 Z-grams.

At times, especially in October 1972 as the Navy was plagued with its race riots, Zumwalt had discovered it was lonely at the top. But, again, he knew what he was doing had to be done to build a stronger Navy for the future. As the Navy's senior military leader, he knew he had to stay the course—regardless of the difficult waters being navigated—to achieve what President Harry Truman had ordered be done in 1948: to end racial segregation within all the armed forces. He committed himself to doing so, regardless of the political fallout.

Today, DOD periodically conducts meetings to address diversity within all the military services. Those updates make it clear the Navy now is where Zumwalt sought to put it—in the vanguard in achieving racial equality.

* * *

In implementing the changes he believed were necessary to provide minorities in the Navy the same opportunities enjoyed by the majority, Zumwalt found the best way to disarm harsh critics was with humor rather than confrontation.

Approaching the end of his tenure as CNO, Zumwalt received a scathing three-page letter from a gentleman from the deep South. It berated Zumwalt for the changes he had made, of which the writer was critical for increasing rights of the minorities at the expense of the majority. He concluded by adding Zumwalt's upcoming departure from office was welcomed as it would spare the Navy further damage.

The tone of the letter was clearly racist. Not wishing to give the writer (whom we will call "Mr. Smith") any moral high ground, Zumwalt responded with a one-sentence response:

"Dear Mr. Smith:

Please be advised that some nut has written me a letter and signed your name to it.

Sincerely,
E. R. Zumwalt, Jr.
Admiral, U.S. Navy"

No further communication was ever received from Mr. Smith.

* * *

Zumwalt's concern about people is evident in the thousands of letters he generated and received both during and after his tour as CNO. One letter in particular shares some insight into how much this character quality was appreciated by those he touched.

As Zumwalt was instituting changes to improve life in the Navy for its sailors, he received a letter from the mother of an 18-year old son. She wrote to tell Zumwalt her son suddenly announced to her that he was going to join the Navy. As he never had previously expressed an interest in serving in the military, she asked why. He responded he had read the Navy had a new admiral in charge who was committed to improving life for his sailors. After her son joined the Navy, the woman wrote to thank Zumwalt for his concern for his enlisted sailors and how it had motivated her own son to join. Zumwalt immediately responded, thanking her for her letter and asking that she keep him informed about the son's naval career. This initiated a chain of communications between the two in which she did keep Zumwalt informed—with every letter she wrote receiving a response. When her son left the Navy ten years later, she continued to write Zumwalt about her son's endeavors and Zumwalt continued to respond, occasionally offering advice for the son as he ventured into the business world. A two year gap in the communications followed—ending with a final letter from the woman's husband. He explained to Zumwalt the gap occurred as his wife, Mary, had died two years earlier. It had taken him that long to get around to going through her belongings. In doing so, he found in her desk some of the things that had meant so much to her during her life—including a stack of letters from Zumwalt. The husband wrote to thank Zumwalt for always taking the time to correspond with her over the years. The husband's only regret, he said, was that Zumwalt never had the chance to meet his Mary. Therefore, he enclosed within that final letter his wife's picture.

* * *

Most great leaders are true visionaries. No one exemplified this more than Zumwalt for the various programs he initiated as CNO. While logical, not all met with success, eventually being abandoned either for political reasons or for want of a champion within the Executive Branch. Such visionary programs often focused on maximizing military capabilities with limited assets.

For example, Zumwalt believed DOD was failing to maximize its air assets by not requiring some, if not all, of the U.S. Air Force's tactical air wings to be carrier capable—i.e., capable of being launched off the Navy's aircraft carriers. Various crises occurring during the early 1970s resulted in Air Force assets being unavailable for lack of airfields in the region, requiring sole use of Navy carrier-based aircraft. Additionally, to maximize underway refueling capabilities for Navy ships, Zumwalt explored using merchant ships for such operations. While the concept proved successful, he could not get anyone within the Executive Branch to push getting the merchant ship construction industry to configure ships during construction with this capability. Yet another vision involved the feasibility of using supertankers during wartime as platforms for Vertical Short Takeoff or Landing (VSTOL) aircraft and anti-submarine helicopters—equipping them with the necessary equipment and armament to protect the ship. While proving technically feasible, politically it was not.

Due to the existing fiscal and domestic political climate at the time, Zumwalt recommended to the Chairman of the Joint Chiefs of Staff that an initiative be undertaken "to break away from rigid boundaries established by traditional service roles and missions...Expansion of cross service missions now might be a good way to begin (addressing decreased funding budgets)." Rejected back in the 1970s, this recommendation remains visionary even today.

* * *

Professor of strategy at the U.S. Naval War College Kenneth Hagan, in his book "*This People's Navy*" published in 1991, says the following about Zumwalt:

"The truly visionary naval leader of the generation spanning Vietnam and the Gorbachev (Soviet navy) revolution was Admiral Elmo R. Zumwalt, Jr. His tactical innovations as the senior naval officer in Vietnam showed an adaptability and practicality that was rare in a navy whose hierarchy had been taught to think in terms of rigid war-fighting doctrines conceived to defeat major powers. Tapped at an early age to become the navy's senior officer, Admiral Zumwalt brought his fresh insights to Washington. For four years, he fought to restructure the navy around new kinds of ships designed from the beginning to fight 'conventional' and limited wars or to intervene effectively in episodes of modern 'gunboat diplomacy.' In the end, he was defeated by a pragmatic alliance formed between key congressman and the navy's two leading interest groups, the aviators and the Rickover-led nuclear-power officers. Still, when the Soviet empire in Eastern Europe began to crumble in 1989 and the American defense budget in 1990 came under its closest congressional scrutiny since the beginning of the Cold War, it began to appear that the harbinger of the American navy of the future was... Elmo Zumwalt."

* * *

Even after retiring from the Navy in 1974, Zumwalt exhibited yet another trait indicative of great leadership—tremendous loyalty to the men and women who had served him so courageously in Vietnam.

As Commander of the U.S. Naval Forces in Vietnam, Zumwalt made decisions giving the Navy a more aggressive role in successfully reducing the enemy's flow of men and material into the South—but it increased Navy casualties. Serving in the narrow waterways of Vietnam, naval personnel stood a 72% change of being killed or wounded during a one-year tour of duty due to the heavy vegetation on riverbanks affording the enemy cover and concealment from which to conduct their highly effective ambushes. Zumwalt ordered the spraying of Agent Orange to defoliate riverbanks, stripping the enemy of this advantage. U.S. Navy casualties dropped twelvefold—to six percent.

Before directing the use of Agent Orange, Zumwalt sought and had been given assurances by the chemical companies manufacturing it that there were no harmful effects on humans. Not until years after the war was it learned this was not the case as thousands of Vietnam veterans exposed to the chemical defoliant were dying from various cancers or were fathering children with birth defects related to it. In a bitter irony for Zumwalt, his older son and namesake—who had commanded a Swift boat in Vietnam—died of Agent Orange-related cancers in 1988.

At the time of the younger Zumwalt's death, the U.S. government did not recognize a correlation between Agent Orange and the numerous cancers from which Vietnam veterans were dying. Regardless of his son's death, Zumwalt firmly believed a wartime commander's responsibilities to his subordinates survived the battlefield. While the Vietnam war was long over and Zumwalt had retired before its end, he believed it was his duty to lead the charge to convince the U.S. government a definite correlation existed between Agent Orange exposure and the cancers laying claim to Vietnam veterans.

Zumwalt, with no medical background, analyzed dozens of U.S. government studies that had found no correlation. In a 1990 pro bono report he submitted to the Secretary of Veterans Affairs as a special advisor, Zumwalt did an analysis that showed many of these studies were flawed, having established parameters at the outset that pre-determined their outcome. For example, some studies' parameters focused on battalion-size units and larger, while it was the company-size units and smaller that were most exposed as they had provided perimeter security where the chemical was heavily used. Additionally, veterans who had more than one Vietnam tour—who would have had a greater chance of exposure—were eliminated from these studies. Finally, Zumwalt found the U.S. government's board of physicians—established after the war to review, every three years, the existing medical evidence concerning Agent Orange exposure—had connections to the chemical companies that had manufactured it. Zumwalt recommended disbanding the board and replacing it with truly independent members. Zumwalt's report determined there were more than two dozen cancers and other harmful effects more likely than not caused by Agent Orange exposure. His initiative directly led to the U.S. government recognizing the correlation and providing benefits to Vietnam veterans.

* * *

When Zumwalt died, among the numerous tributes made to him was one entered into the January 24, 2000 Congressional Record by Senator Russell D. Feingold of Wisconsin who said, "Admiral Zumwalt crusaded for a fair and equal Navy. He fought to promote equality for minorities and women at a time of considerable racial strife in our country and at a time of deeply entrenched institutional racism and sexism in the Navy,... Admiral Elmo Zumwalt was a great naval leader, a visionary and a courageous challenger of the conventional wisdom. We will not see the likes of him again. We mourn his passing and salute his accomplishments."

Thousands, including President and Mrs. Clinton, attended Zumwalt's funeral at the U.S. Naval Academy, where he is buried. The

President, who in 1998 had awarded Zumwalt the Nation's highest civilian medal—the Presidential Medal of Freedom—in part for his leadership of the Navy during a very difficult time, gave a eulogy. In it, he shared a comment made to him by a Filipino White House steward earlier that morning as Clinton prepared to attend Zumwalt's funeral. Zumwalt, said the steward, was the best CNO the Navy had ever had. Clinton went on to describe Zumwalt as truly a "Sailor's Admiral."

* * *

On July 4, 2000, onboard the carrier USS JOHN F. KENNEDY (CV-67) anchored in the Hudson River in New York City, President Bill Clinton announced the Navy was naming a new class of warship to be named after Admiral E. R. Zumwalt, Jr. The lead ship of that class—DDG-1000— would bear his name.

This decision by Clinton was most appropriate. DDG-1000 is unique—unlike any other ship the Navy has ever undertaken to build. It incorporates ten new technologies into a new platform—something never before attempted by the Navy in new ship construction as it usually limits such construction to introducing only one new technology at a time and into a proven, existing platform. Just like Zumwalt's four-year tenure as CNO, the DDG-1000 program has been the subject of much controversy. Reminiscent of the High/Low program of Project 60, heated debate has engulfed the DDG-1000 concerning its perceived higher cost over the lower cost ships of the Burke destroyer program. Diehard critics of the controversial CNO even undertook an unsuccessful initiative— after Clinton's announcement—to strip the ship of Zumwalt's name.

Clearly, Zumwalt had generated emotions both positive and negative because of the wide-ranging changes he had implemented as CNO. Leaders seldom lead without eliciting such emotions. But Zumwalt would have been proud of those critics still working after his death to deny him the honor of having a ship bear his name. As he once told an interviewer querying him about his critics: "I know my changes in the Navy made me a long list of friends and a long list of enemies and, quite frankly, I am equally proud of both."

In May 2008, I had the honor of attending the christening of the USS STOCKDALE (DDG-106) at Bath Iron Works (BIW) in Bath, Maine. While there, I was shown the first piece of steel received by the shipyard that was to be forged into USS ZUMWALT. I have no doubt that sheet of steel, to others at the shipyard, appears no different than a piece of steel forged into any other ship built by BIW in its long, storied history. But to me, it represents something much more magnificent. To me, that piece of metal represents the mettle of a remarkable man, a loving father and a great naval leader, whose name the ship will bear, thus ensuring his legacy continues well into the 21st century.

# # #

James G. Zumwalt, Lieutenant Colonel, U.S. Marine Corps Reserve (Retired), author of *"Bare Feet, Iron Will ~ Stories from the Other Side of Vietnam's Battlefields"* (Fortis Publishing, 2010) is a Marine infantry officer who served in the Vietnam war, the 1989 intervention into Panama and Desert Storm. An author, speaker and business executive, he also currently heads a security consulting firm named after his father—Admiral Zumwalt & Consultants, Inc. He writes extensively on foreign policy and defense issues, having written hundreds of articles for various newspapers, magazines and professional journals. His articles have covered issues of major importance, oftentimes providing readers with unique perspectives that have never appeared elsewhere. This has resulted, on several occasions, in his work being cited by members of Congress and entered into the U.S. Congressional Record. Colonel Zumwalt is featured as one of 56 U.S. military professionals in *"Leading The Way"*, a book by best-selling author Al Santoli, which documents the most critical moments of the interviewees' combat experiences from Vietnam to Somalia. He has also been cited in numerous other books and publications for unique insights based on his research on the Vietnam war, North Korea (a country he has visited ten times and about which he is able to share some very telling observations) and Desert Storm.

1ST Lt. James G. Zumwalt with Admiral Elmo R. Zumwalt, Jr., in 1971 onboard USS MANITOWOC (LST-1180) off the coast of Vietnam

Admiral Elmo R. Zumwalt, Jr. and his wife Mouza Coutelais-du-Roche Zumwalt

Chapter 11

Lloyd "Pete" Bucher (Deceased)
Commander, U.S. Navy
By F. Carl "Skip" Schumacher, Jr.

"I sometimes think great men are like great mountains: one cannot realize their greatness till one stands at some distance from them."

— *Joseph Chamberlin*

Profile

Commander "Pete" Bucher

Commander Lloyd "Pete" Bucher, born in Pocatello, Idaho, in 1925 and given up for adoption, was orphaned at an early age and raised by different family members until he was contacted by Father Flanagan and invited to come to Boy's Town in Nebraska. For the rest of his life he considered it his home. He flourished at Boy's Town, making honor roll each year and playing football, basketball, track and baseball. He enlisted in the U.S. Navy during World War II and reached the rank of Quartermaster Second Class. After leaving the service, he entered the University of Nebraska on a football scholarship and joined the Navy ROTC program. Upon graduation, he was commissioned an Ensign in the

U.S. Naval Reserve and in 1954, was recalled to active duty and served aboard the USS MOUNT MCKINLEY (LCC-7). He then decided to make the Navy a career and was accepted to submarine school at New London, Connecticut. He served aboard many submarines during his career however, he was a conventional submariner not trained in nuclear power and his career options became limited when the submarine force became increasingly populated by nuclear-powered submarines. He screened for command and received orders to an auxiliary surface vessel outfitted for communications and signals intelligence collection – USS PUEBLO (AGER-2).

While monitoring off the coast of North Korea, the PUEBLO came under attack by North Korean forces (four surface craft and aircraft), although the ship was operating in international waters. One crewmember was killed and several wounded including Bucher. North Koreans boarded the ship and took her and the crew to Wonsan, Korea. For the next eleven months, he and his crew were held as POWs, and were starved and tortured. Bucher was tortured and put through a mock firing squad in an effort to make him confess—without success. When the North Koreans threatened to execute his men in front of him, Bucher finally relented. On Dec. 23, 1968, the crew was released. Bucher was subjected to a court of inquiry by the Navy and court martial was recommended but Secretary of the Navy John Chafee intervened on his behalf and no action was taken against him. His next assignment was at the Naval Post Graduate School and a tour as Chief of Staff of Mine Clearing in Haiphong Harbor (Vietnam). After retirement, he became an accomplished artist and a much sought after speaker. He wrote a book detailing his experience and his life, *"Bucher: My Story."* He died Jan. 28, 2004.

Leadership Story

There's no shortage of literature or speakers who teach leadership in crises. But the best sources come from those who have actually been through one. Equally instructive is how these leaders built trust and loyalty before the crisis occurred, and how they behaved afterward.

One shining example of a fearless leader under tremendous duress is Lieutenant Commander Lloyd "Pete" Bucher. As captain of the USS PUEBLO, Pete led his crew of 82 men through an uncertain 11 months in captivity by the North Koreans, and then spent the remaining

36 years of his life advocating for them and ensuring they were duly recognized for their conduct under unimaginable circumstances.

As the ship's captain, Pete had earned the confidence of his crew well before their ill-fated 1968 capture in the Sea of Japan outside of Wonsan, North Korea.

Pete, whose motto in the face of adversity was to "just deal with it," found himself faced with urgent life-and-death decisions while largely kept apart from his crew. They all endured vicious beatings to extort confessions and were subjected to bizarre requests by their captors. In the end, this leader of men managed to keep morale high under the most harrowing of circumstances. And while the Navy blamed and criticized Pete alone for the ship's capture, his crew stood staunchly behind him to the end. As all of them later said, they'd "follow him anywhere."

A U.S. ship in trouble

The spotlight hit Pete at about 12:30 p.m. on Tuesday, Jan. 23, 1968, when several North Korean gunboats closed in surrounding his unarmed ship and opened fire. That opening salvo on the defenseless USS PUEBLO in international waters defied the tradition of freedom of the seas, thus stripping the PUEBLO of the only protection it had.

For Pete that light shone squarely on him, a hitherto unheralded naval officer and that light, and as if through a prism, refracted to reveal Pete's dynamic characteristics. The leader that emerged was a man able to deal with all that life was about to throw him: a one-sided "battle;" aggressive and barbaric captors; a crew looking for support and solace, not to mention medical care; and his own Navy's hostility, which was bent on holding him solely responsible for the PUEBLO's plight.

Massive media attention followed, including countless newspaper, radio and television interviews, magazine cover stories, several books, including Pete's autobiography, and a movie. Consequently, Pete would spend the rest of his life in the public eye, where he met every right wing "bomb them back to the stone-age" fanatic who had an opinion about the PUEBLO's misfortune.

For Pete, it was his crew's well-being and reputations that mattered most. That concern continued until his death in January 2004 at age 77. The story of the capture and confinement of the PUEBLO and her crew belongs to Pete and his crew — the story of how the man in charge dealt with all of this is Pete's alone.

By the end of 1966, Pete, a submarine-qualified officer, had earned the right to command. Not being nuclear-qualified, however, his opportunities were limited to the (then) 26 still active diesel subs, a position he very much desired. Instead he was offered command of an Environmental Research Ship (AGER) something relatively new to the Navy. Though disappointed, Pete set a goal to make the best of the situation. As captain, he could mold the ship into his image. His vision was simple: He was the Commanding Officer of the second of three similar ships, and he would make his command the very best of all three.

What he found as he delved into his job at Bremerton, Wash., was just how difficult this was going to be. Because of secrecy surrounding the ship's real purpose – a spy ship – it was designated as an auxiliary -- and service ships were rarely on front line sea duty, nor were they equipped to deal with what ultimately the crew had to deal with.

Knowing the true mission of his ship, Pete requested proper equipment to support that mission. But many of Pete's requests made no sense to those directly responsible for outfitting the ship and were routinely denied. Pete did not take "no" for an answer and pressed his requests up the chain of command, often talking at odds with them. The problems persisted throughout the ship's commissioning. Secrecy aside, a clear understanding of the ship's mission might have smoothed out the process of properly equipping the PUEBLO. But due to its top-secret status, transparency and communications were seriously hampered. The unending tug of war to get his ship properly fitted for its mission was, to put it mildly, a no-win situation.

Another sticking point was the ship's organizational structure of the crew. The Naval Security Service assigned 29 men to the PUEBLO who reported not to Pete, but to their own Officer-in-Charge, Lieutenant Steve Harris. So, on paper at least, Steve and his men did not report to the captain of the ship, an inefficient and potentially harmful situation.

Fortunately, Steve and Pete worked out an informal agreement where Steve would make his sailors available for regular shipboard chores, such as damage control, firefighting and in-port watch standing – all roles under Pete's command.

Also, the PUEBLO's ultimate command was never identified due to bureaucratic snags. It was not listed among the Seventh Fleet ships. Which command oversaw the PUEBLO's actions? It was never clear.

I ran into my own snags as well. As First Lieutenant, Weapons Officer and Operations Officer, I was responsible for the ship's communications. Due to space limitations, our radios were located just off the bridge, while all of our teletypes and cryptography equipment were in a separate space just off our super-secret Special Operations Department (SOD). And I wasn't yet cleared to enter the SOD hut. So I was unable to ensure all messages to the ship were received and properly routed. Getting the "top secret" clearance I needed would take at least two months. Without the proper clearance, I was not privy to the ship's real mission, although you didn't have to be a rocket scientist to understand we were in the espionage business.

Pete was, from the beginning, a dynamo of a leader. With a barrel chest, bulging eyes and an inquisitive and interested mind he was much more aggressive and assertive than previous officers under whom I had served. What that meant for us was one giant leader with a devoted following. In exchange for that devotion, we benefited from his expertise and his support.

Good leaders also know how to walk the line between allowing subordinates to learn from their mistakes and rescuing them at the first sight of trouble.

For instance, I was already qualified as an Officer of the Deck in my previous assignment, but when I tried to maneuver the PUEBLO using those skills, I almost ran us aground in the San Diego channel. Pete's reaction was typical: "It's got a rudder as big as a barn door, Skip, so you don't need much rudder to turn it. You've got a good helmsman in Behrens – just give him a course to steer and he'll do it." Lesson learned: adapt your skills to the current situation, circumstance or as in this case—to the type of ship and its handling characteristics. Pete had us all practice docking maneuvers to get comfortable with the ship.

Later Pete expounded on his philosophy: "I learned more from my failures than I did from my successes, so I gave you enough room to make a mistake. Learn from it." In his view had he corrected me too soon he would have destroyed my self-confidence. If he waited too long he could have lost his ship. But he knew how to walk that delicate line – and then by training other crewmembers, he ensured that each was prepared to handle the task if called upon.

His support was cemented with the crew after a couple of his sailors were harassed by the San Diego shore patrol for being out of proper uniform. When they returned to the ship around 2 a.m. and their plight learned, Pete grabbed the three of them and visited the local MP Office to express his displeasure. As a Lieutenant Commander, he out-ranked anyone on duty at 4 a.m. and made his point, although the next day he was called on the carpet by his superior for interfering with the MPs' job. He argued the dress code rules were crazy and should be revised. He received some sympathy towards his position, but the matter was simply dropped. His actions inspired the crew. They knew they had a Skipper who cared for them and would support them in all they did. Pete's devotion to his men was one of his great qualities: He expected top-notch work and in exchange would back them completely.

Early on, it was clear Pete didn't pursue the "blame game" when something went wrong – "I can't do my job because you aren't doing yours." "Not at all", was his belief.

Pete acted on two levels. First, as problems arose he did what he could to get assistance from up the chain of command. Usually this resulted in the standard response – no budget for this or that. The two most pressing issues were the need for more destruction equipment and better shredding devices. Neither was authorized in a ship like ours.

On the second level, Pete refused to play the blame game and simply dealt with the situation as it faced him. If they couldn't fix the steering, for instance, stop complaining and rig a manual alternative. (There's always a workaround and Pete usually found it – or didn't rest until all effort to do so was exhausted.) If they wouldn't give us thermal shredding devices and powerful shredders, we'll just use what we have and the hell with 'em.

We worked hard and played hard, and Pete was always the leader. Unknown to me, and certainly unknown to many, were the resources available through Pete's relationship with the submarine branch of the Navy. This is a real "can do" part of the Navy, a place where officers and crew were handpicked and where, because of its size, almost everyone knew everyone else. As a result, submarine repair teams did most of our repairs. And we enjoyed their specialized Officer Clubs and their general camaraderie. Like others, they didn't know exactly what we were up to but had a good idea of the types of missions facing us. So they helped us in any way they could.

Playing the hand, he was dealt

About 11 a.m. on Jan. 23, 1968, a North Korean sub-chaser came out from Wonsan and we exchanged various signals. They asked us to stand by for boarding. We replied we were in international waters conducting oceanographic research. As other North Korean military units joined in, and it became clear this was large-scale harassment; Pete concluded it was time to leave the area and head to the open sea. At 12:32 p.m. the North Koreans opened fire on us, with their first salvo aimed at our pilot house. No warning shot across the bow, just a direct shot at our Command Center.

Though our position in international waters was known by all, once that status was ignored, the PUEBLO was on its own – small, isolated, defenseless and alone. From that point, Pete did what he could to stall -- hoping for time to allow help to arrive, time for the North Koreans to realize our capture would not be easy, as well as time for us to destroy classified documents and materials.

For the North Koreans, time was the enemy, so they used gunfire to prevent us from heading out to sea. One crewmember was killed, three others seriously wounded, 17 (including Pete) less seriously injured by shrapnel. This confrontation lasted for nearly two hours. Our messages were sent as "Critic Pinnacle" which meant automatic routing to the highest commands, including Washington, and designating an incident of international consequence. No reply.

Pete faced horrible choices as the engagement wore on: head for the open sea and take more gunfire or turn the ship towards North Korea. Scuttling, or sinking, the ship was ruled out for two reasons – it would take more than two hours but would disable the ship almost immediately and make us inoperable should help arrive. Worse, should we actually succeed even more of the crew would be lost in the cold Sea of Japan.

During a visit to the crew's mess – turned into our sick bay – Pete saw that about 20 percent of his crew had been injured. With his options narrowing, his crew suffering, and with no indication from the United States of any assistance, Pete concluded that the ship had no defenses. With great reluctance and yet with the hope the North Koreans were still playing the harassing game, Pete stopped the ship and the North Koreans boarded.

Faced with such an unexpected situation Pete acted in the best manner he knew how. He did what he could to stall and called for help, but ultimately had to act on his own for the good of the ship and its crew. While he didn't like anything about it, Pete played the hand he was dealt.

During the first days of our confinement, the North Koreans' major focus was on Pete, and within 36 hours, they obtained the "confession" they sought. Pete was disappointed he didn't hold out longer, but felt the North Koreans were in a position to ultimately get whatever they wanted. Pete also figured the crew would have fewer inhibitions about making their own statements. Lacking direct communication with his crew, Pete believed he had to lead by example. He was decisive under the most trying of circumstances and though separated from his crew, he sent them a solid message: not to endure the brutality when, in his mind, a confession was the only thing close to ensuring their release.

At a point during our captivity, the North Koreans allowed the officers – who were isolated in single rooms – to get together in the evenings, and I spent a lot of time with Pete. Pete, and to some extent the officers as well, spent time with the General in charge of the camp. These sessions often lasted eight to ten hours and were extraordinary on several fronts:

1. First, of course, was our exposure to a top ranked North Korean officer and the opportunity to measure his capabilities. He was extremely well educated, well read and enjoyed discussions ranging from philosophy and literature to politics and world affairs. At the same time, he never deviated from the North Korean party line: the U.S. and South Korea started the Korean War; U.S. foreign policy reflected our desire to rule the world; communism was an infinitely better system than crass capitalism.

2. In all these meetings Pete's position never varied: keep him and release the crew. Stop the needless beatings. Give the crew better medical treatment and more food. Pete was quick to acknowledge any special treatment. For instance, we received an extra ration on Korea Army Day – and expanded it by asking for more on U.S. national holidays – Easter, the Fourth of July, Labor Day, etc. The General at least listened.

3. It was clear as the months went by and these lectures continued that a special relationship developed between Pete and the General. Pete treated him with respect and the General came to realize that Pete's demands for better food and healthcare for his men and for maintaining the proper military chain of command were exactly what a leader should do, regardless of his government's policy. So a grudging respect developed.

4. Finally, Pete came to realize the limitations of the general's interpreter – we naturally called him Silver Lips – and understood that the slang language and Navalese we used in our various writings would be undetected by the North Korean interpreters. So he encouraged the crew to take every advantage to undermine the North Korean's propaganda efforts and the very first "confession" the crew heard defined the ship's location as inconsequential, since "penetration however slight is sufficient

to commit the crime" which the crew immediately recognized as the military's definition of rape.

Pete felt strongly the desire to do all we could to resist our captors and he was the first to realize the enormous value the crew had to the North Koreans as a propaganda tool. Realizing this he showed the crew by his own examples how to lace all we said with double and triple meanings. The crew was, of course, quite talented and accomplished this task with excellence.

In Pete's mind, resisting served two vital purposes. First, it would make the North Koreans look ridiculous to anyone who read our "confessions" or viewed one of our press conferences. While our efforts may have been lost on other Third World countries they certainly rang home for our Western allies.

Secondly, resistance served to unite the crew in a common cause and effort and as they saw their success, it was a significant morale booster. Without Pete's leadership in this effort the 82 men might have ceased being a military unit -- a Navy crew -- and instead, become a demoralized group of despondent individual men lacking a common bond.

Pete insisted on exercising his rights as the commanding officer and demanded the organizational structure of the crew be maintained. He told the general repeatedly that the crew would only comply with their demands if he, as the captain, told them to do it. The General complied, allowing Pete to address the crew from time to time. We had already established informal communications – quick messages dropped and picked up, Morse code tapped through the radiators and quick words in the latrine. These and the chance to communicate with the crew as a whole, made all the difference in morale. We could use slang language, Navy jargon and the "Hawaiian Good Luck sign" (this middle finger gesture of defiance was universally recognized, except by the North Koreans. We termed it the "Hawaiian Good Luck sign," when the North Koreans asked for an explanation about what it meant). None of this was well received by the General, but over time, Pete earned his respect as a leader of men.

We also discussed things we wished we had done on the day of the capture. Pete was disappointed with the lack of publication destruction and blamed himself rather than others. While we had sent several "Pinnacle Critic" messages describing the situation, we had not stressed that we had never violated North Korean territorial waters, nor had we listed the name of the sailor killed. We ran through everything else we might have done, but ultimately, according to Pete, our fate all came down to one assumption: that no nation would dare attack a U.S. ship in international waters.

We knew there would be a Naval Court of Inquiry, and Pete acknowledged that he would be held wholly responsible for the loss of the ship. He was disappointed – all of us were – that there hadn't been a strong military response, since he had been told there would be in support of our mission.

We discussed the prospects for our repatriation, since developments in the talks at Panmunjom for our release were reflected in the way we were treated by the North Koreans. Pete remained insensitive to these nuances, and wouldn't permit himself to anticipate anything about our release. He felt strongly that our country was negotiating in good faith and doing whatever it could to obtain our release. He lived in the present and saw things the way they were – not as he hoped they were.

This focus on the now translated directly into what he could do today to better the crew's living conditions.

Pete consistently worried about the crew – their health and morale – and felt it was our duty to do everything we could to undermine the North Korean's propaganda efforts. Certainly, he remained the leader in this effort, setting personal examples for the whole crew to follow.

Finally, we focused on the need for the officers to provide leadership for the crew. In our discussions we shared our darkest fears -- that we would never be released -- but Pete said repeatedly that we couldn't show that despair to the crew. It was our job to maintain an upbeat and positive attitude, even when we hurt the most.

Pete's defiance of the North Koreans lasted for our entire 11-month captivity, and concluded with his final "farewell" message, broadcast as we left North Korea at Panmunjom, on his desire to "paean" the North Korean army, "paean" the North Korean navy and, most of all to "paean" on the Great Premium Kim Il Sung. Pete was defiant to the end.

Home at last

The Pueblo's Captain:
Lloyd M. Bucher

The story of the crew's confinement and treatment by the North Koreans became Pete's to tell after the crew was finally repatriated. The venue for this was a formal Navy Court of Inquiry; five Admirals hearing testimony from Pete and other witnesses about the events surrounding the PUEBLO's capture. Pete attended every session and was formally charged early on in the proceedings with allowing the North Koreans to capture the ship while he still had the means to resist.

With the Court of Inquiry Pete accepted full responsibility for everything he did with the PUEBLO while he was its captain. It would have been easy to blame others for mistakes in the mission development and on numerous other issues that loomed large – but he never did that.

Pete never ducked accountability even as others – Congress held two hearings blaming everyone from the Chief of Naval Operations on down – looked for blame. That wasn't Pete's style. He held himself fully accountable for everything he did.

During their entire time in North Korea, the crew never lost faith in its government or in the Navy. We never felt we had been abandoned; in fact, we felt strongly that the Navy and the U. S. State Department was doing all it could to obtain our release. Our loyalty to the Navy was absolute and in turn, our expectation was that they would be loyal to us as well. Again, Pete set the example for this shared attitude.

That loyalty wasn't mutual. The Court called several experts to address specific issues leading up to the event: what support was provided to the ship and its mission; was emergency destruction of the amount of documents and publications we had feasible? Who decided we didn't need to know about North Korea's increased level of terrorism and hostility in the days prior to our capture? On all these points, the Navy simply closed ranks and adopted the party line: "no mistakes were made by senior commanders"; Pete and the crew were solely responsible for the loss of the ship.

What did surprise us, however, was the Court's lack of interest in the way the crew had conducted itself during its incarceration. As Pete related it, the North Koreans forced him to sign a "confession" by threatening to kill crewmembers one by one, starting with the youngest. He told the North Koreans that they should release the crew and keep him, but they would have none of it and brought in the youngest crewmember to begin the executions. That was it for Pete and he agreed to their demands.

Bucher, "Skip" Schumacher and Lt. Edward Murphy (PUEBLO's Executive Officer)

From orphan to naval officer

Pete's reaction shouldn't have come as a surprise to anyone who knew him well. Born in Idaho he was orphaned early, raised by relatives and then put in an orphanage until at the age of nine he was able to secure a place at Father Flannigan's Boys Town in Nebraska. Given the life he had been handed, he embraced Boys Town and its philosophy with enthusiasm. At its bedrock, Boys Town not only believes in "the other fellow first" but also has as their motto "he's not heavy, he's my brother." Pete's devotion to his crew and his concerns for them grew right out of that philosophy and, just as he had with the MPs back in San Diego, his priority was always his crew.

Yet the courage of Pete and the crew was largely ignored by the Court, as was their individual heroic conduct during the day of capture. While they were quick to blame Pete and several others for their shortcomings, they were reluctant to praise anyone, least of all Pete, for their conduct. This, too, was simply the Navy way, until a reporter asked the obvious question: Certainly, in all of your testimony you had to uncover someone who had done something right.

The Court made its recommendations and ultimately the Navy did approve individual citations, although nothing was done publicly until after our North Vietnamese POWs were released in 1973.

Pete was always immensely proud of his crew and the job they had done in a horrible and unwinnable situation. His pride lasted for the next 36 years of his life and he and his wife, Rose, helped all of the crew in a proactive way. To his dying day, Pete was most upset by what the North Koreans had done to his men with their barbaric treatment. He never complained about what they had done to him.

In the final analysis, I think Pete was disillusioned by the actions of the Navy after our repatriation. Not only was the Navy unwilling to acknowledge any of its own shortcomings, it also treated the crew as second-rate citizens.

In November 1985, Congress created the Prisoner Of War medal to honor service members who had been held captive by various enemies. Accordingly, the Veteran's Department contacted the families of all former POWs to arrange the presentation of the medals, and contacted all living POWs, including the PUEBLO crew to make certain they received the medals.

The Navy, however, nixed awarding the medal to the PUEBLO crew, claiming we were "illegal detainees" rather than actual POWs, since no war existed at the time. Pete took great exception to this slighting of the crew and on his own initiative arranged for a Special Act of Congress to have the crew included. This effort could only be done by someone devoted to getting the best he possibly could for his crew. Eventually, under Congressional pressure, the Navy did reverse itself and the medals were awarded by the Assistant Secretary of the Navy in a special presentation in San Diego attended by most crewmembers.

Pete's disillusionment with the Navy was somewhat mollified by Admiral Elmo Zumwalt, after he became Chief of Naval Operations in 1970. Unable to find a responsible position through the Navy hierarchy, Pete wrote asking for a clarification of his position – either give me a responsible job or tell me to leave the Navy. Admiral Zumwalt flew Pete to Washington and interviewed him personally for a half an hour, then judged him fully qualified for any billet available to a full Commander. (Admiral Zumwalt – considered by many to be the Sailor's Admiral -- was quite a controversial CNO.) Pete ended his Navy career as the Chief of Staff for the Pacific Minesweeping Force, responsible for removing mines from Haiphong Harbor at the end of the Vietnam War. So for Pete, if not for his crew, there were some amends by the Navy by way of the CNO's personal recognition of the kind of person Pete really was.

More than 40 years after our captivity, the wounds felt by the crew remain unhealed, and after all these years there has been no official recognition of what a great job they did. Despite Congressional Investigations and promises of internal reform, the crew has never been told by anyone in the Navy hierarchy that they did the best they could with a lousy situation.

Pete wrapped up his Navy career in 1972, after completing his tour with the Minesweeping Force. He was in much demand as a speaker to groups nationwide. While most of the audience wanted to hear how the Navy had "done him wrong", Pete focused his talk on what was right with America. Having experienced life in communist North Korea, Pete recognized more than most the values of our freedoms and delivered upbeat and moving commentaries about what a great nation we live in. In addition, Pete was surprisingly able to focus on one of his other loves -- watercolor painting. He was much in demand, specializing in many warship paintings. In truth, the paintings weren't all that great, but with Pete's signature in the corner, they were priceless.

His life ended On Jan. 28, 2004, at age 77. As he would say, he was ridden hard and put up wet. He had led a fulfilling life, full of excitement and he had, he told me, no regrets. His funeral was a big deal, well attended by his crew and his friends from Boys Town. He was laid to rest in Fort Rosencrans National Cemetery, overlooking the San Diego channel and his beloved submarine base.

All of us who knew Pete recognized he was a strong character not likely to come our way again. He was a true and loyal friend, full of life and interests and more than willing to share it all. More than that, though, his leadership got his crew through extraordinarily difficult times and to a man, they credit him with their survival.

At a ceremony at the National Security Agency, the Deputy Director related his experiences of Pete when he conducted the debriefing after our return. He had about 12 Navy Yeomen working for him, transcribing recorded debriefs all night every night for nearly two weeks. When their work was completed, he took his staff out for a beer and asked each of them for their impressions of Pete as a leader and a Skipper. To a man, they all said the same thing: I'd follow him anywhere.

No doubt in reading this you've probably noticed several leadership traits that it would benefit many to emulate. Pete exhibited more than several great leadership qualities that are valuable even if you never have to face a North Korean general with a loaded pistol. Here are just a few:

1. Pete was authentic – he followed his own judgments and wasn't swayed by others just because it was the popular thing to do. Maybe this was a result of his upbringing as an orphan, but wherever it came from, Pete knew himself well and assumed no airs or subterfuge. What you saw is what you got

and what you got was all of Pete. He recognized his own shortcomings and knew what he didn't know. And he wasn't afraid to say so.

2.   He believed in other people and did whatever he could to help them succeed. He was more interested in their accomplishments than in his own, and he strived to build a team pulling together rather than reaching for personal rewards, such as power or money.

3.   He was consistent and clear. He let people know where he stood on any issue, and made clear that his friendship today would be there tomorrow. I think his crew followed him because they knew exactly where he stood at all times. Sure he could be a disciplinarian when needed, but no one every faulted his judgment.

I've often wondered whether good leadership talents are self-taught or learned. I think Pete was more self-taught. He learned from his experiences the importance of loyalty, love and caring (mainly things he missed as a youngster). In the highly disciplined world of the military, he expected his superiors to act accordingly; set the rules, then get out of the way and let others work. It worked for him, it worked for his family and it worked for the crew of the USS PUEBLO.

I am proud to have known him.

# # #

F. Carl (Skip) Schumacher, Jr. was born and raised in St. Louis, Missouri. He attended St. Louis Country Day School then enrolled and graduated from Trinity College (Harford, Conn) with a Bachelor's of Arts degree in Religion. In 1980 received his Masters of Business Administration from Harvard Business School. He received his commission in the U.S. Navy and served in the Navy from 1965 through 1969. He served aboard the cargo carrying, refrigerated stores ship USS VEGA (AF-59) but his most notable naval assignment was as the young Operations Officer aboard the USS PUEBLO (AGER 2), when on January 23, 1968, the ship alone and virtually unarmed was sized international; waters by six combat units the North Korean Navy. One American was killed by shellfire, but the survivors, 80 officers and men and two technicians, were taken into captivity, threaten, beaten, starved, frozen and forced to sign false confessions for the next eleven months. He co-authored (with George C. Wilson, military correspondent and former reporter for the Washington Post) *Bridge of No Return* (1971) which captures his North Korean experience. It is a penetrating analysis of the entire eleven-month ordeal through the outcome of the Court of Inquiry, where the courage, the loyalty of the crew was brought into question. He was awarded the Silver Star and Purple Heart medals and various other citations during his naval career. Once he resigned from the Navy, he has served as president and CEO for various financial service and insurance companies. Over the years, he held several managerial positions and has overseen client relationships totaling more over $6 billion dollars. He has managed several foundations, endowment accounts and organizations. He is currently the founder of the Financial Support Services (St Louis) which provides accounting and record keeping services to individuals, trust companies and not-for-profit organizations. In addition, he has been the past President, Board of Trustees, Mary Institute-Country Day School; President, Board of Trustees, Edgewood Children's Center; a member of the Young Presidents Organization (YPO) and remains active with the USS PUEBLO crew reunions.

March 2003, "Pete" Bucher and Medal of Honor recipient, Tom Norris, U.S. Navy

Chapter 12

Charles B. "Chuck" DeBellevue
Colonel, U.S. Air Force (Retired)

"Wars may be fought with weapons but they are won by men. It is the spirit of the men who follow and the man who leads that gains the victory."
— *General George S. Patton, Jr.*

Profile

Colonel "Chuck" DeBellevue

Colonel Charles "Chuck" DeBellevue is a retired U.S. Air Force officer and graduate of the University of Southwestern Louisiana. Commissioned a Second Lieutenant through the Air Force Reserve Officer Training Corps (AFROTC) program at the university, on graduation he applied and was accepted into undergraduate navigator training (UNT) at Mather Air Force Base (AFB), California in 1969. He completed F-4 combat crew training at Davis-Monthan AFB and was assigned to the 335th Tactical Fighter Squadron. In October 1971, he was sent to the famed 555th Tactical Fighter Squadron ("Triple Nickel"), of the 432nd Tactical Reconnaissance Wing at Udorn Royal Thai AFB, Thailand, flying in an F-4D as the Weapons System Officer (WSO).

On May 10, 1972, he and Capt. Steve Ritchie, the pilot, scored the first of four Mikoyan-Gurevich MiG-21 kills they would achieve. Later, on September 9, Capt. DeBellevue flying with Capt. John Madden scored two MiG-19 kills giving him six MiG kills, the most earned during the war. During his combat tour, he logged 550 combat hours while flying 220 combat missions. After the war, following graduation from undergraduate pilot training (UPT) and upgrade in the F-4, he flew with the 8th Tactical Fighter Squadron. He was then assigned to the 43rd Tactical Fighter Squadron where he serviced as the assistant operations officer before moving to the Alaskan Air Command Deputy for Operations Staff. After graduation from Armed Forces Staff College and a tour at the Pentagon, he was assigned to the 4th Tactical Fighter Wing, where he flew with the 335th Tactical Fighter Squadron, served first as the Assistant Deputy Commander for Maintenance and then as the Assistant Deputy Commander of Operations. Following graduation from Army War College, he served as the 5th Air Force Chief of Staff at Yokota AFB, Japan and as the commander of the 432 Combat Support Group at Misawa Air Base in northern Japan. He commanded the 95th Air Base Wing at Edwards AFB, Calif.

His last assignment in 1998 was commander of AFROTC Detachment 440 at the University of Missouri. He is highly decorated and his military awards include the Air Force Cross, Silver Star Medal (three awards), Distinguished Flying Cross (six awards) and Legion of Merit (three awards). He received the 1972 Mackay Trophy and the Eugene M. Zuckert Achievement Award. Today, he works for the Oklahoma State University Center for Innovation and Economic Development as the liaison to the Oklahoma City Air Logistics Center, serves as the Director of Business Development for SAYtr, a small engineering firm and is Chief Executive Officer of Eagle Support Enterprises — a defense contractor.

Leadership Story

As a young weapon systems officer and pilot in the F-4 and later as a group and wing commander, I always depended on my training and ability to focus on the mission to ensure that the team was successful. There are three situations during my 30 years of active duty in the Air Force that helped me develop my leadership and team building skills to successfully fulfill critical and extremely dangerous missions. Two of the three situations were combat missions in Southeast Asia.

The first was a mission into Hanoi, the capital of North Vietnam. We were early for our TOT (Time Over Target) and decided to delay 10 minutes by holding over Yen Bai Air Base, about 70 miles northwest of Hanoi. Although we were in North Vietnam, both jamming pods were in standby to keep them from radiating a jamming signal. They were repeaters and tended to "talk" to each other, highlighting our position. I was head down in the cockpit making sure, that everything was working and that we were still on schedule. We had just turned outbound holding in a loose route (a relaxed formation) when I got a rattlesnake sound in my headset. At the same time, the RHAW (Radar Homing and Warning) gear was flashing and the azimuth scope had a very strong strobe on it with a moving break on the strobe. All were indications that there was a SA-2 Surface to Air Missile (SAM) in the air. All this happened in the blink of an eye and as I was looking up to see what was going on, I reached down and turned on both jammers. The missile passed through the formation without detonating. Following right behind it was another SA-2. It passed between us without detonating. The jammers had worked. Both missiles detonated about a mile and a half above us.

Had I looked up and then turned the jammers on instead of turning the jammers on as I looked up, either SA-2 SAM would have destroyed at least two F-4s (Lead and number 3) and perhaps all four aircraft in the flight. Lesson Learned: Follow your training and in critical situations—do not hesitate to make a decision and take action.

The second was my last combat mission on 9 September 1972. I was flying with Captain John Madden on a MiG CAP (Combat Air Patrol) in the Lead of Olds Flight. The targets that day were in the Thai Nuyen area and along the Northeast Railroad.

Olds Flight entered its assigned area 30 nautical miles north northwest of Hanoi, near Thud Ridge. They called it Thud Ridge, because the F-105s used to start their attacks on Hanoi from the backside of the ridge, effectively hiding from the SAM radars, until they were up to speed and had a reduced time of exposure to the enemy defenses in the target areas. We received information from allied GCI on MiG activity to the east-northeast. Friendly GCI radar called a MiG-21 heading west toward Phuc Yen Air Base. They told us to orbit Phuc Yen. Phuc Yen was protected by numerous SAM sites and was surrounded by many AAA guns, the same way as Soviet airbases. After being on an easterly heading for a few minutes, Olds 3 called out a SAM at our right 3 o'clock position. We looked in that direction and saw, not a SAM, but a MiG-21. He was below 1000 feet AGL (Above Ground Level), slow; low on gas and about to land at Phuc Yen Airfield, 10 nautical miles northwest of Hanoi, North Vietnam. We immediately turned to engage the MiG. I acquired a radar lock on and we fired two AIM-7 radar missiles. Since we were above the MiG looking down at him, in an aircraft with analog radar in it, the radar transferred lock from the MiG to the biggest target on the radarscope, the ground. The missiles hit the target only in this case, it was the ground. We came in behind the MiG-21 and started to overshoot him on the left.

As we slid past the MIG-21, I noticed that it was one of the new ones the North Vietnamese had gotten from the Russians that could carry four Atoll heat-seeking missiles, and had a 30 mm cannon and an external fuel tank. This one was out of missiles and was missing the centerline fuel tank but still had the internal 30 mm cannon and was extremely dangerous. With the MiG behind and to the right, we started a turn into him at 180 knots. The last thing you want to do is pull out in front of an enemy aircraft - even if he is trying to land. All the MiG driver had to do was rudder the nose of his jet over to us, pull the trigger and he would have gotten a kill and I would not be here today. He did not do that. The MiG driver decided to go around. He began to accelerate and turn into us. We made about three leaves of a horizontal rolling scissors with the MiG, until he was able to pull up out of the fight. The F-4 will not accelerate when it is slow, low to the ground and in a hard turn. You have to get the nose of the aircraft pointed downhill, but at the altitudes we were at, that was not possible. Since we were unable to follow the MiG, we cleared Olds 3 in to press the attack. As soon as he heard us clear him in, he fired two AIM-9E heat-seeking missiles, which guided toward the MiG, but did not appear to hit it. Olds 3 continued to close to gun range. At a distance of approximately 500 feet from the MiG, Captain Tibbets fired a sighter burst to be sure that the 20 mm Gatling gun was shooting where it was aimed. Since everything he fired seemed to hit the MiG, he then squeezed the trigger down tight and fired a long burst into it. The 20 mm shells were observed striking all over the MiG. A few seconds later, an explosion was seen in the after burner section and the pilot ejected from his crippled jet as the MiG rolled off on a wing and crashed near a village north of Phuc Yen. Lesson Learned: When the situation calls for it, utilize your assets and resources to help you accomplish your mission or reach your objective. This can only be done if you understand the capability of those resources and know when and how to use them—or to empower them to take action.

At that time, the element moved back into patrol formation. Olds flight headed back to its orbit point to provide a barrier to the MiG threat. Allied GCI called two MiGs in our area. Olds 1 called a slight turn to meet the MiGs head on. I got one sweep of a blip on the radar, 7 nautical miles and 30 degrees left. The next call was that we had a radar contact, were getting ready to engage, and that the MiGs were approaching slightly offset to the left. Our fuel state was approaching the point that we had to make short work of these two MiGs or not have the fuel to get home. We got a tally-ho or sighting, on the MiGs at left eleven o'clock and started a turn to get behind them. Our wingman gave a frantic call "they're 19s!" meaning that we had the possibility of having a tiger by the tail. Our Intel, in their all-knowing ways, had told us that their best pilots flew the North Vietnamese MiG-19s. They also told us that the only thing that could out turn a MiG-19 was an F-86 with afterburner and maneuvering slats. The fact that the F-86 went out of the inventory long before I came into the service didn't seem to matter.

Olds 3 pulled up to cover us and we started a hard, eight "G" turn at approximately 1500 feet above the ground. We had 90 degrees of turn to go when the MiG-19s jettisoned their external fuel tanks and started a hard turn into us. They were getting down to their fighting configuration. At that point, we knew that they had seen us.

We fired two AIM-9J heat-seeking missiles at the trailing MiG-19. The first missile detonated near the left wing and stabalator of the MiG. The explosion from the AIM-9J started a fire inside the MiG and he left the fight burning. We then switched the attack to the lead MiG-19. The MiG was visible above the rear cockpit canopy bow. After a very hard, high G turn, a loud growl was heard in the headset. This told me that the

AIM-9J saw the heat from the MiG-19's engines. Very shortly after that, we fired the third AIM-9J. At first, the missile looked as if it was going to miss, that it was heading for the sun. But the next thing I saw was the missile heading right for the MiG —hitting it in the afterburner section. The MiG-19 continued on for a few seconds, started a slow roll, and Split S'd into the ground in a large fireball. Even a strong MiG-19 pilot could not perform a Split S from less than 1500 feet.

Olds 3 and 4 moved to a line abreast patrol position as the flight egressed, leaving the area. Olds flight had destroyed three enemy aircraft (1 x MiG-21 and 2 x MiG-19s) without losing any aircraft to the enemy fighters. It was only by keeping focused on the mission and operating as a team, that we were able to ensure everyone got back to Udorn Royal Thai Air Force Base safely.

Captain DeBellevue and his F4 (note: the six stars signifying six enemy planes shot down)

The third situation was not in a combat environment but had the potential to be one. It took place at Misawa Air Base (AB). My job was to get Misawa AB ready for an Operational Readiness Inspection and more importantly, get it ready to fight in place in case war broke out with the Soviet Union. With three days prior notice, I arrived at Misawa Air Base, Japan, to assume command of the 432nd Combat Support Group (CSG). Misawa Air Base (AB) is at the northern end of the main Japanese island of Honshu and just south of Sakhalin Island in the Soviet Union's Far East Military District, on May 15, 1989.

I had direct command of a unit of 1300 personnel and was responsible for a base of 14,000 people. My duties included being the mayor of the base, incident commander for any major accidents or environmental incidents, the federal magistrate, responsible for all the support necessary to maintain a major military base and for the war fighting capability of a base on the edge of the free world (interestingly, I was also the president of the School Board).

I started by meeting with each of my squadron commanders and people who directly reported to me to find out what they did and how I could help them. Misawa AB was also the home to the Northern Air Force of the Japan Air Self Defense Force commanded by a lieutenant general and a fighter wing commanded by a major general. Misawa AB also had major tenants that included an AF Electronic Security Group commanded by a colonel and two Navy commands with Navy captains in charge, a Navy Mobile Mine Magazine with a lieutenant commander in charge and intelligence detachments for the Army with lieutenant colonel in charge and Marines with a major in charge.

I arrived at Misawa prior to the normal summer relocation cycle. I found out that of the 11 O-6s on Misawa, no two of them liked each other. This was not a good sign. Since I was in charge of assigning colonel housing, I knew when the new colonels arrived on base. To meet each colonel, I would walk over to their quarters when they were moving in and welcome them to Misawa Air Base and to the neighborhood. I would bring two beers with me, one of which I offered to the newly arrived colonel. After I introduced myself, I would explain that they would not agree with every decision I made. If they disagreed with a decision I made and sent a complaint thru channels, life would not be very pleasant for them while they were at Misawa. If they had a problem with a decision I made or something I did, they could walk across the street with two beers and we could discuss it.

In the fall of 1989, the Fire Department was involved in an exercise in which they were going to burn an old building built by the Japanese during World War II. The plan was to set it on fire and before it got really going to put it out, regroup and set it on fire again and fight it until it burnt down. The plan was a good one and I was asked if I would like to suit up and go in during the first fire, which I agreed to. By doing so, I gained a lot of respect for the firefighters and the difficulty of the job they do. I also gained their respect. I immersed myself in many of the training programs of the units under my command, gaining a great deal of respect for those who perform the critical support functions necessary for an installation to run well and be able to survive and operate in a combat environment. Again, I also gained their respect. This proved critical during the Operational Readiness Inspection we underwent about a year later and allowed the 432nd Combat Support Group to receive high scores from the PACAF (Pacific Air Force) IG (Inspector General). In fact, the Combat Support Group did better than other groups in the wing.

Lesson Learned: Communicate personally and directly; learn about your personnel's responsibilities, their needs and wants. Define your expectations and how they, in turn, can relate issues and problems back to you so you can help them to be resolved.

* * *

The military prepared me very well for the challenges that I would face in my civilian career. Missions required that I quickly analyze situations and rapidly decide on the proper course of action. I learned a great deal about motivating people in difficult situations, as well as the ability to learn on the fly and make decisions with the best information available. My thought process, when I had to make a difficult leadership decision was to gather the facts, review the situation and courses of action and make a decision. In combat and critical emergencies, indecisiveness will injure or kill people. I have found that making decisions with the best information available at the time is the better solution. If you get better information and need to change decision or modify your course of action, then do it. If you need perfect information to make the absolutely best decision possible, you probably have failed to satisfactorily accomplish the mission and may have increased the danger to your team.

I have successfully applied my leadership experiences in today's corporate environment after I retired from the Air Force. The lessons I learned about leadership, management and how to form a team worked to my great benefit when I entered the civilian workforce and went to work in an area where I lacked background experience. By using what I learned, I was able to take a dysfunctional operation with a large financial loss and turn the operation into such a success that the program is still going strong today, over 10 years later. The ability to make decisions and form a team from the individuals working for you is just as critical to the corporate environment as it was to military operations. Good management is necessary but strong leadership is a requirement. You can go to school to learn management but leadership is learned, by being out in front of your command or program.

I feel that the three most important leadership characteristics in development of a successful leader are the ability to be decisive when the situation demands it, to form a team that is well-trained to perform when the chips are down and to delegate both responsibility and authority. If you provide effective leadership to your team, they will follow you when the mission success requires their support. Colonel Joshua Chamberlain, commander of the 20th Maine Brigade at Gettysburg on July 2, 1863, during the Civil War, exemplified the importance of this. When told by his lieutenants that they were out of ammunition and should they sound retreat. He pulled out his saber, yelled, "Fix Bayonets, Charge" and rushed down the hill to meet the 15th Alabama that was starting their third charge up the hill. His actions prevented the Confederate forces under General Lee from winning the day and set the stage for the end of the war. He was not only decisive but also had trained the 20th Maine very well—and knew their capabilities. Colonel Chamberlain was a schoolteacher prior to the war. The person whose leadership style that I admired the most was the wing commander of the 432nd Tactical Reconnaissance Wing at Udorn Royal Thai Air Force Base in Thailand, Colonel Charles Gabriel. He had two kills in Korea and knew what we were facing when we started flying into the area around Hanoi, North Vietnam on a daily basis. He was a real leader and a gentleman. When he flew in our formations, he flew his position very well, whether in the lead or on the wing. He was someone you would enter Hell with and not ask how he was going to get you out.

Management can be taught. Good managers are necessary for success. The basics of leadership have to be in us, but it is developed by the situations that we are involved in that give us opportunities to grow. We gain experience by taking chances and learning from our decisions, especially those that don't work out as planned.

I hope that these suggestions and observations from my experiences help you on your journey to success. It is not always easy and you will not be successful in everything you attempt. But if you learn and keep trying, you will be far above your peers.

Colonel DeBellevue on Veterans Day at University of Missouri

Chapter 13

Thomas J. Hudner, Jr.
Captain, U.S. Navy (Retired)
Medal of Honor recipient - Korean War

"When I was selected to lead the first mission I was responsible to name who would fly with me. Very simply, I picked the best flyers, men I could trust in the heat of deadly combat. This was serious. Rank, credentials, efficiency reports didn't mean a thing. It would be the guys who could fly and shoot."
> — *Vice Admiral James Stockdale,*
> *Congressional Medal of Honor recipient*

Profile

Captain Tom Hudner

Captain Thomas J. Hudner, Jr. was born in Fall River, Massachusetts and graduated from the U.S. Naval Academy in 1946. That graduating class also included retired Admiral William Crowe (Chairman of the Joint Chiefs of Staff and subsequently Ambassador to England), retired Vice Admiral James. B. Stockdale (Medal of Honor recipient in 1976), retired Vice Admiral Stansfield

Turner (former CIA director) and Jimmy Carter (the 38th President of the United States).

Following service in surface ships and ashore, he attended flight school and was designated a Naval Aviator in August 1949. Later he was assigned to Fighter Squadron 32 (VF-32) aboard the Essex class carrier USS Leyte (CV-32). Tensions erupted into war in June 1950 when the North Korean People's Army crossed the 38th Parallel and attacked South Korea. The Leyte was recalled from duty in the Mediterranean and redirected to the east coast of Korea.

Hudner in the cockpit of his F4U Corsair

On December 4, 1950, while flying his F4U-4 Corsair as wingman for Ensign Jesse L. Brown, the Navy's first black aviator, they were forty-five minutes into an armed reconnaissance mission in support of United Nations operations in far North Korea when Ensign Brown was hit by ground fire. Given the mountainous terrain, he was nevertheless able to crash land his aircraft in a snow-covered area but the airplane hit with such force it bent at the cockpit. Hudner was concerned about smoke rising from the aircraft, the time it would take for a rescue helicopter to arrive and the possibility that the smoke could develop into flames. So he decided to try to land his plane near the Chosin Reservoir in an effort to rescue Ensign Brown. He found Ensign Brown severely wounded and pinned in his cockpit by the buckled fuselage. Hudner worked bravely to free his shipmate, despite severe cold, and having no tools at his disposal apart from a small hand ax. It was to no avail. For his heroism, he was awarded the Medal of Honor by President Harry Truman on Friday, April 13, 1951. He was the first Navy Medal of Honor recipient for actions in the Korean War.

Following his tour with VF-32, he held a variety of training, operational and staff assignments. He commanded Training Squadron 24 (VT-24), and then was Executive Officer of USS KITTY HAWK (CVA-63). He also had a tour as Head of Aviation Training in the Office of the Chief of Naval Operations. He retired in 1973 from the Navy, worked as a management consultant, and was involved with the USO. He then served as Commissioner of the Massachusetts Department of Veterans Service a position he held for ten years before yielding it to another Medal of Honor recipient, retired Navy Captain Thomas Kelley, in April 1999.

Leadership Story

There wasn't much emphasis on leadership when I was growing up. Leadership was a characteristic you either had or you didn't, and it was usually manifested by one's popularity in school or athletics. For example, the captain of a team was always a popular guy, but that didn't mean he was automatically a good leader.

    The first time I was exposed to anything positive about leadership was at the Naval Academy. There, we had leadership classes, which were new to almost every one of us except for those classmates who came in from the fleet or those that had some military schooling. We got examples of leadership right from the beginning in a somewhat structured but rather informal way. These tried to help us develop the qualities of leadership with the eventual goal of making us ready as division officers aboard ship. Midshipman rank structure was based on the grown-up world of commissioned officers with uniforms and positions of responsibility. Going through the Naval Academy was an incredible experience where our leadership was graded.

    I entered the Naval Academy during WWII, in 1943, and graduated in 1946. Each summer after plebe year was a midshipman cruise, but because of the strain put on by the war, we went aboard ship for only a short time; the first year was just down on Chesapeake Bay, the next year we got out into the south Atlantic, cruised around Cuba and had some shore time. On these cruises, assignments were made pretty much the same way enlisted personnel were assigned. Each year they were more senior and contained more responsibility and we were graded at the division officer level. As underclassmen, the upper-class midshipmen graded us on how we performed. The officers on the ship would observe our abilities and we learned from actually leading men in real-time situations—which taught us a lot.

At the time we graduated, the war had been over for about a year. Personnel of all ranks and all services were being discharged as quickly as possible, though everything was still on a wartime basis when we went into the fleet in July of 1946. The Navy was discharging personnel, decommissioning ships and reducing the amount of on-hand material and equipment as some ships were placed in mothballs. Leadership was very important during this time to keep up the morale of the people who wanted to get out but whose time had not yet come to be released.

When I reported to my first ship, my first job was ship's visual signal officer in the communications department. In my division, we had about 30 people. This was my first experience and exposure to the importance of chief petty officers in the Navy and they became critical to my leadership development. Some were relatively short-timers, coming in at the beginning of the war but many were in before the war started. These were the old-timer's that you count on though there were very sharp young petty officers as well. I was very lucky—with a few notable exceptions, all the chiefs I worked with were great. Fantastic teachers and advisors, I was able to work with them very closely and I learned a lot from them. For the most part, they were very competent, good Navy men who insisted upon strict discipline.

Almost all the sailors were draftees. Understandably, some resented being in the Navy, but most were extremely eager to be sailors. Regardless, every one of them served his country. There were all types, from tough guys, to those you could see that if they didn't make careers of the Navy, they would do well in the civilian sector. Today, you run into many of these people, high-level corporate leaders who have been in the military. They start in the Navy or Marine Corps at very low ranks, and it's the military that provides them with the foundation to be the good leaders they are today.

There are people born to be leaders but need to be developed. With proper guidance and coaching, these natural-born leaders utilize their personalities and characteristics to help them to become outstanding leaders. But there are some who have the capabilities of becoming good leaders, but don't have the aggressiveness to develop themselves completely.

A good leader must be honest and of good character as well as having self-confidence, integrity, fairness and courage. More important than just flat-out physical courage is moral courage – the ability to act properly in the face of popular opposition, shame or discouragement.

Probably the most important quality a good leader must have is integrity. Without it, you'll never have the respect of the people working for you or of the people you are working for. And as well as being capable in your job, you must train your subordinates to do their jobs well also. It is most important to surround yourself with the best people possible. If you have incompetent people working for you, regardless of how well you do your job, your success will be nullified.

Being articulate is extremely important. You should be able to speak clearly and effectively. You need to be able to stand up in front of a group of people and to speak well enough so they know what you are talking about. You need to be persuasive in your manner so that people are enthusiastic about doing what you are telling them to do--rather than their taking a ho-hum attitude that they are just receiving another set of orders. Once a job is complete, it is important that your subordinates feel they have accomplished the task, can continue to learn and develop and become invaluable to the organization.

Leadership abilities learned in the military are transferable to the corporate world. You must have discipline in your organization. The top people in a company, from the CEO down through the managers and supervisors at lower levels, must have the obedience of their employees.

The nature of discipline in civilian life differs markedly from that of military discipline. But discipline in each environment serves the same purpose: the means for the successful accomplishment of a determined mission, whether it be winning a battle or winning a contract to create a new product. Without discipline, success of a mission (or a business) is always in doubt.

If you make mistakes, work to recognize what those mistakes are and try to correct them. Make yourself more knowledgeable about the area in which you are working, whether it's knowing what the jobs are or what the circumstances are.

Situations may arise where you are called upon to give your superiors advice. Make sure you do so properly—work to educate yourself so you can provide them with the best advice possible.

I was Deputy, then Commissioner of Veterans Services for the State of Massachusetts for 12 years and I was relied on heavily to increase the benefits for veterans in the state. Every commissioner, like every senior executive, has his own unique style. I worked hard to open lines of communication with Massachusetts veterans.

Part of my responsibilities consisted of working for veterans and getting them what I felt they deserved; however, they had to be reasonable about their demands. It was tough sometimes because I testified before the legislature on behalf of veterans on matters that I didn't personally fully support, but there were those who thought I wasn't working for them at all. What they often didn't realize is that without our support their benefits would probably have been much less. I had the responsibility to veterans not only to try getting them reasonable benefits from the state, but also to try to persuade them (when possible) when in light of fiscal restraints, the legislative action was fair. After a while, they began to realize that I was on their side.

There were some difficult people to deal with sometimes, just as in any work situation. My point in sharing this with you is to say that being a leader isn't about making friends, it's about leading and persuading those under you to do their jobs and do them well. I will say that it was gratifying after I left that job when I'd have people approach me as if I were a friend and not just a former boss.

If I could offer any advice to corporate America, it would be know your job and you need to know the people who are working for you. When I say, know the people who are working for you, I mean really take an interest in them—get to know about their family and personal accomplishments. Know the mission of the corporation so that you can be working all the time for the primary benefit of it and its shareholders. Be able to communicate the mission to your employees. Organize your company or division so everyone knows their job and how it relates to the overall success and operation of the organization. Have measurement points of accomplishments and meeting your goals.

The people working for you have many concerns and doubts, just as you do working for your boss. Job security is extremely important, especially now. It's critical that you try to make working conditions as good as you can for the employees without taking anything away from the company's success. Respect those whose judgment is sound, listen to your subordinates and get to know them as well as you can. Give open praise and credit to others for jobs well done (but don't give them false praise because they will see through that).

Make sure your employees have an opportunity for self-improvement through additional educational and training opportunities. That is one of the most important benefits any organization can provide to their employees. Put it in your budget if it's not already there. It doesn't have to be a lot, but the payoff for doing things like that for an individual is great.

The transition from a military life to the corporate world is often challenging, but a military background is tremendous preparation for a successful career in civilian life.

(At left) Rear Admiral Greg Slavonic and (at right) Tom Hudner, Washington D.C. 2004

Chapter 14

Wesley L. Fox
Colonel, U.S. Marine Corps (Retired)
Medal of Honor recipient - Vietnam War

"Military organizations and success in battle depend on discipline and a high sense of honor."
      — *General Omar N. Bradley*

Profile

Colonel Wesley Fox

Colonel Wesley L. Fox was born near Herndon, Virginia on 30 September 1931. He enlisted in the Marines on 4 August 1950, and served with the 1st Marine Division in the Korean War. Following a number of peacetime assignments, he was commissioned a 2nd Lieutenant in 1966 and served as an Infantry Battalion Advisor with the Vietnamese Marines. On his second Vietnam tour and while Commander of Company A, 1st Battalion, 9th Marines he was involved in an action that resulted in his award of the Medal of Honor. His last active duty assignment was as Commanding Officer, Officer Candidate School, Quantico, Virginia where he retired from active duty on 1 September 1993. In addition, as a 43-year veteran, he is uniquely distinguished by having held all but one enlisted and officer rank from private to colonel. (The exception is Sergeant Major.) He retired only upon reaching the mandatory retirement age of 62. Fox is widely regarded as a legendary hero within the Corps, and his story is known to many Marines. Fox is a graduate of the Marine Corps Amphibious Warfare School, the Marine Command & Staff College, and the U.S. Army War College at Carlisle. He graduated cum laude with a Bachelor of Arts Degree in Business at Western State College, Gunnison, Colorado in June 1977.

1st Lt. Fox, Company Commander of Alpha, 1st Battalion, 9th Marines--taken after the battle on 22 Feb 1969 during *Operation Dewey Canyon* in the A Shau Valley, Vietnam. Fox was awarded the Medal of Honor for his actions during that battle

In addition to the Medal of Honor, his medals and decorations include: the Bronze Star Medal with Combat "V", the Navy Commendation Medal with one Gold Star, the Purple Heart with three Gold Stars in lieu of second through fourth awards, the Combat Action Ribbon, the Presidential Unit Citation, the Good Conduct Medal with four Bronze Stars in lieu of subsequent awards, the National Defense Service Medal with one Bronze star, the Korean Service Medal with three Bronze Stars, the United Nations Service Medal, the Vietnam Service Medal with one Silver Star and one Bronze Star in lieu of subsequent awards, two Vietnamese Crosses of Gallantry, the Vietnamese Honor Medal 1st Class, the Vietnamese Unit Cross of Gallantry with Palm, the Korean Presidential Unit Citation, and the Republic of Vietnam Campaign Medal.

Lt. Col. Fox, battalion commander of 1st Battalion, 6th Marines during a tank assault at 29 Palms, Calif. Sgt. Maj. Homer Hunt is to Col. Fox's right

After retirement he continued to wear the uniform for eight more years as a deputy commandant of cadets for the Virginia Tech Corps of Cadets. During his time at Virginia Tech, Fox spoke of his experiences to America's next generation of military officers, business executives, and civic leaders. His memoirs, *Marine Rifleman: Forty-three Years in the Corp*s, is published by Potomac Books, Inc. His second book, *Courage and Fear*, came out in December 2007. Colonel Fox was featured on the 2003 PBS program American Valor. He is married to the former

Dotti Lou Bossinger of Mattawana, Pennsylvania; they have three daughters: Dixie Lee, Amy Lu, and Nicole Lyn.

Leadership Story

There is not a subject closer to my heart, than leadership, leading, motivating and inspiring others. That fact is covered in my memoir and my second book on handling fear with courage, at best, the Marine version. In addition, I have written a third book specifically on leadership entitled, "*The Essential Elements of Leadership*". Maybe one day a publisher will get that one on the shelf for readers interested in the subject. I was pleased that Admiral Greg Slavonic offered me the opportunity to contribute my thoughts on leadership in his book on the subject. While much of what I have written here is covered in my own leadership book, at least my thoughts will be published and be available to tomorrow's leaders.

I list and provide my thoughts on the essential elements of leadership. Six of them are Care, Personality, Knowledge, Motivation, Commitment and Communication. These are listed or ranked in their importance with "Care" being number one, caring for one's followers in all of the many ways of personal involvement. A leader might be weak or lacking in one or more of these essential elements of leadership. If so, he/she can work hard to make up for it and impress others with his or her ability to lead. A leader missing one of these essential elements is not going to go very far in leading others.

There are those who feel that leaders are made, not born, while others feel that leaders are born, not made. That thought includes those from the past, nineteenth century and earlier, where certain persons were recognized as leaders due to their birthright, e.g. kings and such notables. While that source of leaders is no longer recognized within our society, we do have many people born with the personality of a leader. These people are those who have the personal characteristics that suits leadership, and that position is helped if they know and exercise the traits of a leader (reference the military list of the Fourteen Traits of a Leader).

I feel that leaders come from both sources, born and made; the deciding factor is the desire of the individual. If one wants to be a leader, studies the traits that make a good leader along with the principles of leadership and observes what positively influences him from those leaders over him, he or she can become one. One's personality comes with their birth for the most part, but we all have the final say in whom and what we are.

One must start with a study of human nature if he or she desires to become a leader. They must place themselves in the positions of those whom they would lead in order to have a full understanding of the thoughts, attitudes, emotions, aspirations and ideals of their people in a particular situation. A wanna-be leader can learn much from those in leadership positions over him, focusing on the leaders' actions that motivate him and cause him to want to be involved.

The leader's primary concern should be the morale of his unit or organization. With the right morale, people can do the impossible. Great morale will replace a shortage or lack of material things, and who should know that better than a United States Marine. The Marine Corps during my early years was always short on gear and equipment. Our weapons had already served many Marines earlier. It was a "hand-me-down" environment but we had the spirit, and we made do with what we had, thanks to good leaders.

My battalion commander in the Vietnam War, Lieutenant Colonel George W. Smith had a beautiful statement expressed to us, his company commanders, on what leadership is about; at least in our Marine Corps. I heard him state a number of times, "Teach, train, guide, and take care of your Marines, including their families to the degree that you can, and they will charge right up the enemy's gun barrel for you in a moment's notice and never ask why." I love that expression, and it is so very true of Marines and their leaders, at all levels.

I think of leadership as being able to influence and cause others to reach deep down inside themselves and pull up that something that they didn't know they had. Real, positive leadership has to be before us, provided, and active during the tough times that face us, especially when death is one of the possibilities.

We recognize leadership as caring for, guiding, directing, motivating & inspiring others, especially those for whom we are responsible. If leadership is so important to each of us, to our communities, to our society, and to our country, where can one study the requirements of and learn how to lead? Where can one get an education, a bachelor degree in something so important to us? Don't even think of a masters or a doctorate in leadership, not in our United States! Of course, our military services are very much involved in studying, teaching and exercising leadership. But even our military academies do not offer and provide a degree in recognition of something so important to us as a nation—a bachelor degree in leadership.

I recognized and had real leadership in the Korean War. Though I was familiar with the subject from my earlier involvement with family and friends, my squad leader impressed me with what leading others was all about. Because he was so good at handling us in that tough combat environment, I relate some of his leadership examples here; and provide his full story in my memoir. There is no better example to define leadership than his; leaders don't come any better!

Corporal Myron J. Davis, 596526 U.S. Marine Corps (3rd Squad, 3rd Platoon, Item Company, 3rd Battalion, 5th Marine Regiment, 1st Marine Division), was my squad leader in the Korean War, and he was my first mentor on leadership. I later handled the Marines for whom I was responsible just as Corporal Davis would have done. He caused me to think about the results, where are we going with this issue, and what is the cost? Where do we want to end up and in what condition? What is in the best interest of my Marines, my squad and the Marine Corps?

Corporal Davis impressed me from the start, and he grew in stature with each passing day. A soft-spoken Marine from Pocatello, Idaho, he had the demanding roll of leading Marine riflemen in combat. Because of our respect for him, his first name was always Corporal until it later changed to Sergeant. (At that time most corporals were addressed by their first or last name with no rank.)

Davis had a long, blond, handlebar mustache that was an immediate clue as to how long he had been in combat. Otherwise, in those days Marines did not wear hair on their face. He had a .38 caliber revolver tied low down on his right thigh. The pistol belonged to a Marine buddy of his who was killed as they assaulted across the Han River just outside of Seoul. Davis' purpose was to ensure that the pistol was returned to the father who had mailed it to his son. He stated that he didn't trust the rear echelon people to send it; the pistol would end up in one of their seabags. He didn't wear it just for looks.

As we knocked out and destroyed the enemy bunkers in our assaults on ridgelines in Korea, Corporal Davis many times was the first Marine inside the bunker following the explosion of our clearing grenade. After a while, I became concerned as I realized just how important he was to our squad members and me; I didn't like the thought of us losing him, of having to do without him. So, I, Private First Class Fox, approached the corporal and told him "That's my job!" The Browning automatic rifleman is trained and expected to be the first in the bunker, firing as he moves in.

Davis responded with, "Fox, look how much quicker I can turn this pistol to cover an unexpected threat in a corner of the bunker, compared to you turning that heavy, long barrel rifle." That was a good point, and before I could think of a counter argument, like give me the pistol, he stated, "And no other hand will touch this pistol". End of subject.

We, the members of 3rd Squad, had many ways of knowing that Corporal Davis cared about us. He never used that four-letter word "love" but his every action expressed care. Little things like C-ration issue were a daily reminder of how we rated with him.

At that time, C-rations came with three meals to a box, about the size of a shoebox. Our problem was that we were always on the assault, taking one ridgeline after another, and we didn't need the extra weight of a day's rations of canned food. Example: my Browning automatic rifle and magazines of ammunition weighed forty-one pounds, add on the weight of two grenades, cold weather clothing, back pack with personal items, and a sleeping bag and I was already over-loaded. I didn't need another five pounds of food added to my load. So we were issued one meal for the assault and would re-supply on the objective when secured.

Problem: Some of those meals were not fit to eat, like corned beef hash, ham and lima beans, and sausage patties with gravy. Three of us would have to share a box. Who gets what? "Hell! I had that hash yesterday; I want the beans and franks today!" We would almost fight over a meal that we could eat. Corporal Davis, always issued meals to his three fire team leaders with the guidance to give him the meal that was left. I surely hope he liked corn beef hash, because that is all he ever got. His Marines were always first in his every thought.

My corporal made another strong statement of his concern and care for his Marines. I don't know what the Marines earlier that winter had for a food-heating source in the Frozen Chosin. But in my time, from January to June 1951, our only means for thawing out and heating our c-rations was with a wood fire. (We didn't get the little heat tab until June of that year.)

Well, we had no chance to build a fire in the mornings, as we were moving forward to attack shortly after daylight. After taking our objectives, our first priority was digging our fighting holes followed by clearing the fields of fire. By then it was usually dark, and one doesn't build a fire…that's like shouting to the enemy where to drop his mortars and artillery rounds. "Here I am, drop it on me!"

For the majority of the time, eating our food amounted to chipping the frozen stuff out of the can with a bayonet. One night, I heard Corporal Davis state, "I am going to get a Coleman Burner even if I have to carry it". The next time we moved back into regimental reserve, Corporal Davis showed up with a Coleman stove that he had gotten from some Army unit. And true to his words, he didn't add that weight on to any of his Marines. He carried it. In spite of carrying the stove, he never used it until all of his Marines had finished with it. He loved coffee in the mornings, but many mornings we were moving before he had a chance to make it. Our leader!

The best example of Corporal Davis' performance in leading Marine infantry in combat happened after the rains started. The cold, hard winter finally softened up for us; we had rain instead of snow, our first rain since my arrival in Korea! We had been in the attack for days through rough terrain with little sleep and a 50 percent watch each night (this meant for the two Marines in a fighting hole that one was awake at all times, one hour of sleep followed with a one hour watch throughout the night) and poor rations. (We were provided with C-rations, the problem was thawing them so they could be eaten. This was before Davis got the stove.) Then the rain came.

It rained all night. It was daylight and there was no word on pressing forward, no word to saddle up. Maybe we were going in reserve; we needed sleep, rest and food badly. We stood around drenched and cold, waiting. There were no fires for heating our rations because the wood was also soaked.

Finally, the word came down; we were being relieved by an Army unit. Item Company Marines moved off the line with sodden sleeping bags and clothing. Besides the misery of being physically exhausted, hungry, wet and cold, the rain soaked gear added much to the weight on our backs. But that was almost unnoticeable, we were moving rearward down the ridge. Great!

With high spirits, we moved down the backside of that ridge, thinking of the hot chow, long, un-interrupted sleeps, maybe in tents, and letters from home waiting for us. We were all on a high with everyone talking about what we were about to enjoy, a long rest. However, at the bottom of our ridge, we turned left, moving to the flank and parallel with the main line of resistance. It was clear to all of us that we were again being committed to take an objective that some other unit could not handle or hold one that high command felt would be under an enemy assault, and they couldn't afford to lose. We plodded along knowing that the situation was only going to get worse; there would be no hot chow, no sleep and no letters.

Squad morale was dangerously low; personally, my spirit was right down in the mud with my feet because of my weakened physical condition. I have never been so down in spirit and de-motivated; I realized I no longer cared about anything. Tomorrow was too far off to enter my mind. I would never see it. I felt that it was all over for me; I couldn't do any more, my end was coming.

Thinking these negative thoughts, a voice seeped into my consciousness; someone was singing. After my initial disbelief, I tuned in

Corporal Davis singing, "Never saw the sun shining so bright, never saw things going so right." The words did not fit our situation, and I resented the implication. Then I realized that I really had to listen closely to hear the words; the corporal was not making a show of his singing. He was not being a smart ass. He had read correctly the loss of our team spirit, our morale and our will to continue. Obviously, all Marines felt as I did.

How did Davis read this low morale situation within our squad? Of course, he no doubt had the same feelings of exhaustion and loss of spirit as did his squad members. But his concern was his Marines, and within his squad, there was complete silence; no talking, no one was even bitching! And, that is a heavy, bad signal to Marine squad leaders. If your Marines aren't bitching, you have a major problem.

My thoughts shifted to, "I know his game; this is all part of leadership. He is just trying to make us feel better, raise our spirit." I refused to be influenced — my spirit would stay in the mud at my feet. We trudged on, and the words and tune continued, not forced or obnoxious, but audible if I listened closely enough. Our gloom gradually faded; someone back in the file made a remark, more of a loud bitch, and a little further, down the trail someone responded to the bitch. Shortly, we were all talking, even if it was bitching. The squad spirit returned, and we moved into night bivouac ready to do what had to be done the following day.

Corporal Davis had all of the essential elements of leadership and he continually exercised them. We, his squad members, learned much from him and through his manner of handling us. One person can make a major mental contribution to others with whom he is involved.

* * *

Where can one learn the art of leadership besides in the military? The Jepson School of Leadership Studies in the University of Richmond, Richmond, Virginia is the one institution I know of that awards a bachelor degree in something so important to us all, our society, and our country. I was surprised to learn from the Dean, Sandra Peart, during my visit with the university that there are about a half a dozen other institutions throughout our country that offer a bachelor degree in leadership. I was not aware of this fact and was pleasantly surprised. That is a plus but why so few? Is leadership so hard to teach? Are there so few high school graduates (our young people) interested and wanting to learn leadership that the field of study is not worth an institution's efforts and expense? Could the problem be a lack of motivated and qualified instructors? I doubt either of the two thoughts as the problem. Hopefully, more universities will offer a degree in leadership to those desiring such as there is such a heavy need for positive leadership in our society. Businesses need leaders for forward guidance of the many managers. Our national leader educational source should be unlimited.

* * *

Young Americans, who want to be leaders, today do have sources for getting experience and education in addition to service in the armed forces. Reserve Officer Training Corps is one and involvement in ROTC helps with the higher education financial load.

Virginia Tech's Corps of Cadets has a great leadership program and rewards those desiring such with a minor in leadership upon graduation. Hopefully, in the not too distant future, graduates will walk across the stage and receive a major degree in this very important field. But as of this writing, that degree, in spite of its importance to our society and our country, is not available at Virginia Tech.

The point I want to make here about the Virginia Tech Corps of Cadets is that those desiring the training and the knowledge required to lead successfully receive the full package. Their four years as a cadet starts out with their first year as a follower, pure and simple. The freshman is the lowest element on the totem pole, and they are made keenly aware of such.

In their second year as sophomores, cadets move into leadership positions at the small unit level, as team and squad leaders. As juniors, they move up to the senior sergeants positions, platoon sergeants, first sergeants, sergeants major, and staff positions within the battalions and regimental headquarters. They are officers in their last year in the Corps as seniors; they are the commanders at all levels from regimental commander down to platoon commanders and including all staff officer positions. By their fourth year, they are ready and do a great job in leading, motivating, and guiding the force. They have worked three hard years for the opportunity–learning leadership all the way.

The corps of cadets has three battalions of cadets with a retired military officer, 0-6, (Army, Marine, or Air Force colonel or a Navy captain) known as a Deputy Commandant of Cadets leading and managing each battalion. As a deputy commandant after my Marine active duty time, I continued with the great pleasure of working with young people wanting to be involved with providing guidance, direction and motivation to others.

What really impressed me in my time with the Virginia Tech Corps of Cadets was those individual cadets working for and deserving the top Corps leadership positions. The very best cadets each year were awarded the top command positions following the Command Selection Board's (Board members were retired military officers working for the cadet corps) recommendations and a thorough study of the cadet's past record. Past cadet commander's written evaluations of the subject, candidates were also closely studied; only the best qualified received the command positions.

Some the teaching points I used while at Virginian Tech might be useful so I will share these with you here:

TEACHING POINTS TO MY CADET COMMANDERS

The following points were presented and discussed with new commanders in reference to our getting ready for a new school year and the incoming freshmen (the followers).

- Motivate New Cadets. How? Talk about it.
- Create a desire to be a member of your team.
- Create a feeling of belonging to the team.
- Work with cadets having problems.
- Show "how to do it" by the numbers, (some of us are slower at catching on).

- Sweat with your new cadets, meaning being involved with them.
- Praise in public, call attention to weakness in private.

WHAT NOT TO DO BECAUSE IT DE-MOTIVATES

- Mass punishment
- Public criticism
- Call attention to continued individual foul-ups
- Punish unfairly
- Show favoritism
- Demean by name, race, sex or desires

TO HAVE MEANING TO CADETS, AN ORDER OR ACTION MUST HAVE A PURPOSE.

What is the purpose of the New Cadet's year?

- Training in close order drill, physical fitness, being a member of the team.
- Screening and evaluating leadership potential.
- Level all personalities to a common denominator.
- How? By stress, fatigue, confusion, and the unknown?
- This one could bite us--what is the justification?

THE EVALUATION OF YOUR WORK, YOUR JOB AS THE COMMANDER, IS BASED UPON THE OUTCOME OR RESULTS OF YOUR COMPANY OF NEW CADETS.

How many have you lost?

What are your company's disciplinary problems and what is its motivational level?

Are you approachable with a problem?

What is your purpose here at Tech?

Did the cadets kicked out of the Corps serve their purpose?

Keep in mind--each New Cadet arrives here wanting to do well. Build on that.

SOME UNIQUE LEADERSHIP THOUGHTS PROVIDED IN A CADET LEADERSHIP CLASS:

Your availability in the corps of cadets is as important as your ability.

Your personal actions are so loud that I cannot hear what you say.

Will alcohol help you gain your lifetime objectives?

* * *

I very much enjoyed my time with my cadets, those eight more years involved with leadership added to my 43 years of Marine Corps active duty time. As I still wore my Marine uniforms, kept my hair cut and shoes shined, and leadership was the name of the game, I had a total of 51 years exercising what I had learned from Corporal Davis, 51 years earlier.

Come on, Americans; let's recognize leadership with its importance to our society and country with awards of doctorates in this important field.

Chapter 15

John Paul Jones (Deceased)
Captain, Continental Navy
By Joseph F. Callo

"Leadership: The art of getting someone else to do something you want done because he wants to do it."
— *General Dwight D. Eisenhower*

Profile

Captain John Paul Jones

As an officer of the Continental Navy of the American Revolution, John Paul Jones helped establish the traditions of courage and professionalism that the Sailors of the United States Navy today proudly maintain.

John Paul was born in a humble gardener's cottage in Kirkbean, Kirkcudbrightshire, Scotland, went to sea as a youth, and was a merchant shipmaster by the age of twenty-one. Having taken up residence in Virginia, he volunteered early in the War of Independence to serve in his adopted country's infant navy and raised with his own hands the Continental ensign on board the flagship of the Navy's first fleet. He took the war to the enemy's homeland with daring raids along the British coast and the famous victory of the Bonhomme

Richard over HMS Serapis. After the Bonhomme Richard began taking on water and fires broke out on board, the British commander asked Jones if he had struck his flag. Jones replied, *"I have not yet begun to fight!"* In the end, it was the British commander who surrendered.

Jones is remembered for his indomitable will, his unwillingness to consider surrender when the slightest hope of victory still burned. Throughout his naval career Jones promoted professional standards and training. Sailors of the United States Navy can do no better than to emulate the spirit behind John Paul Jones's stirring declaration: *"I wish to have no connection with any ship that does not sail fast for I intend to go in harm's way."*

Leadership Story

AN INTERVIEW WITH JOHN PAUL JONES

John Paul Jones is the best-known American naval leader of America's War of Independence. He was respected among his fellow countrymen, treated as a mega-celebrity in France and hated in Great Britain, where he was considered a renegade. Writers have referred to him as "a genius prone to adventure," "a knight of the seas," "one chosen by fate," and even "the father of the American Navy." But the more we read about his improbable career and his astonishing accomplishments, the more we suspect that we still don't really know the man. If it were only possible to interview him today and hear his own words, surely there would be much to be learned about leadership in such a dialogue.

For just a while then, stretch your credibility and imagine John Paul Jones on a set in a network television studio. He is sitting at a table in front of the cameras and lights, facing a television newsperson. The interviewer is young, perhaps in her mid-thirties, and very professional. She has a pad with notes in front of her, and has obviously done some homework. John Paul Jones is dressed in the uniform of a Continental Navy captain, with a blue jacket with brass buttons. His tricorn hat is on the table to his right.

The words and ideas Jones speaks in the imaginary interview that follows are based on the character of John Paul Jones as revealed in his own writings, his implausible achievements and the analyses of scholars and writers who have studied his life and times.

* * *

INTERVIEWER: Good evening Captain Jones. Thank you for being a guest on "Lessons in Leadership."

JONES: Good evening; thank you for inviting me.

INTERVIEWER: Our emphasis this evening is of course on leadership, something that continues to be a life-and-death subject for the military, and a crucial issue in business, politics, and other areas of American life. But first, it would be helpful to know just a little about your background. For example, what do you remember about your childhood in Scotland?

JONES: I remember walking along the shoreline of Solway Firth with my older sister. I couldn't have been more than three or four years old. And sometimes my mother would take me with her when she went into Castlethorn at the mouth of the River Nith. I dearly loved being on the waterfront with the ships and the sailors. It made me wonder about the far places they went to when they sailed into the Irish Sea.

When I got a little older, my father built a small boat for me, and I was allowed to paddle it in the inlet near our cottage. I learned quickly that being careless in a boat could have unpleasant consequences. That was how I learned to swim. But as I grew up, and I watched the boats moving up and down the Firth, I kept wondering about the places they came from and went to.

INTERVIEWER: We know from the books that have been written about you that you went to sea at age thirteen in the British merchant marine. What was that like?

JONES: It was the best of times and the worst. When I was apprenticed in the brig *Friendship*, I learned quickly to talk little and learn fast. I also learned to not have to be told something twice. But I liked it when I was able to carry out my duties without someone standing over me, and it was wonderful to go to places that I could only dream of as I grew up on the Arbigland estate where my father was a landscape gardener.

Once the ship's officers and senior crewmembers knew that I would do my share and do it well and that I was not one to be bullied, it was a matter of hard work. I welcomed that and came to understand and respect a job well done. After about a month, when I demonstrated to the first mate that I was a willing worker, he began teaching me things about the ship beyond the regular tasks assigned to me.

INTERVIEWER: Was there anything special that you recall about those first years at sea?

JONES: I can still remember the first bad storm we went through. We were a few days from landfall in the West Indies when the barometer started to dive and the storm caught us. I was fearful, knowing that the only thing between Davey Jones' Locker and me was a hull a few inches thick and my shipmates, who thank God were all good seamen.

We fought the storm through a day and night, and when the sun came out again, I was no longer a lad. I knew from then on, the most important lessons in life I would learn would be taught by the sea itself.

But the best thing was when I was allowed ashore in places like Port-of-Spain in Trinidad, Bridgetown in Barbados, and St. John's in Antigua. The taverns along the waterfronts weren't fancy, but the rum was decent, and the ladies didn't care who you were as long as you had money to spend. But it was how different everything was that was most interesting. There were palm trees and even the water was a different color than Solway Firth. And it never got cold in those places.

My hard work gained increasing responsibilities for me, and with some luck, I was a captain by the time I was twenty-two years old. That was in 1772.

INTERVIEWER: Captain, tell us how you got into the Continental Navy. That must have been a big change in your life, going from captain of your own ship in 1772 to an officer in a struggling new navy in 1775.

JONES: Indeed it was. And it was a troubling event that started that process. It began with an altercation in 1773 with one of my crew in the port of Scarborough, Tobago. He was a troublesome wretch from that island who attacked me with a belaying pin during an argument over wages. I ran the rascal through, and because he was from Tobago, I knew that I would not fare well in a local court. On the advice of close friends, I fled and made my way to Virginia. I was a fugitive, and it was then that I began using the name John Paul Jones instead of my birth name John Paul.

In the American colonies, I was fortunate enough to meet some of the leading men of the time, men like Joseph Hewes, who became the founding leader of the Continental Navy in the Continental Congress. My first acquaintance with Thomas Jefferson also happened at that time in my life.

Well as you know, there was growing turmoil in the colonies and resentment was mounting against those in London who were treating the people of the colonies, as they were foreigners, not Englishmen. The more I learned, the more I took hold of the American cause, and when I realized that war was inevitable, I enlisted as a lieutenant in the Continental Navy and took on the responsibility to commission one of its first ships, the *Alfred*. That was in December 1775. It might be said that I captured the cause of American Liberty before I captured any British ships. And fighting for that cause was what drove me on during the desperate times of the Revolution.

INTERVIEWER: There were some, captain, who said that you fought mostly for glory and even for money.

JONES: They were wrong. There wasn't much prospect for glory to be had in a navy that started with eight ships, and not even one built as a warship. And since we were up against the greatest navy of the time, there wasn't much prospect for prize money either. If it were money I was after, I would have gotten myself a fast ship and a letter of marque and become a privateer. Those people who say that I wanted glory and money just haven't paid attention to what was going on at the time, and they certainly don't know me.

INTERVIEWER: What was the hardest thing about being in the Continental Navy?

JONES: There were no senior naval officers to look up to, and all the officers were people who had influence with Congress. There were some good men who had been captains of merchant ships, but there was no naval experience, no traditions or guidelines that could be passed down to the men who were America's first naval officers. We had to just make it up and make do. After the War, I wrote that our initial efforts to take to the sea against the Royal Navy could have been thought of as madness.

We were all becoming self-made naval officers, and some picked things up faster than others did. From the beginning, I did my best to establish the training and discipline that are essential in a navy or for that matter in any serious enterprise.

Our first effort was to attack New Providence Island, where it was thought there was a supply of gunpowder. Powder was very scarce, and capturing it from the British was the main source of supply. We didn't find much powder there but we got out safely. The most important thing was that we were getting past the first steps in learning how to lead a military force, and in May 1776, I was able to get a command from Congress, the 12-gun *Providence*. She was a small vessel but I was hungry to have my own ship. I wanted both the responsibility and the opportunities that went with even a small ship. Soon I was placed in command of a somewhat larger ship the 24-gun *Alfred*.

INTERVIEWER: What happened with those two ships?

JONES: I attacked the English merchantmen along the coasts of New England and Canada and raided some ports along the British Canadian coast, but I wanted to do much more.

INTERVIEWER: It sounds like what you did was a lot. What do you mean by more?

JONES: It seemed to me that given the disparity between our two navies, it made sense to not just attack English merchant ships and seek allies to take on the Royal Navy at sea. I believed it was important also attack Great Britain itself, and to do it in ways they would not expect. My first proposal along those lines to Congress was to take a small squadron and attack Britain's trade along the west coast of Africa. By moving fast and striking where we wouldn't be expected, we would cost the British government and merchants a lot of money, at the expense of one small, well-manned, aggressively led squadron. But unfortunately, my proposal was turned down.

INTERVIEWER: What happened next?

JONES: Eventually I was assigned to put a new ship in commission, and it was agreed I would take the ship to France, with the intention of mounting an attack against the British Isles. There also was mention of the possibility of getting a new frigate when I got to France. At least that was something that my friends in Congress and Commissioner Benjamin Franklin in Paris talked about. The new ship, an 18-gun sloop of war, was one of the first purpose-built warships in the Continental Navy. She was built in Portsmouth, New Hampshire and named *Ranger*, after the famous Roger's Rangers from that area.

INTERVIEWER: Wasn't it foolhardy to suggest taking a ship that wasn't even as big as a frigate to attack the British homeland?

JONES: Not to my way of thinking. For me it was a lot more sensible than sitting in port waiting for a chance to slip past cruising Royal Navy blockaders. But I have to admit there were many people in Congress and my own navy who thought it was too risky. But we left Portsmouth on the first of November 1777 and got to Nantes in France at the end of December, after a troublesome crossing.

INTERVIEWER: Why do you describe the crossing that way? What was the trouble?

JONES: There were two main problems: I had a new ship that needed many adjustments with her rig and her ballast, and I had a crew that was not prepared for navy discipline. They were all former merchant seamen, fishermen and landsmen. Most of them had been recruited with promises of prize money and adventure. That was why they signed on, and initially that's what drove them. Almost to a man, they were from the area around Portsmouth, but because I was from Virginia and Scotland, I was considered an outsider, even a foreigner.

INTERVIEWER: And they actually challenged your leadership?

JONES: There were times when things came close to mutiny. But I took it one day at a time, and I never backed down. At first, I think they tended to their duties because they figured that eventually, I would have to give in. They were wrong. It was a test of wills, and I knew if I faltered, it would have been chaos in *Ranger*. And I kept thinking of the exceptional opportunity we had, an opportunity to advance America's cause of liberty that outweighed the risks.

INTERVIEWER: Obviously, you made it to France.

JONES: Yes, we got to Nantes at the end of December, but my troubles were not over. I had difficulty getting money to pay the crew, make repairs, even to feed the men. It was hard to keep going, but I kept telling myself that the fight for our liberty was not going to be easy. I just kept pushing on.

Then it got worse. I found out that there would be no new frigate for me. I have to admit that at that point I questioned my own judgment about enlisting in the Continental Navy. I felt that what I was trying to accomplish wasn't understood or appreciated. At one point, I even paid a portion of the wages due to my crew out of my own pocket. It seemed like my civilian leaders didn't really understand or support what I was trying to do. But I never questioned being responsible to America's civilian leaders. It was a special challenge in that regard: I was learning to be a professional naval officer and they were learning how to control the new nation's military forces. I might add that we were developing a relationship that has stood the United States well over the years.

INTERVIEWER: What happened next, captain?

JONES: After I learned that there would not be a larger ship for me, I was able to make the needed improvements to *Ranger* and prepare the ship for action against the enemy. On the tenth of April, we got underway for a deployment into the Irish Sea. I had several things in mind. I wanted to take or destroy any British merchant ships I came across, I wanted to attack the English ashore, and I wanted to capture a British nobleman to trade for the American seamen being held under harsh conditions in British prisons. That was all part of fighting against a much stronger military power in what you call today "asymmetrical warfare."

We managed to take a few prizes before we even got into the Irish Sea, and headed for the English port of Whitehaven, where I planned to get ashore and destroy the shipping in the harbor. I knew the harbor well from my days in the merchant service, and after more trouble with my crew—my officers actually refused to be part of the landing party—I managed to get a landing party together and get ashore at Whitehaven. We spiked the guns that defended the harbor and set a collier that was alongside the pier afire. We could have done even more damage, but a traitor in the landing party actually deserted and ran through the village warning townspeople. I knew there soon would be local militia forces to contend with, so I got the landing party back to *Ranger*.

230 | Chapter 15 - Jones

The most important thing was that it was the first time in a hundred years that an enemy landing party had come ashore and attacked an English port. What was a seemingly modest operation created a lot of anxiety in British ports and in the countryside. And the raid had a very important impact on the British leaders and people. It was a classic example having a major psychological impact with what seemed at first to be a relatively minor effort.

INTERVIEWER: Did you manage to also kidnap the British noble to exchange for Continental Navy sailors imprisoned in Britain?

JONES: No, we actually got ashore on St. Mary's Island, the home of Lord Selkirk, but he was in London. The plan turned into an ignominious event, and to this day, I am embarrassed by losing control of the landing party. They went off on their own and sacked the Selkirk manor of its silver plate. It was a most unprofessional action, and it was a bitter leadership lesson for me. I knew at the time that the landing party had looting on their minds but I rationalized letting the men go off to the manor. I have lived with this mistake.

INTERVIEWER: Was that the end of the deployment against the British Isles?

JONES: By no means! After St. Mary's Island, I was able to precipitate a single ship action against the 20-gun HMS *Drake*. The two ships were evenly matched. They had a few more guns, but we had somewhat heavier guns. Our 18 guns were nine-pounders and theirs were six-pounders. They had a larger crew, and my opponent, Commander George Burdon, was an experienced Royal Navy officer. And I have to admit that *Drake's* gunners were the better trained.

We got in a good first broadside, however, as we raked *Drake* by managing to quickly cross her bow. The combat went on for about an hour, but when *Drake's* captain and first lieutenant were wounded at almost the same time, their sailing master decided it was time to strike their colors, and the battle was over. Our more aggressive tactics overcame their better gunnery. Counting those from *Drake* and the merchant ships we either captured or sank, we returned to Brest with *Drake* as a prize and more than 200 prisoners!

INTERVIEWER: That sounds like an amazing accomplishment for a Continental Navy ship. I imagine your welcome back at Brest by the French officials and the American commissioners in Paris must have been gratifying.

JONES: Sadly, it was not. Although word of the accomplishments in *Ranger* had preceded us back to France, when I made an official report to Commissioner Franklin and the other American commissioners in Paris, I received the most astonishing response from Commissioner Arthur Lee. His letter made absolutely no mention of what we achieved but instead went into administrative details about the expense of supplying and maintaining *Ranger*. I was even rebuked for having created an inconvenient situation when I placed my first lieutenant, an officer by the name of Simpson, under arrest at the end of the deployment for disobeying a direct order. I will never forget my anger at the time.

At the moment I finished reading the letter from Commissioner Lee, I was the closest I ever came to resigning my commission in the Continental Navy. I knew full well that if I had been captured at any time during the voyage, I would have been hung by the British as a rebel and a pirate. But I risked all for the cause and got nary a nod from my leaders.

INTERVIEWER: What kept you from quitting?

JONES: I waited for my rage to subside. Then as I thought about it realized that, for better or worse, it was important that I acknowledge that it was the civilian leaders of our government that were to control the Navy and other military forces. But most important was the fight for American liberty, which was still very much in doubt at that point. It was a very difficult decision for me, but it was the right one. I'm not a patient man, that's certain, but I was learning that sometimes being right isn't enough. I realized that our civilian leaders were not having an easy time trying to secure allies and financial support in Europe.

INTERVIEWER: Obviously, your career didn't end when you returned to Brest in *Ranger* in May of 1778. Did you go back to sea in *Ranger*?

JONES: No. She went back to America for the court martial of the officer I had arrested. I was, as they say, beached—a naval captain without a ship.

INTERVIEWER: What happened when you were stuck without a ship?

JONES: The first thing I had to deal with was the matter of my first lieutenant, and as I said, eventually Simpson was sent back to America in *Ranger,* and there the charges against him were dropped. Then he was actually sent back to sea in command of *Ranger*. His career was undistinguished. He was soon captured by the British, and subsequently he returned to the merchant service and was drowned at sea. *Ranger* was sold by the Royal Navy as a merchant ship. For my money, Simpson ended as he deserved but *Ranger* deserved better. She was a good ship.

INTERVIEWER: What did you do at that point? You were stuck in France without a ship. To whom did you turn; what were your options?

JONES: I renewed my efforts with the Commissioners, the French naval leaders, and even the French King to get another ship. After all, I had proved that I could attack the British homeland, and I didn't want to go back to America and start arguing all over for the means of more offensive action against the British Isles.

INTERVIEWER: Why was offensive action against the British homeland so important? After all the armies that were fighting were fighting in America.

JONES: What was most important was that what I had done in *Ranger* got us inside the British decision cycle.

INTERVIEWER: Inside the British decision cycle, what does that mean?

JONES: It means that the British were reacting to what *we* were doing militarily. We had started them thinking about what they had to do to react to *us*, rather than the reverse. That's an important strategic aspect of war that many historians miss. And I would point out in connection with these points: the probability of winning a war if you are permanently on the defense is virtually nil.

INTERVIEWER: How did you go about getting another ship?

JONES: I kept making my case with the American Commissioners in Paris—at the time they included Benjamin Franklin, John Adams and Arthur Lee—the French Minister of Marine and even the French King himself. The main problems were funding and politics, and those two elements were tightly intertwined. It was a difficult struggle for someone not schooled in the subtleties of such situations, and it was clear that there were times when I was considered a bother by the Commissioners and the Continental Congress. But I did the one thing I was good at; I persevered. I simply would not be defeated in my efforts.

INTERVIEWER: Did you make enemies and did you have to compromise?

JONES: I didn't mind the enemies, but with my personality, making compromises was very, very difficult. But I kept falling back on the idea that it was liberty for America that was paramount. I didn't realize it at the time, but I suspect that it was Mr. Franklin who finally made the difference, and he did it behind the scenes. I was battering on people; he was cajoling them quietly. As a result, I finally got a ship, and in honor of Franklin and my French benefactors, I named her *Bonhomme Richard*. She wasn't all that I thought I needed for my next mission, but that was one of the compromises I alluded to a few moments ago. The ship that the French provided to me was a converted, 14-year-old French eastindiaman. She wasn't fast and she wasn't nimble, but she was a frigate and a large one at that, with 40 guns. Most important I would take her to sea with a small squadron!

INTERVIEWER: Besides *Bonhome Richard* what were the ships in your squadron?

JONES: I had the new 36-gun American frigate *Alliance,* with a captain who was described by Commissioner Adams as "a man with an embarrassed mind." I also had three French ships that were, with their French captains, placed under American Flags and assigned to my squadron: the 26-gun small frigate *Pallas,* the 12-gun brig *Vengeance* and the 12-gun cutter *le Cerf.* Two American privateers also agreed to join my squadron. It was encouraging to be commodore of a squadron at that point, but there also were some very troubling aspects of the situation.

INTERVIEWER: I can see where the squadron you had was a very big step beyond your situation when you were attacking the British Isles in *Ranger.* What were the problems you had?

JONES: The problems had to do with command and control. Specifically my authority as commodore of the squadron was seriously compromised. Since the French had provided *Bonhomme Richard* and three of the other four naval ships, I had to defer to them on a number of basic matters. The problem became acute what the French Minister of Marine Antoine de Sartine sent a representative, Jacques Donatien Le Ray de Chaumont, to facilitate our preparations for our mission. Monsieur Chaumont was a civilian and the first thing he did was to begin working directly with the captains of the individual ships. This undercut my authority and created chaos in our preparations. As if that wasn't bad enough, Monsieur Chaumont presented me with an agreement that, among other things, said that each of the captains in my squadron could act on his own, if he disagreed with my orders.

INTERVIEWER: Did you refuse to sail under the conditions set up by the French?

JONES: No, despite the fact that the arrangement proposed by the French caused me considerable trouble during the deployment, I knew that the importance of the mission came first, and that I would never get to sea unless I agreed to Monsieur Chaumont's terms. Despite the fact that I knew the agreement seriously compromised my authority—in fact, it almost wrecked the mission—I signed the agreement. I knew that if I did not, I would never get to sea.

On the positive side, my orders from Commissioner Franklin, in contrast to the muddled command authority I had, gave me hope of success. Franklin's orders were brief. I was ordered to take my squadron to the west coast of Ireland and then proceed northeast around the tip of Scotland, finally southeast along the coasts of Scotland and England, while distressing the enemy as much as possible along the way. And that in the end is exactly what we did.

INTERVIEWER: Can you tell us some of the specifics of what you did?

JONES: We attacked British merchant ships as we went along the coasts and that roiled the countryside. There was a lot of fear that we would actually go ashore to raid, as we had done at Whitehaven in *Ranger*. There were local and London newspaper stories about our presence and that caused militias to be mobilized. In addition, the Royal Navy had to devote assets to a search for us.

When we finally got to the English coast off Yorkshire, we met a major Baltic convoy loaded with naval materiel that the Royal Navy sorely needed. There were two Royal Navy ships escorting the convoy and they managed to herd the merchant ships into Scarborough. The lead escort ship, the 44-gun frigate HMS *Serapis*, positioned herself between the merchant ships and us, and the result was a bloody single-ship battle between *Serapis* and *Bonhomme Richard*.

INTERVIEWER: That was the famous Battle off Flamborough Head in 1779?

JONES: Yes, it was the 22nd of September to be exact. My opponent was Captain Richard Pearson, a thirty-year veteran of the Royal Navy. His ship was new and had a coppered bottom. She was faster and more nimble, and I have to admit her gunnery was better than ours was. At first, Captain Pearson maneuvered *Serapis* skillfully around us and we were getting the worst of things, but then the ships came together and that changed matters. It became a bloody slugging match between the two of us, but grappled together as we were, I was able to use my larger number of embarked French soldiers in *Bonhomme Richard's* tops and rigging. They swept the weather decks of *Serapis* almost clear. But poor *Bonhomme Richard* was suffering badly. The enemy's guns were actually firing through one side of her hull and out the other. At one point, the ship's carpenter reported to me that we were actually sinking.

INTERVIEWER: Was that the point when Captain Pearson shouted over asking if you would strike your colors?

JONES: Yes and my response was "I have not yet begun to fight."

INTERVIEWER: Captain, there are many historians who claim that those were not the exact words you used when you shouted back to Captain Pearson. What do you say to them?

JONES: The first thing I would say is "Please be serious!" The second is "You can be damn sure that with cannon and musket fire flying, I didn't have time to write down my words for posterity. But what I am sure of is that those words are very close to what I said, and here is what is important, they are *exactly* what I was *thinking.*" I was determined that I would not surrender.

INTERVIEWER: What changed the course of the battle?

JONES: At one point, one of my sailors perched on a yardarm dropped a grenade though one of *Serapis'* hatches onto her gun deck. The grenade's explosion set off powder accumulated for the guns and wiped out the remaining guns and many of the men on the gun deck. At that point, it was Captain Pearson's turn to contemplate striking his colors. The convoy for which he was responsible was safely into Scarborough, and he decided to stop the carnage. It was a rational act, and there was no dishonor in it.

INTERVIEWER: In fact, didn't the British knight Captain Pearson for his performance that day? Did that bother you? After all, he surrendered to you.

JONES: Not in the least, in fact when I heard that he had been made a knight after the action, I said that if we meet in combat again, I'd make him a Lord.

INTERVIEWER: We are almost out of time, but before we finish I want to ask, what were the most important things about your leadership—the things that led to your achievements?

JONES: The most important was that I believed in what I was fighting for. And I was absolutely determined to succeed in the cause of American liberty.

INTERVIEWER: There are other questions I would like to ask Captain, for example about your service in the Russian Navy and the romances in your life, but unfortunately, we are out of time. So, I will simply say goodnight and thank you Captain Jones.

JONES: Thank you.

# # #

Joseph F. Callo, Rear Admiral, U.S. Navy Reserve (Retired), was commissioned from the Yale University Naval Reserve Officers Training Corps. Upon commissioning, Rear Admiral Callo was assigned to sea duty with the Atlantic Amphibious Force. After two years, he returned to civilian life and subsequently returned to active duty for a special assignment in the Pre-Commissioning Detail of USS SARATOGA (CVA-60). Upon the commissioning of the ship, he again returned to civilian life and went on to hold senior positions with major advertising agencies and was also an award-winning television producer for NBC and PBS television programs. As an adjunct associate professor at St. John's University in New York City, he taught advertising, marketing, and writing for the mass media.

His most recent book is the award-winning *John Paul Jones: America's First Sea Warrior,* and he has written three books about the Royal Navy's Admiral Lord Nelson. He is a *Naval History Magazine* Author of the Year and is a frequent contributor of articles to major publications.

A Final Word

"If we work in marble, it will perish; if we work upon brass, time will efface it; if we rear temples, they will crumble into dust; but if we work upon immortal minds and instill in them just principles, we are then engraving upon tablets which no time will efface, but will brighten and brighten to all eternity."
— Daniel Webster

Each chapter of this book provides a range of perspectives on leadership from a unique and diverse group of individuals. Each individual has a different background, and in some cases provides different approaches to leading—but all have, through personal effort, accomplished much in their life and for this country. All are veterans—some of the finest in our military history as a Nation. One of the common threads tying them all together is a military tradition that instilled them with structure and a framework within which to operate. Because of the very nature of the dangers and responsibilities of military service, it breeds strong leadership. It is a career in which the ultimate scorecard is clear-cut—for in war, you win or you lose, you survive or you die.

But human nature is such that not all military personnel make good leaders. Ineffective or poor military leadership is at best a drain of our Nations' resources in men, women and materiel; at worst, it is fatal. The mistakes made by civilian leadership rarely have the life and death consequences of mistakes made by military leadership. In recent times, however, we have seen how mistakes by business leaders can bring financial devastation upon the lives of those trusting in their leadership.

The military offers a unique opportunity to mold strong leaders. To serve in the military, at its simplest perhaps philosophical level, is to be part of the whole. A component that works for the greater good—a whole that is stronger than the sum of its parts. This is something those in uniform understand. For 235 years, in our country, inculcated in every recruit or cadet in boot camps, military schools & programs and service academies—whether enlisted or officer—each individual knows others depend on them to do their jobs and do them well because very often, lives depend on it. The outcome of battles and wars depend on it. Our Nation depends on it.

Politics and the corporate world are far more forgiving—though flawed leadership in these arenas can and often do have calamitous results and far reaching repercussions as witnessed in recent years. CEOs would do well to embrace more of the sense that we truly are "all in this together." I hope that this book will be seen by such corporate leaders as a vehicle for understanding it is "all for one and one for all."

What lessons of strong leadership can be extracted from this book and applied to those serving in the public and private sectors?

The top seven lessons follow:

1) **Leaders must be self-less.** Corporate and government leaders need to come back to the honest realization that they are stewards of the trust that the marketplace or voters have given them. One will know this has happened when such leaders make decisions based on the common good—not purely for the betterment of certain individuals or for self. Should contrary conduct be observed—if a public official, one should vote to remove them—if at a corporate level, one should vote with your wallet and boycott that company's products and/or services.

2) **Leaders must believe in those they lead and just as important— must respect them.** In the military, one does not go far if one fails to grasp this concept. It is evident in government and corporate America that too often little respect passes from the top down. CEOs, corporate boards, executive management, senators, congressional representatives—the entire chain of leadership at its highest-levels are rife with a lack of respect for the vast majority of people driving our economy and selflessly serving our Nation.

3) **Leaders must establish a tradition and culture that is sustainable (only through its merits).** The way to eliminate mediocrity is to decide it is no longer acceptable. Make changes so that those responsible in part or full for an organization's poor performance are no longer rewarded or are no longer part of the equation. Create a value-based tradition and culture that eliminates any opportunities for leaders, management and people in positions of authority to develop a sense of entitlement.

4) **Leaders must step forward.** To lead means to step out front—to lead by example. "Leader" is not just a title. It does not mean one becomes a leader through delegation, though many ride that horse as long as it carries them. Be a leader who is judged by the example you make and the successes your people (or constituents) attain.

5) **Leaders must have a plan that makes sense—that they then execute.** This goes back to structure. Being headless or clueless does not get it done in the military—and commands operating that way rarely retain the same leadership for very long. Leaders in corporate America and government need to create and execute plans designed to correct problems, cure deficiencies in any system and move things forward positively. True leaders (and those responsible for giving them such positions) should not tolerate smokescreens designed to obfuscate and perpetuate their nice little sinecure.

6) **Leaders must embody the meaning behind "Esse Quam Videri".** Latin for *"to be rather than to seem to be,"* this means true leadership requires character traits of personal honesty, integrity and steadfastness. Too many of Americas corporate leaders, do not have such traits. They sell the public or market at large on their "Potemkin Village." Many Americans rely too much, on a leader's "packaging" rather than on his/her "substance. We have

a duty to identify leaders with real substance, and then supporting them with our business or vote.

7) **Leaders must be accountable.** When things go wrong, true leaders do not waste time finger pointing or continually dissecting a problem or issue to the point that they fail to get around to finding and applying a viable solution. Real leaders need to address the current issues. But they also must think long-term as they shoulder the blame and—though it may bow their back—keep moving forward.

Yes. These things seem obvious ... and they are. It is not rocket science. John D. Rockefeller once said, *"The secret of success is to do common things, uncommonly well"*. Fixing our leadership problems, getting America (in all facets) back on track is not that complicated. We just need to return to fundamentals—i.e., those basics upon which we relied in the past to make us a great Nation are the same upon which we should rely in the future. Somewhere during the past 30-plus years, we lost our way on a slippery slope. We strayed from our strengths and put our faith in false princes.

But we can fix this. We can come back and do what is right. We just need to get back up one more time than we are knocked down. That is the real strength of our country and our people.

It is time to stand up—and lead—again.

About Greg Slavonic

Rear Admiral Greg Slavonic

Rear Admiral Greg Slavonic, U.S. Navy (Retired) born in Great Bend, Kansas, and raised in Oklahoma City, most recently served as the U.S. Navy's Deputy to the Chief of Information in Washington, D.C., and Director of Public Affairs (Reserve) from June 2001 to 2005. In this duel role, he served as principal advisor to the Chief of Information having responsibility for formulating strategic communications counsel to the leadership of the Department of the Navy. As part of his duties, he established and maintained professional working relationships and liaison with Navy Secretariat officers, other Department of Defense commands and activities within the Pentagon and in the Washington Capitol Region. In addition, he was responsible for the training and readiness of more than 500 public affairs reservists assigned to 26 different units across the United States.

In June 2004, Slavonic deployed to support Operation Enduring Freedom II, Baghdad, Iraq. Assigned to the Multinational Force-Iraq (MNF-I) staff; he served as the senior strategic communications and public affairs officer for Commanding General for MNF-I, and directed daily operations of the Combined Press Information Center (CPIC). He worked closely with the White House and served as senior on-scene military coordinator for the first court appearance by Saddam Hussein, plus eleven other high value detainees including Ali Hassan al Majid al-Tikriti ("Chemical Ali"). He led a crisis action team to the Babylon archaeological site numerous times to gather facts to defuse negative media coverage of MNF-I operations at the historical site. He was the first U.S. Navy flag officer assigned to MNF-I and the highest-ranking public affairs officer in Iraq.

In November 1990, Slavonic deployed to Operations Desert Shield and Desert Storm. He was assigned to the staff of General H. Norman Schwarzkopf at U.S. Central Command and served at the Joint Information Bureau in Dhahran, Saudi Arabia. During his tour in the Arabian Gulf Theater, Rear Admiral Slavonic served as a Chief of Navy News desk and senior Combat Media Escort officer. This included escorting four Combat Correspondent Pools (CCP). Of note, he was aboard USS CURTS (FFG-38) to document the processing and interrogation of more than 40 Iraqi prisoners. Then was aboard the amphibious assault ship USS TRIPOLI (LPH-10) when she struck an Iraqi underwater tethered mine causing extensive damage, flooding, and nearly sinking the ship.

After graduating with a Bachelor of Science degree from Oklahoma State University, Slavonic enlisted in the Navy. After completing boot camp and Signalman "A" school, he received orders to the aircraft carrier USS CONSTELLATION (CVA-64) and completed two western Pacific deployments in support of combat operations in Vietnam. Slavonic affiliated with the Navy Reserve and received a commission as a restricted line officer in public affairs. In 1976, he earned a Master's degree from the University of Central Oklahoma. His military decorations include Bronze Star Medal (two awards), Legion of Merit, Presidential Unit Commendation, Combat Action Ribbon and numerous other campaign and service awards.

Slavonic served four commanding officer tours, staff public affairs officer for the Commander, Readiness Command Eleven and was a key member of the commissioning committee for the nuclear-powered, fast-attack submarine USS OKLAHOMA CITY (SSN-723). His civilian employment includes over 30 years in media and management as account executive with *The (Daily) Oklahoma*; advertising director for *The Journal Record*, general manager for the *Oklahoma Gazette* and senior account executive with KFOR-TV (NBC affiliate.)

He has served on numerous boards and held many key leadership positions including co-chair and the lead effort to raise $1.1 million dollars for building a USS OKLAHOMA Memorial at Pearl Harbor. He was chair of the Oklahoma War on Terror Memorial; chair for the selection committee for the Jim Thorpe Award (Outstanding Defensive Back), minority partner for the Oklahoma City Cavalry professional basketball team and has received the "Distinguished Former

Student" Award presented by the University of Central Oklahoma. Slavonic is one of only five graduates in Oklahoma State University history to attain the rank of Rear Admiral and is a member of Kappa Sigma Fraternity.

He is a former adjunct professor in the Department of Journalism & Broadcasting at University of Central Oklahoma and taught Leadership Development in the Meinders School of Business at Oklahoma City University. He co-authored the book – *"Jim Thorpe Award – The First 20 Years."*

He is currently the Principal Leader, Strategic Communications & Public Affairs for CSC (formerly Computer Sciences Corporation); a Washington D.C. based Defense Company and serves on the Board of Directors for Avalon Correctional Services, Inc.

He and his wife Molly have three children and two grandchildren and reside in Oklahoma City.

His website is www.TheAdmiralSpeaks.com.

CPSIA information can be obtained at www.ICGtesting.com
Printed in the USA
LVOW061351171012

303236LV00005B/3/P